28

ESSAYS IN EUROPEAN HISTORY

Selected from the Annual Meetings of the Southern Historical Association, 1986-1987

Edited by
June K. Burton

UNIVERSITY
PRESS OF
AMERICA

Lanham • New York • London

European History Section
of the
Southern Historical Association

Copyright © 1989 by

University Press of America,® Inc.

4720 Boston Way
Lanham, MD 20706

3 Henrietta Street
London WC2E 8LU England

Printed in the United States of America

British Cataloging in Publication Information Available

Library of Congress Cataloging–in–Publication data

Essays in European history : selected from the annual meetings of the
Southern Historical Association, 1986–1987 / edited by June K. Burton.
p.   cm.
"Co–published by arrangement with the European History Section of
the Southern Historical Association"– –T.p. verso.
Includes bibliographies.
1. Europe– –History– –1789–1900. 2. Europe– –History– –20th century.
I. Burton, June K. II. Southern Historical Association. European
History Section.
D353.E87   1988   88–37939 CIP
940.2– –dc19
ISBN 0–8191–7279–0 (alk. paper)
ISBN 0–8191–7280–4 (pbk. : alk. paper)

Co-published by arrangement with the
European History Section of the Southern
Historical Association

All University Press of America books are produced on acid-free paper.
The paper used in this publication meets the minimum requirements of American
National Standard for Information Sciences—Permanence of Paper for Printed Library
Materials, ANSI Z39.48–1984.   ∞

Contents

Preface

This volume appears as the product of efforts made by the executive committee of the European History Section of the Southern Historical Association over a period of several years to enhance the prestige of the organization and the quality of the program of the annual meetings. The original intent was to sponsor a scholarly journal appearing annually; however, too few submissions were received for 1986 to make that feasible while maintaining the principle of selectivity. Hence, the first volume of essays covers, in addition to the Joseph Mathews Addresses delivered at the European Section luncheons and the John L. Snell prize-winning seminar paper, submissions from the programs for the years 1986 and 1987. Future volumes may eventually appear annually if quality can be maintained.

The name for this publication was chosen carefully to cover the variety of papers typically presented at one of our annual meetings. While the speeches of senior scholars Peter Gay and William H. McNeill, for example, were presented when both authors were nearing completion of significant book length biographies, other authors' papers are initial explorations or smaller projects. Also, some topics and methodologies are more interdisciplinary than others. The word "essays" in the title is meant to establish a flexible editorial policy of considering quality contributions from all kinds of historians who may be at different stages in their careers.

In 1986 the section's officers accepted the offer of The University of Akron Department of History to sponsor this publication for a three-year period. Accordingly, the founding editors were chosen to serve three-year terms. Future plans for the journal were left in abeyance until after the appearance of the first volume makes evaluation possible.

[vi]

Part I

The Joseph J. Mathews Address

Presented at the European History Section Luncheon

November 14, 1986

Charlotte, North Carolina

Psychoanalyzing the Psychoanalyst:

Writing the Freud Biography

Peter Gay

All biography is in some measure autobiography. I must therefore begin with myself. I have spent perhaps as much as fifteen years trying not to write a biography of Freud. I had long felt the temptation to write that biography, and I thought myself well equipped to do so: I can read German and, even better, I can read Freud's handwriting. There is no difficulty seeing why the temptation to tackle such a life should be strong. The man is fascinating. His ideas are controversial. His life presents intriguing puzzles. The standard biography, Ernest Jones's three volumes dating from the mid-1950s is, for all its enormous merit, flawed and dated. Moreover, the stakes in writing such a biography are high; for reasons I want to discuss below, the stature of the man appears to be linked in the public mind with the stature of his thought.

Still, for all these years I did not succumb to the temptation, for the countervailing forces were stronger. Freud himself had done the utmost to obstruct his biographers by repeatedly destroying the kind of evidence that such biographers must rely on. In April 1885, he wrote to his fiancée, Martha Bernays, that he had, as he put it, "almost completed an undertaking which a number of people, still unborn but fated to misfortune, will feel severely." Little did I know, when I first read those lines some years ago, that I would be among those fated to the misfortune he predicted. He had explicitly his biographers in mind. "I have destroyed all my notes of the last fourteen years," he wrote, "as well as letters, scientific extracts, and manuscripts of my works. Among letters, only family letters have been spared." In later years, he repeated this destructive gesture more than once, the last time in April 1938, while he was sitting in Vienna waiting for the Nazis to give him a permit to emigrate. He went over his papers and tried to throw away as many of them as possible. His daughter Anna as well as Princess Marie Bonaparte were present at this trying moment and, as they reported later, fished materials out of the waste paper basket for posterity: they were the historian's true friends.

Marie Bonaparte proved the historian's true friend in yet another way. The most fascinating and, from the point of view of the history of psychoanalysis, the most significant correspondence that Freud ever carried on was, of course, with his intimate in Berlin, the ear--nose--and throat specialist Wilhelm Fliess. To him Freud wrote the most detailed letters, beginning in the late 1880s right through 1900 and beyond, long letters and exhaustive memoranda in which he outlined the evolution of his ideas. The 1890s, as you well know, were a critical time for the development of psychoanalytic thinking. It was the decade in which Freud discovered the dynamic unconscious, the sexual aetiology of the neuroses, the Oedipus complex, the way to the interpretation of dreams and, reluctantly, infantile sexuality.

It was the decade, too, of his self-analysis. And all this one could reexperience, in the most satisfying detail, in the scores of letters he sent to his friend, the only man in the 1890s, Freud thought, who understood the revolution that he, Freud, was making. But gradually the friendship waned, the two men quarreled, and after 1904 never wrote to one another again.

Now, to recall a familiar episode: in the mid-1930s, Fliess's widow sold these letters to a book dealer in Berlin who intelligently enough, got in touch with Marie Bonaparte. She bought the letters with the greatest possible excitement, but felt constrained to tell Freud about her fortunate discovery. He begged her to destroy them, offered to pay part of the expense, but she, much as she adored her former analyst, disobeyed. He belonged to history, she told him, and to burn those letters would be the equivalent of destroying Eckermann's conversations with Goethe, or those dialogues in which Plato tells us about the life and fate of Socrates, philosopher and pederast. We have reason to be grateful to her--the writing of a Freud biography would be infinitely poorer without those letters to Fliess. If it had been up to Freud, his biographer would not have that resource.

Freud, I must add, obstructed his biographers in yet another, even subtler way, and this is where psychoanalyzing the psychoanalyst may take its root. Many of his writings, including his masterpiece, The Interpretation of Dreams, are partly autobiographical. In the dream book, as he liked to call it, he did not hesitate to gloss those of his dreams he reported with fascinating and revealing biographical information. It is from the dream book that the biographer may glean revealing details about Freud's childhood: how his father predicted to his eldest son, when one night he invaded the parental bedroom, that he would never amount to anything; how, when he was eleven or twelve, he went with his parents to Vienna's famous amusement park, the Prater, and, sitting with them at a restaurant table, he had an itinerant beggar poet predict a great future for him. The biographer learns much else from those pages. But again and again, whenever Freud thinks he is on the verge of revealing too much, he will stop, and argue a little defensively that he has told the world more than most human beings ever have. Thus, in The Interpretation of Dreams, he excised virtually everything about his sexual life, which clearly governed many of his nocturnal wishes. As a fearless researcher, he exposed aspects of his innermost being, including some very unpleasant material. But as a good bourgeois, he valued his privacy immensely.

Unwittingly--I think it was unwittingly--Freud built still higher fences around himself. He made some memorable comments that could only mislead his biographers. Here is one of them: "If one has been the undisputed darling of his mother, one retains throughout life that feeling of conquest, that confidence in success, which not rarely draws real success in its wake." Freud offered this aperçu in a paper on Goethe's childhood, but since he had said it before, and since it seemed to fit his own life so well, Freud's biographers have unhesitatingly applied the saying to the making of his own character.

6

After all, his mother used to refer to him adoringly as her "Golden Sigi." But one thing I was to discover when I finally decided to write Freud's life, obstructions or not, was that his psychological relationship to his mother was immensely complex; not merely far from exhausted by this confident talk of conquest and success, but gravely misrepresented by it. I shall return to this point.

Again, in a much-quoted letter to Wilhelm Fliess of February 1, 1900, Freud said of himself: "I am not a man of science at all, not an observer, not an experimenter, not a thinker. I am nothing but a conquistador by temperament, an adventurer, if you want to translate this term, with all the inquisitiveness, daring, and tenacity of such a man." We may grant Freud his conquistador's temperament, but to follow him by denying him the stature of a scientist, observer or thinker is to distort his spirit by obeying his letter. It is one thing to treat his pronouncements with respect -- the responsible historian can do no less. It is quite another thing to treat his pronouncements as gospel. Freud, the biographer must discover, was not his own best judge. Fortunately, what he said about all humans in the Dora Case applies to him, too: try as people may, they cannot keep secrets, and if their lips are sealed, they chatter with their fingertips, and confessions ooze out from every pore.

Freud also issued some grim general warnings that gave me further pause. Near the end of his life, he asked his good friend, the German novelist Arnold Zweig, who had offered to write Freud's biography, to desist. "Whoever turns biographer," he cautioned Zweig, "commits himself to lies, to concealment, to hypocrisy, to embellishments, and even to dissembling his own lack of understanding, for biographical truth is not to be had, and even if one had it, one could not use it." That was vehement enough, indeed too vehement, and that alone did not deter me. Nor did another, even better known statement of Freud's, that he placed strategically into a biographical essay of his own, the famous paper on a childhood memory of Leonard da Vinci. "Biographers," he wrote--it was in 1910--"are fixated on their hero in a quite particular way." What Freud meant was plain enough: the biographer is likely to choose his subject in the first place because he admires him and has great affection for him; hence, the temptation to idealize is virtually irresistible.

I thought that I might be able to control the infatuation with my subject enough to write a fair-minded life of Freud, warts and all. Naturally, I must leave the verdict to my future readers. Here let me only say that my confidence proved, as I wrote, too easy. Freud, I discovered, had a point. Some time ago, the history graduate students at Yale invited me to speak to them about the biography on which I am now engaged. When I got ready to give my talk, I was nearing the end of my first draft. The time I was working on was was spring, 1938; the situation of Freud and his family, and of all Jews in Austria, exceedingly precarious. And when I started my paper for the graduate students, I found myself saying things I had not planned to say: "This is not a good time for me to be speaking to you," I said. "The Nazis have just marched into Austria, and I am very upset." This was more than just an oratorical device to entertain my audience. I really was suffering for the victims of the Nazis. I had done a good deal of reading about the cheerful, indeed ecstatic way that the Austrians had greeted Hitler and his troops, about the casual and sadistic violence offered to Jews, young and old, in the streets of Vienna and elsewhere in Austria. The Nazi occupation appeared to liberate a streak of imaginative violence in thousands of Austrians. Late in March, Anna Freud was summoned to Gestapo headquarters; and Freud's physician, Max Schur, whom all the Freuds trusted, gave her veronal, in case her captors undertook to torture her. Freud, not an emotional man, spent the day pacing up and down in his study, ceaselessly smoking his cigars. He was very upset. And so was I. I could now understand what Flaubert meant with his famous exclamation, "Emma Bovary, c'est moi!" I could understand, too, from my own experience, what Flaubert had gone through when he decided to have Emma Bovary poison herself. He threw up his dinner after he finished that passage and was sick for three days. I was not quite so badly off, but I suffered with Freud's suffering. How objective can so involved a biographer be? The whole enterprise, far more than I had anticipated, became an internal combat between the professional discipline I had so painfully acquired over the years, and the emotions that rose up within me against my will.

But Freud was not alone in making the life of his biographer virtually impossible. Ernest Jones, after all, had enjoyed privileges that no other student of Freud's life enjoyed: close enough to visit the Freud family, Freud's loyal associate through decades of hard struggles in the establishment of psychoanalysis, he was given access to practically everything that was later closed to others. Jones saw Freud's letters to his fiancée, to his most intimate associates like Sandor Ferenczi of Budapest, and to others. He quoted from them, copiously, but there was no way of checking his translations, or of moving beyond the snippets he was willing to share with the world. As those of you will recall who have read Janet Malcolm's brilliant profile in the New Yorker, "Trouble in the Freud Archives," the man in charge of giving permission to other researchers, the eminent psychoanalyst Dr. Kurt Eissler, did not believe that there was anything to be gained by publishing anything--I mean, anything--of Freud's that Freud himself had not intended for publication.

It was Eissler whom I confronted as long ago as 1968 to ask for a change of policy. He was extremely courteous, listened to my case with attention, gave me a book he had written--and said no. I had gone to him as the representative of three historians; none of us, including myself, had any intention at the time of writing the life of Freud, but the principle of secrecy, which only breeds rumors, was one we hoped to persuade Eissler to modify--in vain. Fortunately, there were trickles of publications. In the 1960s, Ernst Freud brought out several volumes of his father's letters: a general collection that included some two dozen of Freud's early passionate letters to his fiancée, and exchanges with his principal lieutenant in Berlin, Karl Abraham and to his Swiss friend, the Protestant pastor Oska Pfister. But these were truncated, expurgated, highly selected editions,

8

offering scanty and unsatisfactory indications of what had been left out and where--well-meaning, amateurish editing calculated to whet the biographer's appetite without in any way satisfying it. A potential biographer of Freud did not know what he did not know.

2

You may wonder why I plunged ahead with my life of Freud even so. To begin with, I perceived Jones's classic biography as a challenge. It was honestly but awkwardly written, mixing personal reminiscences with long quotations from correspondence and technical discussions. Unable to integrate life and work satisfactorily, Jones would tear them apart and discuss them in widely separated sections. Besides, his biography was, for all of Jones's heroic efforts at objectivity, too partisan for comfort. How partisan was almost impossible to establish, because the proof texts were unavailable to other scholars. But Jones made charges against former disciples of Freud--notably against Alfred Adler, Carl Jung, Otto Rank, and as well as against Sandor Ferenczi -- attributing to them ill will and even dubious mental health, charges that might be true but sounded like special pleading. Later writers, more sympathetic to the men they conceived to be Jones's victims, denounced his work in the strongest terms as tendentious. The possibility of writing a better biography than Jones's, even with sources still largely restricted, was a spur to ambition.

But then, as I have said, there were trickles of new information, editions of letters that beckoned biographers to go beyond Jones. the most tantalizing was the publication, in 1950, of Freud's letters to Fliess, of which I have already spoken. But it was an open question whether this was an invitation to the biographer, or yet another obstruction in his path. For the Fliess letters had been ruthlessly cut, and while the editors suggested that the cuts were necessary to reduce repetition and to respect the physician's professional obligation to discretion, it gave no ideas of the riches withheld. Jones, who had of course seen those letters, was no help here. But then something happened. In 1966, in a festschrift for Heinz Harmann, the most eminent refugee psychoanalytic theorist then in the United States, Max Schur published a long piece entitled "Some Additional 'Day Residues' of 'The Specimen Dream of Psychoanalysis.'" For this psychoanalytic audience, such a title must have set off all sorts of clanging bells. For general readers, though, assuming that any of them would ever see this festschrift, the article would have appeared most innocuous, quite technical, wholly unexciting. In fact, the paper was explosive; it disclosed for the first time a significant portion of Freud's letters to Fliess that their editors had withheld a decade and a half before. This portion did not merely enrich what we already knew about Freud's missives to his friend; it also managed to elucidate the famous Irma Dream, which Freud had incompletely interpreted in his Interpretation of Dreams. It showed that following that notorious bit of incompetent medical malpractice, in which Fliess had almost killed Freud's patient Emma Eckstein--who was at least in part Irma--Freud had done his utmost to exculpate his friend. He had gone so far as to shift the blame for Fliess's leaving a long strip of gauze in Emma Eckstein's nose from the guilty party, Dr. Fliess, to the innocent victim, Emma Eckstein. This addition to our knowledge of Freud's way of thinking and feeling made him less perfect and more human.

There was, then, something to go on, but still not enough. Gradually, with the 1970s, bits of Freud's life were revealed one after the other. The most significant portions of his inner world remained secret; Dr. Eissler firmly argued against publishing more. He even objected, strongly, to the publication of the fascinating and valuable correspondence between Freud and Jung, which first came out in 1974. Yet slowly, drop by drop, the pool of our knowledge about Freud was slowly filling up. It was not yet large enough to force me to take up my assignment. But, as I look back, I can see now that, more or less unconsciously, I inched closer and closer. In 1976, I became a candidate in the Western New England Institute for Psychoanalysis, and for seven years did my training analysis, took my courses, did a bit of clinical work, and finally graduated. If this did not prepare me for the biography I had been avoiding, I do not know what would. But even this was not yet enough. What persuaded me that the time had come was two things. First, the rash of publications--speculative essays, new biographies, conjectural papers, most of them embroidered with the most sensational claims--seemed to call for a response, and I was immodest enough to think that I was the person to offer that response. And secondly, my new position in the psychoanalytic profession gave me an understanding of how the Freud papers were being managed and gave me, too, access to analysts involved with setting policy for releasing certain hitherto restricted documents. My confidence was not misplaced. And so now that more and more material is being given over to the public domain, I felt I could safely go ahead. There was enough new to say. And with this, I can finally move away from autobiography to biography.

3

This seems to be open season on Freud. Attacks on Freud, of course, are nothing new. In the first decade of this century, when he was publishing his epoch-making books on dreams and sexuality, word was out that Freud was a sensualist and, at the very least, a charlatan. In recent years, the intensity and the range of abuse have increased, until they have become a scandal of real interest to the cultural historian. Freud has been freely called liar, opportunist, plagiarist, adulterer, even pedophile. One of the most elaborate reconstructions of his middle years by Peter Swales has Freud carrying on a love affair with his sister-in-law Minna Bernays, and taking her to Italy for an abortion. I may note that I find Swales's work as fascinating as it is unconvincing; the love affair, unless in the coming months I find more persuasive evidence, will not be in my biography. Another such reconstruction, far more malicious, it seems to me, is Frederick Crews's attempt to portray Freud as a self-serving fabulist.

I want to stay with Crews's charge for a moment, because it strikes me as characteristic for the contemporary mood. Besides, it is an interesting story. According to Crews, Freud made up out of whole cloth an important anecdote about that historic patient, Anna O. Anna O., as you know, the founding patient of psychoanalysis, was not Freud's patient, of course, but that of Freud's close paternal friend, Josef Breuer, from whom Freud elicited the details in several confidential conversations.

Now, according to Freud, the therapy of Anna O. ended with a dramatic incident. Virtually cured, after her physician had said good-by, Anna O. suddenly lapsed into a monumental hysterical attack that showed all the symptoms of a false pregnancy. This was Dr. Breuer's baby, she said, that she was carrying to term. One can see why Freud thought so highly of this story, thought it in fact historic. First, because it documented the lengths to which hysterical conversions can be pushed. And secondly, because it demonstrated Breuer's unwillingness, or inability, to pursue a highly provocative clue to the end; somehow, Freud saw, hysteria was linked to sexuality and its discontents. It would be precisely Freud's merit to have had the courage of Breuer's medical experience and to found psychoanalysis in large measure on what he had learned from Breuer about Anna O.

Freud offered a straightforward version of this episode in a letter to Stefan Zweig. Now, Crews argues that Freud "cajoled" Breuer into publishing the case history of Anna O., and "dramatize[d] his superiority to Breuer," by telling "Jones and others" a "memorable tale," namely the tale of Anna O.'s false pregnancy. What shall we say? We are confronted with a melodramatic report about Anna O. We know that Freud told some of it. We know that Jones told more. But what is the skeptical historian entitled to say about it? There are only too many possibilities. First: the story--except for the part about the second honeymoon, which is Jones's--may have been true. Anna O. may have had such an episode. Secondly: the story may be partially true, but embroidered by Breuer in frightened recollection, misremembered or misreported for reasons beyond Breuer's conscious control. Third: Breuer may have made up the story, lying to Freud about the episode. Fourth: Freud may have misremembered Breuer's report or conflated that report with other experiences, but done so quite innocently, at least on the level of consciousness. Fifth: Freud may have lied. Sixth: Jones, hearing some story about Anna O., may have told it more sensationally than required by strict veracity, but have done so without intent to deceive. We must not forget that he heard the story many years after it happened, and then wrote it down a number of years later. It all happened, or didn't happen, in 1881; he probably learned of it about fifty years later--Freud's letter to Stefan Zweig, at least, dates from 1932.

I will not bore you with some of the other possibilities and combinations. What matters is that Crews has chosen to take from this menu of possible versions, on the basis of no independent evidence, and misusing the Ellenberger article, the one that is most discreditable to Freud. Why?

This is not the place to psychoanalyze Crews; I agree with Freud that what he calls wild analysis, especially when designed to discredit an opponent, is neither a respectable nor, for that matter, a very instructive activity. Let me now move, rather, to other instances. In late May, 1937, Alfred Adler died suddenly at Aberdeen. Now for thirty-five years and more, Freud and Adler had been enemies--it is not too strong a word. Adler had of course been one of Freud's earliest adherents, an original member of the little group who began meeting in Freud's apartment every Wednesday night from the fall of 1902 on. But the two men had parted in anger and remained angry; for Freud, Adler had made a career out of betraying psychoanalysis. When Arnold Zweig wrote to Freud about Adler's death, and appeared moved, Freud replied coolly: "I don't understand your sympathy for Adler. For a Jew boy out of a Viennese suburb, a death in Aberdeen is an unheard-of career in itself and a proof of how far he had got on."

Freud's derisive phrasing has invited a good deal of critical comment. Ellenberger, the historian of psychology we have encountered before in connection with the Anna O. case, waxed indignant: "Could Freud have forgotten that he himself had been a 'Jew boy out of a Viennese suburb?'". To which Dr. Eissler has answered, reasonably enough, that unlike Adler, Freud had not forgotten his Judaism: it was Adler, after all, who had converted to Protestanism, not Freud. Moreover, to be precise, Freud had neither been born, nor ever lived, in a suburb of Vienna. But what matters is the translation of the term "Judenbube." To make it, as Ernest Jones does in his biography, "Jew boy," is to give it a racist resonance it does not have in the original. Freud's comment--"For a Jewish boy out of a Viennese suburb"--is derisive and unfeeling enough without being burdened by a mistranslation (innocently offered by his admirer Jones, and tendentiously taken up by Freud's denigrators).

Here is the final instance, less grave, doubtless, but no less instructive. At the psychoanalytic Congress at Weimar, held in 1911, the participants posed for the usual group photograph and, as usual, the ladies sat and the gentlemen stood. Freud stands near the center, not far from Jung. Paul Roazen, a prolific biographer of Freud and his followers, the kind of admirer of Freud that makes denigrators redundant, has paid particular attention to this photograph, and commented: "Jung can be seen crouching forward next to Freud. Mounted on a box, the master stands out as the leader of his group." There may have been a box under Freud's feet or not; it is far more likely, as Eissler rightly notes, that the photographer asked the very tall Jung to stoop a little that the analyst behind him not be obscured. The innuendo that Freud was too vain to let reality intrude is obvious, but unjust. As Eissler also, again rightly, notes, Freud had himself photographed with Jung, and other taller men, more than once and seems not to have minded. But in such matters, refutation never catches up with the charges: in a recent biography of Freud by J. N. Isbister, we read the same sentence about the box, virtually in

Roazen's language, without even a footnote to identify the source. Improbable myth has become definitive fact.

Why this need for what I am calling open season on Freud? Why this passion for finding flaws in Freud, or real vices? Why must his biographers concentrate on seeing him as a giant with feet of clay-- clay all the way up to his neck? This fashion--for it has become a fashion--goes far beyond the debunking mania that hit biographical writings everywhere after 1900, in reaction against the hero-worshiping lives and letters so common in the nineteenth century. Freud seems to invite this sort of treatment. It is worth asking why.

The answer reaches beyond biography, just as the fashion reaches beyond Freud's life to the whole psychoanalytic construction of mind. Some of his most wild-eyed critics started out as awestruck adorers, who, unable to bear the evidence of Freud's imperfections, have visited their disenchantment on him ever since. But this open season on Freud, I repeat, is not just a biographical vagary of a few critics. There can be no doubt that, more than other great figures in the history of Western culture, Freud seems condemned to stand under an obligation to perfection. No one acquainted with the psychopathology of a Newton or a Darwin, a Beethoven or a Schumann, a Keats or a Kafka, would venture to suggest that their neuroses damaged their creations or in any way reduced their stature. In contrast, Freud's failings, real or imagined, have been proffered as conclusive evidence for the bankruptcy of psychoanalysis.

This is precisely the point. It has become commonplace to strike at psychoanalysis by striking at its founder, as though the successful blackening of his character would be the ruin of his work. It is not too hard to see why this should be. Freud is identified more closely with a whole movement in psychology than any other psychologist has ever been with any other psychology. Hence the passion for debunking him is intimately related to Freud's enterprise. After all, he hit humans more smartly, aroused their defenses more drastically, than any other poet or philosopher or scientist. Only Charles Darwin can measure himself with Freud on this score. It was his fate, Freud would say with rather quizzical satisfaction, "to agitate the sleep of mankind." And much of mankind has responded by pulling the covers over its head, muttering curses against the insistent intruder who would wake it. To be sure, we all live in a psychoanalytic universe now; we speak Freud whether we know it or not, talking of repressions or projections, of ambivalence and neurosis, of narcissism and sibling rivalry. But, as Freud rather glumly predicted, this support has been more damaging than outright opposition. Cocktail party psychoanalysis, glib, merely verbal endorsement, has served to soften down, to weaken, to betray Freud's tough-minded message.

But the appeal of the attacks is easy to understand. It is harder to imagine a liar, a plagiarist, a tyrant, discovering truths about the human mind than it is, say, to imagine a philanderer, a narcissist, a voluptuary, a bigot (I am thinking, of course, of Richard Wagner) writing memorable music. Still, the interplay between character and work is never unproblematic. Late in life, when Marie Bonaparte declared Freud to be a mixture of Pasteur and Kant, he demurred, much as he enjoyed the compliment: "Not because I am modest, not at all. I have a high opinion of what I have discovered, but not of myself. Great discoverers are not necessarily great men." Even Columbus had really been an adventurer, a great explorer but not a great man. "So you see that one may find great things without it meaning that one is really great." The debate is really idle, but Freud's point remains a shrewd caution against conflating origins with results. In a discipline as subjective in its materials, as openly autobiographical as Freud's depth psychology, there are bound to be subtle influences of the founder's mind on his creation. Yet the validity of psychoanalytic propositions does not depend on what we discover about their originator. Freud might have been the perfect gentleman and still propagated a fundamentally flawed psychology; he might have been a very catalogue of defects, even of vices, and still be the greatest psychologist who ever lived.

4

I want to conclude with some thoughts on where I now stand. What I have discovered in my reading of Freud? Remember, as I speak to you, that I am still in the midst of my researches, that it is quite possible that new discoveries will complicate, enlarge, or invalidate what I am about to tell you.

What I have to offer you, briefly, is a negative finding (if there is such a thing), two observations, and one conjecture. The negative finding is that there is no material of any sort, at least none that I have come across, to substantiate the charge that Freud had a love affair with his sister-in-law. Hence the picturesque sequence that would make such a scene: Minna Bernays and Freud moving around Ascona in search of an abortionist, will have to be scratched from any future truthful film about Freud.

But, as I think my first observation will show, there is enough interesting material left. Freud was a good hater. There were times when he got angry and could be appeased: there were episodes with Ernest Jones that suggest a certain prudent flexibility on his part. When he was seriously annoyed to find Karl Abraham lending himself and his prestige to the making of a film about psychoanalysis, he was also supple enough not to take the whole affair too seriously. But in general, when Freud got mad, he stayed mad. I have already cited his unfeeling response to news of Adler's death. I can cite other instances; he enjoyed name-calling. Fliess was paranoid. Jung was brutal. Stekel was a swine: ein Schwein. In fact, Freud liked that epithet so much that he used it in English. Stekel, he wrote to Ernest Jones, is a pig.

One good, which is to say, revealing instance of Freud's gift for strong language and real hatred is his relation to Americans. Everyone knows that Freud was anti-American; even the loyal Ernest Jones found himself noting that Freud's sentiments were so extreme and so irrational that they must have had nothing to do with the Americans

14

themselves. He called his stomach complaints his American dyspepsia, thought that as a result of his American visit even his handwriting had deteriorated. Now it is true that the Americans gave Freud a good deal to worry about, most notably, after 1925, their consistent and unbending opposition to lay analysis. Woodrow Wilson, Freud's least favorite politician was, of course, an American, a pious prophet all too typical, he thought, of the hypocritical fanaticism the Americans were only too likely to produce. But while all this is well known, the fact remains that the Americans stuck in Freud's craw even before he ever visited the United States. The Americans, he wrote early in 1909, when he was dissatisified with the financial conditions that G. Stanley Hall was offering him to come to Clark for its conference, the Americans are good only for getting us money, not for costing us money. He liked <u>that</u> formulation enough to repeat it in the the 1920s. The very quality he thought most American, namely exploitativeness, he exhibited in the highest degree--to the Americans. When his American analysand H. W. Frink, whom Freud wanted to take over the leadership of psychoanalysis in the United States, had a psychotic breakdown, Freud treated that not as a personal tragedy but as a typical form of American behavior. "What is the use of Americans if they bring no money?" he wrote to Ernest Jones in September 1924. "They are not good for anything else. My attempt at giving them a chief in the person of Frink which has so sadly miscarried is the last thing I will ever do for them had I to live ... one hundred years." When he said, in a famous observation in his <u>Interpretation of Dreams</u>, that he had always arranged it to have one friend and one enemy, one may take the Americans as one of those enemies.

The second observation has to do with his working habits. It is no mystery, I think, that Freud was obsessive about his schedule. As his son Martin once put it, his mother Martha liked and inculcated promptness with a vigor rare among the lackadaisical Viennese. he could have said the same thing, more strongly about his father. As his friends and acquaintances well knew, he grew impatient, downright worried, when they did not reply to his letters promptly. He once sent a letter to Ferenczi, dismayed at Ferenczi's silence, consisting entirely, between salutation and signature, of three large questions marks. More important: work was a kind of torment to him--a necessary torment. Problems came to him as the grain of sand comes to the oyster: an irritant from which a pearl might or might not grow. But without the irritant, the pearl would never even get started. I mean the term "torment" quite literally, Freud used that language over and over. He is tormented by the mystery of the tragic school, tormented by the problem of Macbeth, tormented by the resemblance of the opening scene in <u>King Lear</u>, the scene of the three caskets in the <u>Merchant of Venice</u>, and the judgment of Paris. He is tormented by the mysteries of female sexuality. It is as though an idea would get him in its grip and let him rest only after he has somehow discharged it. Psychology, he once told Fliess, was his tyrant. This feeling, the need for closure, was more than interest or even fascination. It is a pressure urging for discharge. Work, then, appears as a response to some inner turmoil, perhaps as a defense against guilt and depression.

15

This last, very tentative formulation brings me to the conjecture. It has to do with Freud's sense of guilt. I come back to Freud's statement that I quoted early on in my talk, about the man who, having been the undisputed darling of his mother, had acquired a secure sense of success. I suggested then that this was misleading when we apply it to Freud. And so it is: as some students of Freud have noted before me, Freud has very little to say about mothers. This neglect is particularly blatant in his great case histories. Dora's mother is merely the woman with the housewife psychosis. Little Hans's mother is suspected (not by Freud but by her husband) of being the cause of Hans's phobia, but as the case progresses, she is demoted from her central position. The Rat Man's mother appears very fleetingly as the woman whom he consults before he starts analysis. The Wolf Man's mother has her role to play, but a small one; she is just the woman with whom the all-important Wolf Man's father has intercourse. And Schreber's mother? For all we know, he never had one.

Now it is risky to argue from silence. But there is something to Sherlock Holmes's famous remark that the dog that did not bark in the night may be very significant. It was a father's death that Freud described as the post poignant loss of a man's life. He had not then experienced his mother's death, to be sure. But he seems not even to have considered that that death, too, could be very poignant indeed.

This silence, or perhaps better, this astonishing neglect, is particularly striking in view of Freud's general theory of sexual and aggressive development. Why this failure? While Freud analyzed his relationship to his father thoroughly, exhaustively, he never did the same for his relationship to his mother. There is that famous scene, so significantly misdescribed in a famous letter to Fliess about seeing his mother nudam on the train when he was not quite four, and having his erotic emotions toward matrem awakened. In that same scene, Freud recalled his little brother, eleven months his junior, whose early death he had wished for and greeted with wicked delight.

There is indirect evidence, too, that Freud was anything but secure about his mother's love. In one of his later papers, Freud vividly delineates the stormy sibling rivalry, the unappeasable jealousy that little girls—girls, note, not boys—feel at the regular appearance of new brothers and sisters who, one and all, ruin the monopoly position that the eldest had once enjoyed. The precise instance Freud offers is that of a first-born who at eleven months is presented with a sibling. This specificity is worthy of Freud's Psychopathology of Everyday Life. As I have just noted, it was precisely when Freud was eleven months old that his mother presented him with that hated little brother Julius, the one he wished dead and, in his mind, succeeded in killing. I submit, then, that his obsessive mode of working was in part a stratagem of defense and an act of restitution. He did not just wish to show his father (as he himself had put it) that he would amount to something after all. He also wished to show his mother that he was, after all, worthy of her unstinted and undivided love.

16

This is where I am now. I find it fascinating work, and will continue to find it fascinating even if I have to modify some of my conclusions. This is the main reason why I am devoting all the hours at my disposal to the writing of this biography. It helps that there should be sufficient new and sufficiently important material to enrich and complicate my sense of what Freud really was. But beyond this, I am enjoying myself as I have not enjoyed myself before. And until I am done I can say, with Flaubert, <u>Sigmund Freud, c'est moi!</u>

Yale University
November 1986

17

Selected Papers From the 1986 Annual Meeting

Allied Psychological Interpretations
of Germans and Nazis
During and After World War II*

Louise E. Hoffman

If the "German Question" attracted much attention in the West
during and after the First World War, it became a matter of obsessive
interest during and after the Second. For no one was the issue more
important than for psychologists, psychiatrists, and psychoanalysts,
who were refining and extending their disciplines and attempting to
establish their authority beyond the clinic and the laboratory in
social and political arenas and in the interpretation of history and
culture. In the United States and, to a lesser extent, in Great
Britain, many of them entered wartime military and governmental
agencies responsible for intelligence-gathering and analysis and for
post-war planning. Thus, academic and clinical behavioral scientists
largely displaced the military officers who had offered amateur
psychological appreciations of the defeated enemy after the Great War.[1]

The theories and methods brought to bear by these later
investigators were more varied than before, and in some respects more
sophisticated. Like their predecessors, though, the behavioral experts
of the Second World War era often expressed extra-scientific attitudes
in their analysis of Germans and Nazis. However, unlike the obscure
military attachés of the early 1920s, they influenced the subsequent
trend of psychohistorical discussion of Nazism and German history:
their war-time research found its way into peace-time publication, and
they returned to academic and professional positions from which many of
them continued and extended such research. The collaboration within
wartime agencies of specialists in various disciplines and schools
fostered interdisciplinary research, a trend that continued in the
post-war era. Psychohistory was but one of the beneficiaries of
wartime psychological research.

This discussion is concerned with two categories of wartime
psychological studies on Germany and National Socialism: first,
background reports, often speculative, written for the Office of
Strategic Studies (OSS) and other agencies, generally during the first
half of the war; and second, assessments of prisoners of war and other
groups of Germans, conducted primarily by military psychiatrists late
in the war and immediately thereafter. Justified in the short run by
policy needs of wartime and occupation authorities, these works
generally also express professional interests intended for the longer
term. In them, psychoanalytic concepts and empirical survey techniques
found innovative applications. Yet often they also reveal the older
idea of national character, a perspective which (despite refinements)
tended to perpetuate a view of German history and society as inherently
pathological.

One notable difference in the background of wartime psychology in the 1940s, as compared with the era of the First World War, is the arrival of Continental theories--and their practitioners--in Great Britain and the United States. For example, Gustav Marc Gilbert, later prison psychologist at Nuremburg, had written his dissertation at Columbia University on Gestalt approaches to the psychology of perception.[2] Central European psychoanalysts, of course, had emigrated en masse, often to the U.S. or Great Britain; they and other intellectual refugees often brought with them direct experience of Nazism, as Bruno Bettelheim did.[3]

Another change was due to the growth in the social and behavioral sciences during the inter-war period. Their practitioners were more able to participate in the war effort in the 1940s than they had been during the Great War, and they had greater ambitions. The U.S. mobilization of 1916-1918 was considerable for its time, but behavioral scientists then concentrated almost entirely on implementing psychological testing programs for the Army.[4] By the Second World War, though, leading psychiatrists and behavioral scientists in the U.S. envisioned much broader efforts to add psychological understanding to a wide range of official activities and policies. Working again through the National Research Council, American psychologists established an Emergency Committee in Psychology and a Subcommittee on Survey and Planning for Psychology, chaired by Robert Yerkes, which reported that, "It seems probably that the present conflict will do for social psychology ... what the first World War did for intelligence testing."[5]

One outward and visible demonstration of these changes is the development of the OSS, its Psychology Division, and the work of the scholars connected with it. From Colonel (later General) William Donovan's office of Coordinator of Information (COI) emerged the OSS, whose advent reflected the previous decline of U.S. military intelligence.[6] Donovan valued specialized expertise and, as is well-known, his agency became a haven for academic experts.[7] He was willing, even eager, to try innovative approaches in pursuing his goal of a unified intelligence service. He set out to recruit the best talent, including Harvard historian William L. Langer as head of the OSS Research and Analysis Branch. Later, as President of the American Historical Association in 1957, Langer called for historians to undertake psychoanalytic study of the past;[8] and his psychoanalyst brother Walter Langer wrote the wartime analysis of Hitler later published as The Mind of Adolf Hitler, and discussed below.[9] Although Donovan's Board of Analysts, who were his main talent scouts in 1941, included no psychologists, it did include William Langer; and by the autumn of 1941, Donovan had created a Psychology Division for the OSS, along with divisions in economics and geography, to supplement the research efforts of the regional staffs working at the Library of Congress.[10]

The Psychology Division's original mandate was very broad: "to collect and correlate all available data pertinent to psychological factors operative in the national and international scene." By early 1942, however, its focus had shifted from domestic to foreign topics.[11]

Much of its work was psychological only in a very broad sense, providing socio-cultural background for agencies concerned with morale and psychological warfare.[12] Its projected Abnormal and Clinical Section never materialized; the staff included only social psychologists, no clinical psychologists or psychoanalysts.[13] Despite these limitations, the Division's chief, psychologist Robert C. Tryon of the University of California, proposed a project similar to one attempted by the Army's Military Intelligence Division (MID) twenty years earlier: a systematic social-psychological study of belligerent nations, particularly the Axis powers.[14] Staff psychologists outlined a general framework for such analyses; Tryon forwarded it to his superiors in January of 1942, arguing that psychological understanding of social and historical experiences, common patterns of child-rearing and personality development--in short, the elements of what we now call psychohistory--would be important in conducting morale research and other practical wartime projects. He likened the approach to comparative national psychology, and accordingly suggested as a consultant Geoffrey Gorer of Yale's Institute of Human Relations, a specialist in national character studies; and he secured the agreement of Harvard social psychologist Gordon Allport to coordinate research assistance among civilian scholars.[15]

The short-term aims of Tryon's plan resembled those of the MID: to provide analysis of practical use in evaluating intelligence data and formulating military or governmental policy. Unlike the MID's staff of the 1920s, however, Tryon had longer-term scholarly interests in mind as well, including the encouragement of interdisciplinary collaboration. Ultimately his plan, like the MID's, was abandoned; the Psychology Division's staff was never large enough to support such a grandiose undertaking, and more immediate wartime needs intervened. The Division nonetheless did sponsor some studies of both collective national psychology and the psychodynamics of hostile leaders, especially Germans. The most interesting of these were written by external consultants--scholars such as Walter Langer who were unwilling to abandon their civilian careers, or who were refugee aliens, such as Erik Erikson.

At Donovan's request, Erikson wrote an evaluation of German and Nazi mentality which furnished material and ideas for his early published works in psychohistory.[16] He set out to apply recent approaches in ego and social psychology and psychoanalytic cultural anthropology to the problems of understanding Nazism's appeal to Germans and, eventually, of reorienting German attitudes after the war. The result is an amalgam of national character concepts refined by psychoanalysis, social behavior linked with the psychobiography of Hitler. National character, Erikson maintained, did indeed exist, but not as an absolute entity; instead, it derived from specific historical and geographic experiences, which were transmitted through child-rearing practices. In particular, Nazism's success depended on the crises in German culture after the Great War, on the Party's ability to generate attitudes and symbols responsive to the crisis, and especially on the concrete embodiment of widespread anxieties and desires in one person, "in the case history and in the myth of Adolph [sic] Hitler."[17] Nazi insistence on pursuit of Lebensraum exemplified

23

"a collective reaction to the nation's ... geopolitical situation," which, despite some historical justification, had "an essentially magic meaning" and gave rise to "irrational mental attitudes which do not easily yield to reorientation." Far from revealing inherent strength, Erikson said, these aggressive policies betrayed "a morbid suggestibility and a deep insecurity," which in turn sought "undoing" and repression in aggressive warfare.[18]

Notwithstanding his disavowal of "the belief in German's uniqueness," though, Erikson did reiterate earlier stereotypes when he identified two sorts of Germans predominating in twentieth century political life: adherents of "a hysterical kind of cosmopolitanism," and their opponents, the narrowest nationalists. The former was "a voluntary exile, a potential suicide or psychotic;" the latter, "sadistic rather than masochistic," and militaristic and arrogant. Both types were politically immature, and when "the few statesmen capable of dignity, realism, and vision, broke under the strain or were murdered," Germans "began to listen to Hitler's imagery which, for the first time in Reichs-German history, corresponded to what is most genuinely German in every German."[19] This argument bears an uncomfortable resemblance to the old dualistic stereotype of Germans as either good (humane, cosmopolitan) or bad (militaristic, overbearing). It serves a heuristic purpose, however, in linking the psychic mechanisms of leader and followers, a goal of many interpreters of Nazism during the 1930s and 1940s.[20]

Erikson devoted most of his paper to analyzing Hitler's imagery, its biographical sources, and its emotional appeal to Germans. Like many observers of the time, he relied almost entirely on Mein Kampf for primary evidence of Hitler's personality, although he recognized the pitfalls of this procedure. Mein Kampf, he said, is an Oedipal fairy tale: on both the familial and the political levels, "the beloved mother betrays the longing son for an unworthy, senile tyrant," and the son retaliates through unceasing rebellion against adult authority. The legend's wide appeal means that the author "primarily reveals the German national character, himself only incidentally," It derives from recent German social experiences in which fathers often expressed their psychic insecurity in sadistically harsh behavior, adolescents were cut off from the traditional escape of Wanderschaft, and growing up meant guilty capitulation to paternal values. Hitler offered an alternate identity: the "adolescent who never gave in."[21]

Erikson employed his psychohistorical analysis of Germans and Nazis to suggest particular propaganda strategies for reinforcing psychically mature--i.e. democratic--attitudes among Germans during and after the war.[22] Whether those responsible for U.S. psychological warfare ever knew of his study, much less found it useful, is questionable. Stripped of some of its more egregious stereotypes, though, it did lead directly to Erikson's published work on Hitler and the Germans and exemplified his emerging emphasis on social identity, which has found extensive application in psychohistorical literature.[23]

Whatever the merits of Erikson's interpretation, his prediction of Hitler's fate proved faulty. "Some day," he forecast, "it may be his worst fate and punishment that with all his hysterical gifts he cannot become insane or commit suicide when it would be most appropriate to do so. For the shrewd exploitation of one's own hysteria has its limits."[24] A more accurate psychobiographical prognosticator was Walter C. Langer, who undertook a much more extensive and systematic study of Hitler, also as a consultant employed directly by Donovan.[25]

Like the Psychology Division staff, Langer initially investigated domestic issues (especially the morale of young men and their probably response to a military draft), and shifted to overseas subjects only in 1942. Like Robert Tryon, he began with an ambitious plan: to establish "a Psychoanalytic Field Unit at Cambridge, Massachusetts," which would "draw on the talents of many experienced psychoanalysts" in order to conduct "exploration of pertinent problems." But the Bureau of the Budget refused to fund what must have appeared to be a duplicate of the Psychology Division, so Langer conducted his work on a reduced scale as a consultant.[26]

In 1943, Donovan asked Walter Langer to provide a psychological profile of Hitler, in order to guide Allied leaders and propagandists and to attempt some prediction of his likely future behavior.[27] One of Langer's original collaborators was Harvard psychologist Henry A. Murray, who as director of the OSS Assessment School established criteria for evaluating and predicting candidates' character traits and likely responses to stress.[28] The principal innovation of Langer's study was its attempt to improve the reliability of its analysis by carrying out a comprehensive survey of available sources on Hitler and conducting interviews with people who had come into contact with him. The effort was necessarily flawed, as Robert Waite and Hans Gatzke have pointed out;[29] but it was probably the most systematic of its time.

As might be expected of a practicing psychoanalyst, Langer took a diagnostic approach to his subject, and so, despite his expanded data base, his portrait of Hitler continues in the tradition of psychopathological studies in biography already established before the war, and still evident today.[30] He acknowledged that diagnosis was inadequate, for both intellectual and military purposes, but offered only the sketchiest explanation of Hitler's influence: "It was not only Hitler, the madman, who created German madness, but German madness that created Hitler." The madness was not uniquely German, as Nazism expressed "a state of mind existing ... not only in Germany, but to a smaller degree in all civilized countries." Unlike Erikson, Langer did not provide a historical context for his analysis. He did suggest future psychoanalytic study of influential leaders to supplement investigations of social groups and their dynamics, since in the leaders "we can expect to find the pertinent factors in an exaggerated form. . . . "[31] As Langer's study remained classified long after the war, and as Langer himself did not pursue psychohistorical research, his report on Hitler had no such immediate sequels as did Erikson's; yet it did eventually contribute to Robert G. L. Waite's explanations of Hitler's career.[32]

In addition to the works already mentioned, Donovan indirectly brought about another psychoanalytic study of Nazism, written late in the war for the Office of War Information (OWI). Originally part of Donovan's COI, OWI became the domestic twin of OSS. Although it lacked a psychological unit and did not adopt any systematic psychological approach to its task, it did employ some psychoanalytically-oriented researchers. Its Experimental Division for the Study of War Time Communications, which collected German press materials and radio intercepts, was headed by Harold D. Lasswell--a noted political scientist whose own work was psychoanalytically informed and who had published a pioneering article on the psychology of Nazism.[33] The study in question was written by Paul Kecskemeti and Nathan Leites and, since it was not classified, soon found its way into a scholarly journal.[34]

Their central hypothesis was that, "a distinctive type of character structure in the Nazi variant of German culture approximates ... the 'compulsive character' of psychoanalytic theory."[35] This personality type strongly resembled the "anal character" type that Freud had defined decades earlier.[36] Freud conceived of character types as constellations of traits derived from similar experiences;[37] the concepts had proved useful since the 1920s to ego and social psychologists seeking to integrate Freud's original libido psychology, which emphasized the childhood origins of inherent drives, with their interest in adult experience and the effects of social structure and historical experience on the personalities of individuals and groups.[38] In Escape from Freedom, published the preceding year, Erich Fromm had associated Nazism with sado-masochistic character traits and explained the emergence of this personality type as a reaction against modernity in all of Western culture and a particular product of German history from Luther onward.[39]

Kecskemeti's and Leites's discussion, though, is essentially static, ostensibly concerned only with the "Nazi variant of German culture" under the Hitler regime. This character structure they found "more widely diffused among lower middle class persons than among persons higher up or lower down in the class system," and typical also of Protestant, urban males who had been adolescents during the Weimar era.[40] Interpreting Nazism as a petty bourgeois phenomenon, they echoed writers (such as Fromm and Wilhelm Reich) who combined psychoanalytic and Marxist perspectives and emphasized the psychic impact of economic Deklassierung among Germans affected by inter-war inflation and depression.[41] At the same time, they unintentionally gave new form to an earlier stereotype about Germans: their argument consists mainly of describing dualistic qualities, such as conformist behavior masking repressed rebellion. Explaining these qualities as products of especially strong ambivalence, they produced an updated version of the old view of German "national character," according to which Germans are bifurcated beings incapable of moderation.[42]

While the war continued, research on Germany was often speculative, as opportunities for direct empirical or clinical study were rare. An exception to this rule was provided by the armed services: psychological or psychiatric survey and assessment of prisoners of war. Military psychiatrists in the First World War had engaged mainly in treating casualties, and psychologists in testing personnel; by the 1940s at least some of them were evaluating captured enemies. The most spectacular such case from the early war years was Rudolf Hess, who flew almost literally into the arms of the British Army, which provided him with a host of physicians and psychiatrists to enliven his captivity.[43]

Hess's case was controversial but unproductive of larger understanding. The more important work was less newsworthy: administration of questionnaires and psychiatric interviews to large groups of ordinary prisoners of war. Such methods provided results that were quantifiable, a result much desired by empirically-oriented American researchers.[44] Although primitive by later standards, these questionnaires nonetheless allowed investigators to gauge the frequency, depth, and distribution of particular attitudes, and to correlate them with basic demographic data (such as age and occupation) and environmental circumstances (such as the war situation at the time).

One such study commenced in late 1943 in Italy and continued in Great Britain and France after D-Day. Initiated by the Psychological Warfare Branch of the U.S. Fifth Army, it was extended by the Psychological Warfare Division of SHAEF (Supreme Headquarters, Allied Expeditionary Force) with some staff from OWI's Overseas Branch, including psychologists Jerome Bruner, Donald McGranahan (previously of the OSS Psychology Division), Morris Janowitz, and Heinz L. Ansbacher, who published the results.[45] This and similar studies were intended not only to help propaganda intelligence officers undermine enemy morale, but also to prepare the way for remodeling German collective psychology after the war. Psychological understanding of widespread social attitudes in their historical context was to assist Allied authorities project and control future events, and thereby transform German history.

Not only POWs were subject to these studies. In schemes to reshape Germany for the future, young people were of course a special concern; they were the focus, for example, of another questionnaire survey conducted in western Germany after V-E Day by Donald McGranahan and Morris Janowitz with the Intelligence Section of the Information Control Division of USAFET (U.S. Armed Forces, European Theater).[46] The British psychoanalyst Roger Ernle Money-Kyrle, working for the German Personnel Branch of the Allied Control Commission in 1946, pursued a more general investigation of the "German problem," its roots and possible solution, while assessing individual Germans under consideration for high positions in the new west German domestic administration.[47]

The most notable British scholar involved in this research was psychiatrist Henry V. Dicks, a wartime Lieutenant Colonel in the Royal Army Medical Corps who organized or supervised a great many studies, including the one just mentioned, on behalf of the Intelligence Section of the British Psychological Warfare Directorate. Pursuing the same general aims as their American counterparts, Dicks and his colleagues relied less on quantitative techniques such as opinion sampling,[48] preferring systematic psychiatric interrogation. He combined the methods of clinical psychoanalysis, statistical evaluation, and social

27

anthropology which, he said, "have gradually converged to enable us to attack the problem of 'national character' with methods which are slowly approaching the canons of [a] science."[49]

Out of the range of possibilities, Dicks argued, each society selects some to foster. "From the process of institutionalized moulding by the social forces acting upon the children of a given community there results a basic personality."[50] The German personality he described includes elements of both the compulsive and the sado-masochistic characters identified by earlier writers: "Our typical German is earnest, industrious, meticulous, over-respectful to authority, docile and kowtowing, tense and over-polite, but a little martinet and unpleasantly ferocious in his dealings with those he can dominate." He is prone to "rigidity of outlook, ... nationalist arrogance and self-adulation especially when in the mass, and ... jealous accusations of all his neighbours of evil designs against his innocent nation..." According to Dicks, the "emotional anarchy" of the Weimar era destroyed what little interest in democracy Germans had developed--and yet "there are reasonable Germans."[51]

The pejorative terminology aside, Dick's discussion presents another application of the social character concept. But he parted company with most of his predecessors, attributing the pattern of "psychological compensations and reactions of Germans" to the "prevalent educational patterns of their élite and of those who aped that élite," rather than to the frustrations of the lower middle classes. And, unlike the theorists of petit-bourgeois facism, he offered no explanation of its socio-economic or historical roots, except for a vague and tautological suggestion.[52] Arguing that "no significant proportion of fanatical Nazis was found to be suffering from gross mental disability in the clinical sense," Dicks concluded that, "we are dealing with a group problem, not with an individual disease."[53] As he struggled to comprehend that problem, he oscillated among a variety of interpretations: Fromm's, Erikson's, and, in his post-war articles derived from the POW project, a classification scheme markedly similar to the famous "F" scale of Adorno's Authoritarian Personality.[54]

Dicks did introduce one new element into the ongoing discussion, albeit quietly. Virtually alone among writers on psychosocial or psychohistorical topics during this period, he made reference to the theories of Melanie Klein, especially her belief that emotional deprivations in infancy could produce psychically crippled adults.[55] Twenty more years would pass before psychohistorians began to assimilate the ideas of Klein and the British school on object-relations.[56] Dicks himself continued to wrestle with the origins of Nazi ideology and mass murder. Interviews with imprisoned SS men reinforced his conviction that, "If there is clinically recognizable 'insanity,' it is to be sought in the unchecked proliferation of this megalomanic fantasy system translated by the Party's ruling elite into a policy of state." How, then, to proceed? In general, he recommended that investigators "no longer falsely separate the intrapersonal and the group aspects if we aim to construct realistic models of social behaviour and process." More specifically, he proposed examination of "the latent capacities of 'ordinary' men to harbour and, under given conditions to activate, <u>murderousness</u>, and--when the given conditions have ceased to operate--to return to inconspicuous, 'ordinarily' law-abiding reasonable existence."[59] Psychiatrists and psychologists ignorant of the political and historical context of the subject could only misuse psychopathological diagnoses and obscure the issue.

World War II, then, provided great impetus to social psychology, psychohistory, and interdisciplinary social science research. The "German question" was urgent and enduring and attracted investigators of diverse orientations, many of whom pursued or inspired continuing psychological interpretations after the war. Geoffrey Gorer, speaking in 1947, lauded these researchers for having been "willing to risk their scientific reputations in an attempt to give an objective description of the characters of our enemies...."[58] In fact, while some of these studies earned considerable criticism, many scholars established or enhanced their reputations, benefitting from official sponsorship of their research, from wartime collaboration with specialists in other disciplines, and from contacts made during government service. They helped to shift the focus of psychohistorical interest from biography to collective processes. Their work was committed rather than objective, but remains important for understanding the history of psychological and psychohistorical thought.

Pennsylvania State University
at Harrisburg
November 1986

Notes

*I am indebted to Professor Joseph Bendersky of Virginia Commonwealth University, who first proposed the project which yielded this paper; to archivists John Taylor of the Miliary Reference Division, National Archives and Records Administration, whose expertise was invaluable in locating many of the necessary documents, and John Slonaker of the U.S. Army Military History Institute, Carlisle Barracks, Pennsylvania; and to James Capshew, historian at NASA's Goddard Space Flight Center, for conveying some of his extensive knowledge of the American psychological profession during World War II.

[1]Joseph W. Bendersky, "Psychohistory before Hitler: U.S. Military Psychological Reports on Germany after World War I," paper delivered at the Southern Historical Association annual meeting, Charlotte, N.C., November 1986.

[2]G. M. Gilbert, <u>Dynamic Psychophysics and the Phi Phenomenon</u> (New York: Archives of Psychology #237, 1939).

[3]Bruno Bettelheim, "Individual and Mass Behavior in Extreme Situations," Journal of Abnormal and Social Psychology 38 (1943): 417-51, derives from Bettelheim's own experiences in a Nazi concentration camp during the 1930s.

[4]Robert M. Yerkes, "Psychology in Relation to the War," Psychological Review 25 (1918): 85-115. This was Yerkes's presidential address to the American Psychological Association, delivered while he was still a Major in the Army Sanitary Corps, Ernest R. Hilgard, ed., American Psychology in Historical Perspective (Washington, D.C.: American Psychological Association, 1978), 165-66.

[5]Edwin G. Boring et al., "First Report of the Subcommittee on Survey and Planning for Psychology," Psychological Bulletin 39 (1942): 620. Karl M. Dallenbach surveys the range of this body's activites in "The Emergency Committee in Psychology, National Research Council," American Journal of Psychology 59 (1946): 496-582. See also Steuart Henderson Britt (wartime editor of the Psychological Bulletin's section on "Psychology and the War") and Jane D. Morgan, "Military Psychologists in World War II," American Psychologist 1 (1946): 423-37; and Walter S. Hunter (wartime chief of Applied Psychology, National Defense Research Council, "Psychology in the War," American Psychologist 1 (1946): 479-92.

[6]Bruce Woodward Bidwell, History of the Military Intelligence Division, Department of the Army General Staff, Part III: Peacetime Problems (1919 - 7 Dec. 1941), Department of the Army, 1959-1961; and Capt. P. M. Robinett, "Military Intelligence Organization," World War I to Sept. 1937, U.S. Army, General Staff, G-2, 1938; both in the archives of the U.S. Army Military History Institute, Carlisle Barracks, Pennsylvania. Corey Ford, Donovan of OSS (Boston: Little, Brown, 1970), 129-30.

[7]U.S. War Department, Strategic Services Unit, History Project, chief historian Kermit Roosevelt, War Report of the OSS (New York: Walker, 1976), 1: 48-50.

[8]William L. Langer, "The Next Assignment," American Historical Review 63 (1958): 283-304. Langer's own scholarship was and remained impeccably orthodox. For an investigation of "the problem--why did this conservative diplomatic historian advocate psychoanalytic research among historians?" see Peter Loewenberg, "The Psychobiographical Background to Psychohistory: The Langer Family and the Dynamics of Shame and Success," Decoding the Past: The Psychohistorical Approach (New York: Knopf, 1983), 81-95.

[9]Walter C. Langer, The Mind of Adolf Hitler: The Secret Wartime Report (New York: Basic Books, 1972).

[10]War Report of the OSS I: 50, 205. Office of Strategic Services, Research and Analysis Branch, Psychology Division: 3 boxes, Record Group 226, Military Reference Dvision, U.S. National Archives (hereafer OSS PD). Staff pscyhologists in the Division over the next two years included E. Y. Hartshorne, in charge of Central European Studies; C. M. Louttit; Donald V. MCGranahan; and about a dozen others, mostly recruited from major universities. Because of their access to classified material, only U.S. citizens could be hired, although others (including émigré resident aliens) could serve as consultants.

[11]OSS PD: "The Psychology Division," memorandum, unsigned, undated: Box I, folder 42; and Carleton Scofield, letter to Donald P. Marquis, 13 Sept. 1942: Box I, Sept. 1942 correspondence folder.

[12]OSS PD: Robert C. Tryon, memorandum to William L. Langer, 5 Nov. 1941: Box I, folder 42.

[13]OSS PD: "Statement of Functions of the Psychology Division," unsigned, 7 Oct. 1941: Box I, folder 42; and Carleton Scofield, memorandum to Paul Hurlbut, 7 Oct. 1942, pp. 1-2: Box I, Oct. 1942 correspondence folder.

[14]Bendersky, "Psychohistory before Hitler," passim.

[15]OSS PD: Robert C. Tryon, memoranda to James Baxter of 7, 10, and 16 Jan. 1942, and Buford H. Junker et al., "Social and Psychological Analysis of a Nation," 30 page typescript: both in Box I, folder 42. Tryon, memorandum to Baxter, 24 Jan. 1942, p. 5: Box, I, folder 43.

[16]Erik H. Erikson, "On Nazi Mentality," 31 page undated typescript (1941 or early 1942), forwarded with cover memorandum from Nelson Poynter to Robert Tryon, 7 July 1942: OSS PD, Box 1, July 1942 correspondence folder.

[17]Ibid., 1.

[18]Ibid., 3-4.

[19]Ibid., 4-6.

[20]On this literature, see Louise E. Hoffman, "Psychoanalytic Interpretations of Adolf Hitler and Nazism, 1933-1945: A Prelude to Psychohistory," Psychohistory Review 11 (1982): 73-78.

[21]Erikson, "On Nazi Mentality," 1, 6, 8, 10-13.

[22]Ibid., 30-31.

[23]Erikson, "Hitler's imagery and German Youth," Psychiatry 5 (1942): 475-93; "Ego Development and Historical Change," The Psychoanalytic Study of the Child 2 (1946): 359-96; and Childhood and Society (New York: Norton, 1950).

[24]Erikson, "On Nazi Mentality," 6-7.

[25]In this instance, the initiative came from Walter Langer, who proposed to Donovan that psychoanalysis could provide understanding of "the unconscious and irrational forces which were far more potent" than conscious ones in psychological-warfare campaigns. William Langer apparently had no direct role in the project at first, although his position in the office of Coordinator of Information, soon to become the OSS, could have eased his brother's reception by Donovan at a time when many proposals and offers of assistance were arriving from both real and self-styled experts. Walter Langer, Introduction to The Mind of Adolf Hitler, 14.

[26]Ibid., 17-18. Apparently someone at OSS found a way to evade the Budget Bureau's decision, as the Psychology Division's quarterly summary of its "Budget Situation" for the period ending 31 March 1942 noted that $17,000 officially allocated to the Division was not available to it, but was earmarked for the "Psychoanalytic Section"-- presumably Langer's project. OSS PD: Box III, folder 81.

[27]Walter Langer, Introduction to The Mind of Adolf Hitler, 19.

[28]Corey Ford, Donovan of OSS, 132. Before withdrawing from the project, Murray submitted a report entitled "An Analysis of the Personality of Adolph [sic] Hitler, with predictions of His Future Behavior and Suggestions for Dealing with Him Now and after Germany's Surrender."

[29]Robert G. L. Waite, Afterword to Langer, The Mind of Adolf Hitler, 232-37. Hans W. Gatzke, "Hitler and Psychohistory," American Historical Review 78 (1973): 394-401. See also responses by William L. Langer, Walter C. Langer, Waite, and Geoffrey Cocks, with Gatzke's rejoinder, in American Historical Review 78 (1973): 1155-63.

[30]Louise E. Hoffman, "Early Psychobiography, 1900-1930: Some Reconsiderations," Biography 7 (1984): 342-43.

[31]Walter C. Langer, The Mind of Adolf Hitler, 144-45. This view closely parallels Freud's description of the psychic functions of leaders in Group Psychology and the Analysis of the Ego (1921), in Standard Edition of the Complete Psychological Works of Sigmund Freud (hereafter cited as SE), ed. James Strachey (London: Hogarth, 1953-1966) 18: 129-30.

[32]Waite, "Adolf Hitler's Guilt Feelings: A Problem in History and Psychology," Journal of Interdisciplinary History 1 (1971): 229-49; "Adolf Hitler's Anti-Semitism: A Study in History and Psychoanalysis," in The Psychoanalytic Interpretation of History, ed. Benjamin B. Wolman (New York, 1971), 203-29; The Psychopathic God: Adolf Hitler (New York: Basic Books, 1977); and Afterword to Walter C. Langer, The Mind of Adolf Hitler, 223, 228-32.

[33]Harold D. Lasswell, "The Psychology of Hitlerism," Political Quarterly 4 (1933): 373-84; Psychopathology and Politics (Chicago: University of Chicago Press, 1930); World Politics and Personal Insecurity (1935; rpt. New York: Free Press, 1965); and, unusual for its time and forum, "The Influence of Prosperity and Depression upon Social Thought," a paper applying Freudian ego psychology to explain recent economic experience and presented to the American Historical Association in December 1933 (The Editors, "Urbana Meeting," American Historical Review 39 [1934]: 424-25).

[34]P[aul] Kecskemeti and N[athan] Leites, Some Psychological Hypotheses on Nazi Germany (Washington, D.C.: Experimental Division for the Study of War Time Communications, Document No. 60, 1945); a revised version was published under the same title in the Journal of Social Psychology 28 (1948): 141-66.

[35]Kecskemeti and Leites, Some Psychological Hypotheses, 1.

[36]Sigmund Freud, "Character and Anal Erotism" (1908), SE 9: 167-75.

[37]Freud, "Some Character Types Met With in Psycho-Analytic Work (Those Wrecked by Success)" (1915), in Collected Papers (London: Hogarth Press, 1949): 318-46.

[38]Two important early theorists of character analysis were Wilhelm Reich and Erich Fromm, both of whom drew on Marxian as well as Freudian theory in their work. Reich, Der triebhafte Charakter (Vienna: International Psychoanalytischer Verlag, 1925), and Charakteranalyse: Technik und Grundlagen für studierende und praktizierende Analytiker (Vienna: Verlag für Sexualpolitik, 1933); and Fromm, "Die psychoanalytische Charakterologie und ihre Bedeutung für die Sozialpsychologie," Zeitschrift für Sozialforschung 1 (1932): 253-77.

[39]Fromm, Escape from Freedom (New York: Holt, Rinehart and Winston, 1941), Chapter 6. See also his methodological appendix on "Character and the Social Process," 304-27. Fromm had been recommended as a consultant to the OSS Psychology Division by E. Y. Hartshorne, the Division's Central European specialist, who considered Escape From Freedom "about the best thing done by anybody on Nazi psychology." There is, however, no record of Fromm's having served in that capacity. OSS PD: Hartshorne, letter to Robert C. McKay, 1 Sept. 1941: Box 1, folder 42.

[40]Kecskemeti and Leites, Some Psychological Hypotheses, 3.

[41]Lasswell expressed such a view in "The Psychology of Hitlerism," as did Fromm in Escape from Freedom. See also Wilhelm Reich, Massenpsychologie des Faschismus; Zur Sexualökonomie der politischen Reaktion und zur proletarischen Sexualpolitik, 2d ed. (Copenhagen: Verlag für Sexualpolitik, 1933); Frederick L. Schuman, The Nazi Dictatorship: A Study in Sexual Pathology and the Politics of Facisim

(New York: Knopf, 1935); and the Frankfurt School's collective Studien über Autorität und Familie (Paris: F. Alcan, 1936). Only decades later has this explanation been effectively challenged: see especially Richard F. Hamilton, Who Voted for Hitler? (Princeton: Princeton University Press, 1982), and Peter H. Merkl, Political Violence under the Swastika: 581 Early Nazis (Princeton: Princeton University Press, 1975), especially Part One.

[42]See psychoanalyst Henry Lowenfeld's critical review of Kecskemeti and Leites in Psychoanalytic Quarterly 16 (1947): 256-58.

[43]John Rawlings Rees, ed., The Case of Rudolf Hess: A Problem in Diagnosis and Forensic Psychiatry (New York: Norton, 1948).

[44]Donald G. Marquis describes American psychologists' eagerness to apply their empirical techniques in "Social Psychologists in National War Agencies," Psychological Bulletin 41 (1944): 115.

[45]H. L. Ansbacher, "Attitudes of German Prisoners of War: A Study of the Dynamics of National-Socialistic Followership," Psychological Monographs 61 (1948): 1-42.

[46]Donald V. McGranahan and Morris Janowitz, "Studies of German Youth," Journal of Abnormal and Social Psychology 41 (1946): 3-14.

[47]R. Money-Kyrle, "Some Aspects of State and Character in Germany," in Psychoanalysis and Culture: Essays in Honor of Géza Róheim, ed. G. B. Wilbur and W. Muensterberger (New York: International Universities Press, 1951), 280-93. He had already established his interest in psychobiography and political psychology before the war, and continued in the latter vein after it: "A Psycho-Analytic study of the Voices of Joan of Arc," British Journal of Medical Psychology 13 (1933): 63-81; "The Development of War: A Psychological Approach," ibid. 16 (1937): 219-16; and Psychoanalysis and Politics: A Contribution to the Psychology of Politics and Morals (London: Duckworth, 1951).

[48]H. V. Dicks, "National Socialism as a Psychological Problem," Directorate of Army Psychiatry, Research Memorandum 45/03/12 (London: War Office, Jan. 1945): National Archives, Military Reference Division, Record Group 226, Document 112809.

[49]H. V. Dicks, "Some Psychological Studies of the German Character," in Psychological Factors of Peace and War, ed. T. H. Pear (New York: Philosophical Library, 1950), 195-96. See also his "Personality Traits and National Socialist Ideology," Human Relations 3 (1950): 111-54.

[50]Dicks, "Some Psychological Studies," p. 197; emphasis in original.

[51]Ibid., 199.

[52]Ibid., 204, 215-16.

[53]Dicks, "National Socialism as a Psychological Problem," 2.

[54]Dicks, "Some Psychological Studies," 211-12; "Personality Traits," 118-21, 140. T. W. Adorno, Else Frenkel-Brunswik, et al., The Authoritarian Personality (New York: Harper and Row, 1949).

[55]Dicks, "Personality Traits," 131, 137, 140-41.

[56]E.g., Peter Loewenberg, "The Unsuccessful Adolescence of Heimrich Himmler," American Historical Review 76 (1971): 612-41; and "The Psychohistorical Origins of the Nazi Youth Cohort," ibid.: 1457-1502. Louise E. Hoffman, "Object-Relations Theory and Psychohistory," Bulletin of the Menninger Clinic 49 (1985): 113-23.

[57]H. V. Dicks, Licensed Mass Murder: A Socio-Psychological Study of Some SS Killers (New York: Basic Books, 1972), 19, 230-31. Dicks was a major participant in the "Tavistock Group," which promoted the integration of personality psychiatry and the social sciences; see his Fifty Years of the Tavistock Clinic (London: Routledge and Kegan Paul, 1970).

[58]Geoffrey Gorer, "The Scientific Study of National Character," 1947, cited in Dicks, "Psychological Studies," 198.

London Quakers and the Business of Abolition:

A Case for Collective Biography

Judith Jennings

The British slave trade was abolished by Act of Parliament in 1807, and historians ever since have been studying abolitionists and their activities. In 1808, Thomas Clarkson attempted to recognize all abolitionists, inside Parliament and out, and remarked repeatedly on the participation of Quakers in the public campaign against the slave trade.[1] Yet despite his efforts, many historians then and since have focused almost exclusively on the parliamentary activities of William Wilberforce and the Evangelicals of the Clapham Sect.[2]

In 1944, Eric Williams challenged the orthodoxy of the Evangelical interpretation by insisting on examining the economic interests of abolitionists.[3] Currently, David Brion Davis is taking another look at abolitionists to understand better "the ideological functions and implications of the British and American anti-slavery movements."[4] Davis has achieved a remarkable synthesis, but he has recognized the need for more detailed and systematic information about individual abolitionists.[5]

A major problem confronting historians from Clarkson to Davis is how to select which abolitionists to study from the literally hundreds involved. One way is to begin at the beginning. According to Thomas Clarkson, the first public association in Great Britain to oppose slavery and the slave trade was formed by a group of six London Friends in July 1783.[6] Davis, too, pointed to the group and the importance of their early activities.[7]

Who were these men and what brought them together in 1783? How did their common Quaker beliefs relate to their commitment to abolition? What did they do for a living? Where did they live? What did they think? The answers to these questions reveal much about the individual characteristics of each as well as their collective effort to bring the slave trade to an end. A composite profile of their lives and activities is one way to increase our understanding of the nature of abolitionism. Moreover, since there has been little recent scholarship on the British Quaker organization in the late eighteenth century,[8] a study of this group provides a useful sampling of the interests and concerns of some Friends. Finally, the business activities of the men illustrate many of the economic developments in the London of their day, particularly about the commercialization observed by Neil McKendrick, John Brewer and H. J. Plumb.[9]

Quakers, like other religious radicals, were perfectionists, mystics and millenarians, who stressed the spiritual equality of all and tried to live by the Golden Rule. Yet Quakers combined pragmatism with piety. George Fox gave advice on business practice as well as on moral conduct and, with Margaret Fell, forged a nation-wide organization of local meetings, capped by the London Meeting for Sufferings, to protect the safety and interests of Friends. By the mid-eighteenth century, Quakers were gaining respectability in Britain and political power in Pennsylvania.[10]

George Fox taught that "every man is enlightened by the Divine Light of Christ"[11] and, although interpretations by later Friends varied, many groups of American Quakers came to see slavery and the slave trade as incompatible with that belief.[12] The British organization did not take up the cause until 1783 when the American Revolution raised the spectre of God's judgment on a sinful nation and ended all possibility of a purely colonial solution.[13] In May 1783, the London Yearly Meeting directed the Meeting for Sufferings to "take this affair under their care," and on 20 June 1783, the Meeting for Sufferings officially appointed a twenty-three member Committee on the Slave Trade.[14]

On 7 July 1783, six London Friends met unofficially, according to Clarkson, "to consider what steps could by them be taken for the Relief and Liberation of the Negro Slaves in the West Indies, and the Discouragement of the Slave Trade on the Coast of Africa." Clarkson's account is confirmed by manuscript minutes of this and subsequent meetings found at the Friends Reference Library in London.[15] Other letters, diaries and printed memoirs at the Friends Reference Library document much about the lives of the six men and show that although they came from different social backgrounds and geographical locations, they were closely connected by 1783. Brief profiles of each provide a basis for comparing their similarities and differences.

By 1783 William Dillwyn, an American, had established a new life and career in London. Of Welsh Quaker ancestry, he was born in Pennsylvania in 1743. He attended the Philadelphia school kept by Anthony Benezet, a Quaker known on both sides of the Atlantic as a opponent of slavery and the slave trade. As an adult, Dillwyn traveled through the southern American colonies on business, observing slavery in practice.

Dillwyn came to Britain in 1774, furnished with letters of introduction from Benezet to Anglican and Methodist abolitionists as well as to Friends. Traveling through northern England, he visited factories, mills and hospitals. Arriving in London in November 1774, he met Samuel Hoare and Joseph Woods among Friends there. He left London in September 1775, but returned during the American Revolution. By 1783, he had become a London resident, married a Quaker heiress, established a firm and built a large home in Walthamstow.[16]

John Lloyd was British-born but, like Dillwyn, knew slavery first-hand. Lloyd was born in Birmingham in 1751, the son of a wealthy Quaker iron manufacturer and banker. He attended Quaker school in Worcester and afterwards went into the tobacco business with his brother-in-law. He traveled to America on business between 1775 and 1777 and witnessed the reality of slavery. By 1783, he had returned to

London and married the daughter of a prominent Quaker. Prospering in the tobacco business, he settled in Bartholomew Close, no far from Lombard Street.[17]

While George Harrison had not crossed the Atlantic, he had crossed social and career boundaries to get to London by 1783. Harrison was born in Kendal, Westmoreland in 1747, the son of a shoemaker. Distinguishing himself at a Quaker school, he was sent to public Grammar School and subsequently spent six months at the Dissenting Academy at Warrington. By the time he was twenty-three, Harrison was established in London as a warehouseman, traveling frequently to the country on business. In 1777, he married the daughter of a wealthy Plymouth Quaker although he settled in the City of London, where he frequented the Exchange and conducted financial transactions for his father-in-law.[18]

Thomas Knowles, like George Harrison, was from the country and rose in rank through education. Born in Knaresborough, Yorkshire in 1734, Knowles lived for a time in Mildenhall before marrying and settling in Birmingham as an apothecary. In 1771, at age thirty-seven Knowles went to Edinburgh to study medicine, and took a degree at Leyden one year later. Returning to London, he set up practice in Lombard Street, developing a profitable clientele among Friends, including the family of John Lloyd. By 1783, he was a member of the Medical Society of London and a licentiate of the Royal College of Physicians.[19]

Samuel Hoare was the son of an Irish landowner who had come to London and solidified his fortune by marrying well. Hoare was born in 1751 in Stoke Newington and attended the same Quaker school as George Harrison who was four years his senior. He studies briefly at a seminary in London before being apprenticed to a woolen manufacturer in Norwich. By 1772, he had completed his apprenticeship and returned to London to join the banking firm of Bland and Barnett of Lombard Street. In 1776, he married a Keswick Quaker with a fortune of her own. The two returned to London to live in Old Broad Street until she died suddenly after childbirth in 1783.[20]

Joseph Woods was, like Samuel Hoare, London-born, but came from a very different background. His father was a pastry cook who sold venison pies in White Hart Court, just off Lombard Street. Like these other five Friends, Woods was educated at a Quaker school. He became a woolen draper, and in 1769 married Margaret Hoare, the eldest sister of Samuel. After his father died, Woods moved his business to the White Hart Court location. There, in addition to selling cloth, he wrote essays for The Gentleman's Magazine and other publications, corresponded about issues and ideas of the day and, with William Dillwyn, served as a purchasing agent for the Library Company of Philadelphia.[21]

Religion was, of course, a strong tie binding the six men. All of them had been born into Quaker families, and many of them were third generation Friends. Living and working near one another in London,

39

they would likely have attended the same weekly Meetings for worship and participated in the same Monthly and Quarterly Meetings as well.

All except Joseph Woods were leaders within the central Quaker organization. Woods was a loyal and devoted Friend, but he declined to take an active role in the business of the Quaker organization. By 1783, the other five had attended London Yearly Meeting as representatives of their local meetings. All five also were members of the Meeting for Sufferings and had been named to the official Committee on the Slave Trade appointed that year.[22]

All six were products of Quaker homes and schools. As Samuel Hoare wrote in 1771, they had been "early initiated in virtuous sentiments."[23] Like other Quaker boys, they learned merchant's accounts and methods of bookkeeping along with morals. Writing in the mid-eighteenth century, a much-admired Quaker school teacher advised boys, "But chiefly strive to gain a Hand/ For Business, with a just Command/ When Figures Exercise your Quill/ Then ask your Care and all your skill."[24]

Mindful of their lessons, by 1783 all six men prospered in businesses. Testaments to the magnetic attractions of London, most of them clustered around Lombard Street, the chief shopping center in the hear of the City. As successful businessmen, they partook of many of the pleasures of their day. Woods frequented the Carolina Coffee House, belonged to an evening drinking club and in the summer months took his family to Margate, Hastings or another of the increasingly popular resort towns. Samuel Hoare, his more affluent brother-in-law, went frequently to Bath and kept a country house. John Lloyd visited Margate and had a rural retreat. Finally, Thomas Knowles' wife, Molly, was welcomed in Bath.[25]

Since the mid-eighteenth century, the Quaker organization had found it necessary repeatedly to warn Friends against the dangers of wealth and lures of luxury. Moreover, according to contemporaries, many London merchants and tradesmen were purchasing more and living better. For example, a writer in the Gentleman's Magazine wondered at the rapidly rising living standards of London merchants in 1783, and a later contributor to The Lady's Magazine grumbled about the lavish life styles of merchant families.[26]

John Brewer has argued that during the last quarter of the eighteenth century "the middling sort of bourgeoisie began to distinguish themselves socially and politically from the patrician elite and the labouring poor," and these six Quakers certainly were remarkably mobile both geographically and socially. They were among the increasingly numerous middle ranks of society; and Joseph Woods, for one, was acutely conscious of his place in the social hierarchy. In 1776, he described to a friend the "pliant Obsequious Civility (read Servility if you wish) of a Tradesman." As Joseph Woods knew and John Brewer noted, for men of the middle ranks, good manners meant good business.[27]

The men were aware of the duties as well as the pleasures of their place. All six were family men, dutiful sons, doting fathers and devoted husbands. They had all married late and well. Their family life was filled with fondness, but, like society, was essentially hierarchical. Joseph Woods had no sympathy for notions of women's equality and after his death was described as being of "masculine understanding."[28]

These, then, were the men who gathered on 7 July 1783. They were all Quakers, but they were closely bound by ties of kinship and friendship as well as by religious brotherhood. All were well-educated and were actively involved in London businesses. All had leisure time and liquid capital, and all were acquainted with American slavery either directly or through their Quaker connections.

Thomas Clarkson writes that at their first meeting the men "conceived it necessary that the public mind should be enlightened." The manuscript minutes show that their first action was to seek the regular admission of articles in the General Evening Post, a London newspaper. The men realized, as John Brewer has indicated, that London newspapers were becoming increasingly important in shaping political and economic ideas of the day.[29]

Clarkson went on to say that "It was not known to the world that such an association existed."[30] The secrecy was undoubtedly designed to avoid the scrutiny which the Quaker organization applied to all publications by Friends. Nevertheless, by acting independently of the Quaker organization, these well-educated and successful businessmen could also appeal to the like-minded and similarly situated of all religious backgrounds.

The printer of the Post agreed to consider periodic publications, and the men met frequently between July and November of 1783 to choose essays for submission. Convening in the evenings at their London homes, the men cooperated as systematically as each must have operated his business. They divided tasks, assigned duties and made reports. All articles selected for publication were neatly recorded and coded to indicate when and where they would be published.

The group did not, at first, try to construct new arguments but rather marshalled existing evidence from a variety of sources. They selected extracts from American and French publications and from accounts by various travelers to Africa and the new world. They mined the works of Blackstone, Montesquieu, Hume and Adam Smith for legal, philosophic and economic arguments and borrowed from a sermon by a British Bishop.

In September 1783, a second London paper, Lloyd's Evening Post, agreed to print regular articles. Those selected for that paper were mainly literary works, including an elegy by Shenstone and letters by Ignatius Sancho. The group also selected accounts by travelers to the West Indies, letters from Americans and the words of another British Bishop.

In addition, the six used their country contacts to try to secure publications in provincial papers. Samuel Hoare wrote to printers in Norwich and Bath, while Knowles wrote to those in Yorkshire and Liverpool. Dillwyn wrote to papers in Bristol, Cork, Dublin and Kent,[31] while Harrison wrote to Sherborne and Newcastle Upon Tyne. The provincial press, too, was becoming more important in national politics and economics, and commentaries on social morality and commerce were frequently mingled on the pages of country papers.[32]

Meanwhile, in September 1783, the Meeting for Sufferings Committee on the Slave Trade directed William Dillwyn and John Lloyd to prepare "a short address to the publick on this important subject." By October, the two had completed The Case of our Fellow Creatures, the Oppressed Africans, respectfully recommended to the Serious Consideration of the Legislature of Great Britain by the people called Quakers.[33]

Addressing Members of Parliament, Dillwyn and Lloyd tried to reconcile the claims of Christianity with considerations of interest. They argued that slavery and the slave trade were contrary to justice and humanity and that abolition was "consistent with sound policy." Contending that commerce in African produce would be more profitable than the trade in slaves, they concluded that Parliament should end the British slave trade and extend such relief to those already enslaved "as justice and mercy may dictate."[34]

The Meeting for Sufferings approved the fifteen page statement, and in late 1783 and early 1784, the Committee on the Slave Trade presented copies to Members of Parliament. In June, the Meeting for Sufferings decided that The Case should be "circulated as generally as may be throughout the nation." Between July and December, 1784, members of the Committee presented The Case to justices of the peace, clergymen, members of corporations, educators and others throughout England of "abilities and influence."[35]

At the same time, Joseph Woods drew up Thoughts on the Slavery of Negroes in thirty-two pages. Convening on 6 July 1784, the association read and approved it for publication. Like the earlier articles published by the group, the essay was to appear anonymously and there was nothing in it to mark it as peculiarly Quaker.[36]

Woods, like Dillwyn and Lloyd, began by calling forth "the Humanity of the Present Age," but, unlike them, his appeal was not overtly connected with any specific religious creed. He insisted on the humanity of the Africans, believing that they "are neither deficient in the feelings of humanity, nor the powers of understanding." He argued simply yet effectively "for their common humanity, their right to be treated as men."

Woods did not argue, as Dillwyn and Lloyd had, that the abolition of the slave trade might be economically beneficial to British commerce. Instead, he insisted that considerations of humanity must be weighed against calculations of profit. "What is the price" he asked,

42

"or indeed the existence, of the articles cultivated by slaves, in comparison with the slavery and oppression by which they are produced?" To Woods the issue was clear. "The objection from motives of commercial policy, amounts to this, that the claims of religion and morality ought to be subservient to those of avarice and luxury." Living in a world of rapid commercialization, Woods was striving to define the moral limits of commerce.

He was convinced that liberty was one item which should not be bought and sold by British businessmen. Referring to Cicero and Montesquieu, he maintained that "No right exists ... to alienate from another his liberty, so as to sell him for a slave, and therefore every purchase of a slave is in contradiction to the original inherent rights of mankind." The British slave trade was a clear case of economic wrong-doing which should be remedied by Parliament. "The first measure which presents itself to the wish of humanity," Woods declared, was "the legislative abolition of the slave trade."

For Woods, as for Dillwyn and Lloyd, the question of slavery itself was more complex, involving as it did the property rights of British colonials. Slavery could be abolished only gradually, Woods concluded, because it was "too deeply entangled with motives of interest and habits of power ...." If slaves could not be liberated, then they should at least be educated and paid for their work, he contended. Woods cited in support of this point Montesquieu's dictum that reason, not avarice, must govern labor.

Woods and his colleagues were applying humanitarian standards to the commercial practices of slavery and the slave trade and although their humanitarianism was deeply felt and deeply rooted in Christianity, it was essentially masculine and definitely hierarchical. Humanity, as Woods made plain, was a matter of man's duty to man, and while Africans were fellow men and spiritual equals, they were not earthly equals. Conscious of his own place in British society, Woods described them as "helpless," "miserable" and "objects of compassion." He did, at first, try to counter the idea of "The inferiority which is attributed to the whole race of Negroes." But, he was willing, to concede the issue by "Granting the inferiority contended for ...."[37]

To Joseph Woods and the association of six, abolishing the slave trade meant exercizing humanity without recognizing equality, it meant affirming the principle of liberty without extending it to slaves. Mirroring the manners and morals of British society, abolitionism was becoming more of a matter of defining British rights than of defending African ones.

With the decision to publish the essay by Woods, the circle of abolitionists widened and James Phillips, another Quaker acquaintance, was drawn in. Like Knowles and Harrison, Phillips was from the country and had come to London to seek his fortune. Born in Cornwall in 1744, he attended Quaker school in Rochester and by 1768 had come to London and married.

In 1775, Phillips became the chief publisher of Friends books in London by taking over the business in George Yard, just off Lombard Street. By 1776, he was well-acquainted with Joseph Woods and, like Dillwyn and Lloyd, had close business and personal connections in Pennsylvania. As printer for the Quaker organization, Phillips could be assured of a certain minimum market and international distribution through Friends' meetings. He printed and distributed all official Quaker documents originating in London and had printed The Case, written by Dillwyn and Lloyd.[38]

When he published the anonymous Thoughts on the Slavery of Negroes in 1784, Phillips could not have had a guaranteed market since the work had not been sanctioned by the Quaker organization. He might have published it at his own risk or more likely, the cost of publication was covered by the group of six who had authorized the printing. By pooling their resources, as Brewer showed, men of the middle ranks could exercise charity and accomplish reforms without the assistance of an aristocratic patron.[39].

In 1784 the six London Friends ordered two thousand copies of the essay by Joseph Woods and directed that they be distributed in Bristol and Liverpool,[40] to Anglican abolitionists and to Quakers in Virginia and Rhode Island. The next year, James Phillips published a second edition.[41] Thomas Clarkson wrote that Thoughts "contained a Sober and dispassionate appeal to the reason of all, without offending the prejudices of any," and believed that the essay was "most useful to the cause which it intended to serve."[42]

By publishing and distributing the essay by Woods, the association of six was appealing not just to Quaker but to men like themselves of humanitarian morals, manners of the middle ranks and business mentalities. By sponsoring their own publication, the group was helping to give abolition a nonsectarian voice. As abolition was becoming a business for James Phillips, it was becoming an issue to the reading public.

The fragmentary copy of the records of the six London Friends ends with the publication of Thoughts in 1784, yet the activities of these Quaker abolitionists did not. Thomas Knowles died in 1786, but James Phillips and the other five went on to become founding members of the nondenominational London Committee for the Abolition of the Slave Trade, established in 1787. All except Phillips lived to see the success of the abolition effort in 1807.

Many of the characteristics of the nation-wide movement to end the British slave trade between 1787 and 1807 as conducted by the London Abolition Committee can be seen in the activities of these Friends in 1783-1784: the importance of publications financed by subscriptions, the appeal to the influential of all religions, the plea for a humanitarianism based on Christian morality but on no specific Christian creed, the shifting focus from slavery to the slave trade,[43] and a concern for defining the moral limits of economic activities.

D. B. Davis has shown that after 1783-84 organized abolitionism, never a Quaker monopoly, became increasingly popular in Britain, France and the United States. James Walvin has also demonstrated that abolition quickly gained widespread popularity in Britain outside London.[44] The early Quaker activities and arguments against the slave trade were effective not because they were different, but because they drew on the common concerns and ideas of many British businessmen. By combining Quaker precepts with practical experience in business, London Quakers were able to translate their unique moral perceptions into widely-accepted social action.

As David Brion Davis has suggested, abolitionism was becoming a shared ideology, part of the mentality of many of those in the middle ranks. Like all ideologies, Davis, explained, abolitionism "focused attention on new problems" while it "camouflaged others and ... defined new conceptions of social reality."[45] Speaking for the association of six in 1784, Joseph Woods focused attention on the immediate problems of the slave trade yet masked the long range problem of a deep-seated paternalism based on ideas of race, class and gender. The origins and the success as well as the limitations and long-term consequences of the movement to abolish the British slave trade owe much, as Thomas Clarkson and D.B. Davis recognized, to these London businessmen and the abolitionism they formulated in the years 1783 and 1784.

Kentucky Humanities Council
November 1986

Notes

[1] Thomas Clarkson, The History of the Rise, Progress and Accomplishment of the Abolition of the Slave Trade, 2 vols., 1st ed., new impression (London: Cass, 1968).

[2] Robert Issac and Samuel Wilberforce, The Life of William Wilberforce, 2 vols. (Philadelphia: Henry Perkins, 1841). Reginald Coupland, Wilberforce (Oxford: Clarendon University Press, 1928). E. M. Howse, Saints in Politics (London: Allen and Unwin, 1971).

[3] Eric Williams, Capitalism and Slavery (Chapel Hill: University of North Carolina Press, 1944).

[4] David Brion Davis, The Problem of Slavery in the Age of Revolution (Ithaca: Cornell University Press, 1975), 13.

[5] David Brion Davis, The Problem of Slavery in Western Culture (Ithaca: Cornell University Press, 1966). The Problem of Slavery in the Age of Revolution. Slavery and Human Progress (Oxford: University Press, 1984).

[6] Clarkson, History of the Abolition, 1:125.

[7] Davis, Slavery in the Age of Revolution, 213-54.

[8] Rufus Jones, The Later Period of Quakerism, 2 vols (London: Macmillan, 1921), remains the standard work.

[9] Neil McKendrick, John Brewer and J. H. Plumb, The Birth of a Consumer Society: The Commercialization of Eighteenth-Century England (Bloomington: Indiana University Press, 1982).

[10] Christopher Hill, The World Turned Upside Down (New York: Viking Press, 1972). Hugh Barbour, The Quakers in Puritan England (New Haven: Yale University Press, 1964). William C. Braithwaite, The Beginnings of Quakerism, 2d ed. (Cambridge: University Press, 1961). Richard T. Vann, The Social Development of English Quakerism, 1655-1755 (Cambridge, Mass.: Harvard University Press, 1969). N. C. Hunt, Two Early Political Associations (Oxford: Clarendon Press, 1961). Sidney James, A People Among People: Quaker Benevolence in Eighteenth-Century America (Cambridge, Mass.: Harvard University Press, 1963). Jack Marietta, The Reform of American Quakerism (Philadelphia: University of Pennsylvania Press, 1984).

[11] Braithwaite, Beginnings, 35.

[12] Thomas Drake, Quakers and Slavery in America (New Haven: Yale University Press, 1950). Jean Soderlund, Quakers and Slavery: A Divided Society (Princeton, New Jersey: Princeton University Press, 1985).

[13] J. Jennings, "Mid-Eighteenth Century British Quakerism and the Response to the Problem of Slaery," Quaker History (Spring 1977) 66, no. 1:23-40. "The American Revolution and the Testimony of British Quakers Against the Slave Trade," Quaker History (Fall 1981) 70, no. 2:99-103.

[14] London Yearly Meeting, "Minutes of the Yearly Meeting held in London," Vols. 16-17, Friends Reference Library, Friends House, London. London Meeting for Sufferings, "Minutes of the Meeting for Sufferings," Vols. 35-36, Friends Reference Library, Friends House, London.

[15] Clarkson, History of the Abolition, 1:123-25. Thompson-Clarkson Manuscripts, "Minutes of the Association of Six," Friends Reference Library, Friends House, London.

[16] Dictionary of Quaker Biography, "William Dillwyn," Friends Reference Library, Friends House, London. Microfilm, "Journals of William Dillwyn," Friends Reference Library, Friends House, London. T. Mardy Rees, A History of Quakers in Wales and their Emigration to North America (Carmarthen: W. Spurrell and Son, 1925), 248-49. Davis, Slavery in the Age of Revolution, 233-35.

[17] Dictionary of Quaker Biography, "John Lloyd," Friends Reference Library, Friends House, London. Lloyd MSS 5463, "Diary of John Lloyd, 1778-1811," Friends Reference Library, Friends House, London.

[18] [George Harrison], Memoir of William Cookworthy (London: William and Frederick Cash, 1854), 107-8, 133-38, 146-49.

[19] Dictionary of Quaker Biography, "Thomas Knowles," Friends Reference Library, Friends House, London. "Mrs. Knowles," The Lady's Monthly Museum (November 1803) 2:288-94.

[20] Joseph Joshua Green, "Biographical and Historical Notices of Jonathan Gurnell," Friends Reference Library, Friends House, London. Sarah and Hannah Hoare, Memoirs of Samuel Hoare (London: Headley Brothers, 1911), 1-6, 12, 18, 61.

[21] Dictionary of Quaker Biography, "Joseph Woods," Friends Reference Library, Friends House, London. Matthews MSS, "Letters from Joseph Woods to William Matthews, 1774-1812," Friends Reference Library, Friends House, London. Margaret Hoare Woods, "Journal," 7 vols., Box O, Friends Reference Library, Friends House, London. Gentlemen's Magazine 82 (Jan.-June 1812) :669. Austin Gray, Benjamin Franklin's Library (New York: Macmillan, 1936), 52-53. "Correspondence from Joseph Woods," Library Company, Philadelphia.

[22] "Minutes of the Yearly Meeting," Vol. 17. "Minutes of the Meeting for Sufferings," Vol. 36. Matthews MSS.

[23] Hoare, Memoirs, 63.

[24] William Massey of Wandsworth, Instructions for a Boarding School, Friends Tracts, E:92. Friends Reference Library, Friends House, London.

[25] J. William Frost, ed., The Records and Recollections of James Jenkins (New York: Edwin Mellen Press, 1984). Matthews MSS. Margaret Hoare Woods, "Journal." Hoare, Memoirs. Lloyd "Diary." JT MSS 346, "William Matthews to Molly Knowles, 1 December 1779," Friends Reference Library, Friends House, London.

[26] Jennings, "Mid-Eighteenth Century British Quakerism." Gentlemen's Magazine, (Jan.-June 1784) 54:92-93. The Lady's Magazine, (Apr. 1792) 23:201-03.

[27] Matthews MSS, "Woods to Matthews, 9 January 1776." McKendrick, Brewer, Plumb, Consumer Society, 197, 215. Brewer writes, "This is a subject as yet unexplored, but it might well prove that the values espoused to obtain a creditworthy society may have had just as significant a social impact as those intended to secure an industrious and compliant labour force." Consumer Society, 215.

[28] Matthews MSS. Gentlemen's Magazine (July-Dec. 1812) 82:99.

[29] Clarkson, History of the Abolition, 1:123. "Minutes of the Association of Six." McKendrick, Brewer, Plumb, Consumer Society, 257.

[30] Clarkson, History of the Abolition, 1:123.

[31] "Minutes of the Association of Six."

[32] McKendrick, Brewer and Plumb, Consumer Society, 217.

[33] "Minutes of the Meeting for Sufferings Committee on the Slave Trade, Sept.-Oct. 1783."

[34] [William Dillwyn and John Lloyd], The Case of our Fellow Creatures, London: James Phillips, 1783.

[35] "Minutes of the Meeting for Sufferings," Vols. 36-37. "Minutes of the Committee on the Slave Trade, October 1783-December 1784.

[36] "Minutes of the Association of Six."

[37] [Joseph Woods], Thoughts on the Slavery of the Negroes (London: James Phillips, 1784).

[38] Dictionary of Quaker Biography, "James Phillips," Friends Reference Library, Friends House, London. Frost, Jenkins. Russell Mortimer, "Quaker Printers, 1750-1850," Journal of Friends Historical Society (1962-1964) 50, no. 3:100-14. Gibson MSS, 6 vols., Letters to James Phillips, Friends Reference Library, Friends House, London. "Minutes of the Meeting for Sufferings," Vol. 36, 37.

[39] McKendrick, Brewer, Plumb, Consumer Society, 224.

[40] "Minutes of the Association of Six."

[41] [Joseph Woods], Thoughts on the Slavery of the Negores (London: James Phillips, 1785).

[42] Clarkson, History of the Abolition, 1:125.

[43] Add MSS, Minutes of the London Abolition Committeee, British Library, London.

[44] Davis, Problem of Slavery in the Age of Revolution. James Walvin, England, Slaves and Freedom, 1776-1838 (Jackson, Miss.: University Press of Mississippi, 1986).

[45] Davis, Slavery in the Age of Revolution, 350.

48

The Experience of Motherhood in Early-Victorian England

Nancy Fix Anderson

It is now generally accepted that motherhood as a profession was created in the late-eighteenth and early-nineteenth centuries, largely as a result of the industrial revolution, which removed productive work from the home.[1] Women of the propertied classes, left functionless, filled the void with the new social role of motherhood, a role buttressed by the romantic Rousseauian emphasis on the importance of childhood. Mothering had, of course, always been a woman's duty. What was new in the early-Victorian period was that motherhood, especially among the middle classes, became a woman's major responsibility, and, as befitting its professionalization, required training and instruction in the form of child care manuals and other advice books which then flooded the market.[2]

Another factor in this new motherhood was the separation of the domestic world of women and children from the male sphere of work. The absence of the father from the home, at least during the day, allowed greater domestic authority for the mother. The father still had legal control over his children, a power only slightly amended by the Infant's Custody Act of 1839, which provided for the possibility of maternal custody of children under seven years of age in cases of separation or divorce. Nevertheless, despite patriarchal family law, it was mothers who assumed the primary obligations of parenting, while fathers were delegated to the more distancing responsibility of financial support.

The ideology of Victorian motherhood has been the subject of much historical scholarship. This study will turn the problem around and examine not prescriptive or external views of motherhood, but rather how mothers themselves experienced their role. Previous investigations of Victorian parental feelings towards children have generally not differentiated between the mother and the father and have focused on attitudes rather than actual experience.[3] Patricia Branca, in Silent Sisterhood: Middle-Class Women in the Victorian Home, acknowledged the importance of treating motherhood "from the viewpoint of the mother herself,"[4] but she then confined her study to an analysis of the prescriptive literature. To examine actual maternal feelings and experiences, I have drawn on letters, diaries, autobiographies, and biographies of middle-class women who were mothers of young children in the first half of the nineteenth century, when the glorification of motherhood was first in full bloom.[5] (Working-class women did not have the luxury of making motherhood a profession, and the aristocracy was, for the most part, unaffected by the early Victorian professionalization of work, even of motherhood.)

This analysis of early-Victorian motherhood is based on a psychoanalytic perspective on the psychology of motherhood and, in particular, on the perhaps universal ambivalence mothers feel towards their children. Maternal love and attachment commonly coexist with the mother's often unconscious angry feels of resentment that her body and her life have been invaded.[6] In most mothers there is an inner conflict between one's sense of self and concern for the child, a conflict ostensibly resolved, when motherhood was professionalized, by maternal self-sacrifice. This resolution, however, involving a women's loss of identity and lonely isolation with small children, had damaging psychological consequences, as exposed for the post-World War II period by Betty Friedan in The Feminine Mystique, and more recently by Adrienne Rich in her angry autobiographical indictment of full-time motherhood, Of Woman Born.

The painful results of the professionalization of motherhood in our own society stand in sharp contrast to the experience of the first professional mothers. Early-Victorian English social conditions allowed for the possibility of self -- as well as maternal fulfillment for middle-class women. There was a new intimacy and involvement between mothers and their children, but without suffocating exclusivity. The key to this balance was in the class structure. Middle-class mothers usually had two or more live-in servants, including a nursery maid, so that the mothers could enjoy the pleasures without many of the burdens of mothering. The nursery maids did not take over the role of the mother -- the institution of the Nanny as surrogate mother did not emerge until after 1850;[7] they merely assisted and relieved the mother from the pressures of constant child care. There were certainly many agonizing aspects of Victorian middle-class mothering, most especially the frequent uncontrolled pregnancies, often well into middle age, and the still-high maternal and child mortality. Nevertheless, the mothers were often able to achieve a balance between their own needs and the demands of their children that is rare in modern western society.

The early-Victorian middle-class experience of motherhood began with childbirth in the home. A licensed male doctor was usually in attendance, which, despite the sentimentalization of the midwife and the increased risk of puerperal fever, was an advantage in difficult births. Chloroform was not used until the 1850s, but the presence of a female support group,[8] usually one's mother, sisters, or aunts, eased the pains of labor.[8] The mother was also assisted by a "monthly nurse," who arrived the week before and stayed about three weeks after the birth.

Middle-class mother commonly breastfed their own babies. It was no longer socially acceptable to use a wet nurse except in emergency situations, and bottle-feeding, although introduced in about 1800, was infrequently used until later in the century. Breastfeeding, a natural process, can nevertheless involve pain and difficulties, but the mother had the monthly nurse to help her expel milk from overfull breasts, make salves for cracked nipples, and relieve other physical problems. Moreover, assisted by a nursery maid in addition to the monthly nurse, the mother could enjoy nursing her baby without the exhaustion of other aspects of infant care. Elizabeth Gaskell, for example, with apparent contentment and pleasure, described in a letter her routine of breastfeeding her youngest child while the nursery maid bathed the other children.[9]

Victorian prudery did not extend to breastfeeding, for it was seen as a natural part of a woman's life, as evidenced by the frequency and ease with which it was mentioned in letters and other personal writings. William Gladstone, who reported without inhibition to friends about his wife's breastfeeding, also apparently felt comfortable, as he recorded in his diary, helping the nurse rub his wife's distended breasts, to keep them "from getting into an obstinate state."[10]

Breastfeeding not only bonds a mother and child, it is also for both a source of sensuous erotic pleasure.[11] The common (although now challenged) image of the sexless Victorian woman must be qualified by an awareness of the (unconscious) sexual experience of the nursing mother. The psychoanalyst Helene Deutsch, writing in the twentieth century, observed that some mothers are unable to handle the erotic feelings of nursing;[12] but, among the early-Victorian women investigated for this study it was apparently not an inhibition. A nursing mother can feel drained and even devoured by her baby, so much so that Isabella Beeton, who breastfed all her babies, wrote in her Book of Household Management of the "baby vampire," and of the "exhausting process of lactation." Moreover, Patricia Branca has suggested that breastfeeding could not have been very satisfying to mothers, else they would not have so readily adopted bottlefeeding in the last half of the nineteenth century. Nevertheless, except when there were special difficulties, the early-Victorian mothers recounted their experiences of breastfeedings in terms of pleasurable intimacy.[13]

After the babies were weaned the mothers generally remained actively involved in their upbringing; but, assisted by a nursery maid, they did not need to maintain constant supervision. Mrs. Eliza Warren, in How I Managed My Children from Infancy to Marriage, described raising her first-born child in poorer circumstances without adequate help. Frustrated and frazzled by her child's constant crying, she felt her love for him "literally dying out; now, as I held him, I almost shook him." When she could afford to hire an experienced nurse, her life and her baby's became much easier.[14]

The mother's primary responsibility for her children was not in day-to-day physical care, but rather in their moral training. As that instructor of early-Victorian women Mrs. John Sandford pronounced, a mother "must give the tone to character; she must infuse the principle; she must communicate those first lessons which are never forgotten, and which bring forth fruit, good or evil, according as the seed may be."[15] It was this responsibility which, except for concern about their children's health, caused the greatest maternal anxiety. The mother saw herself as responsible for the salvation of her child's soul. It was indeed, as Catherine Gladstone said, a heavy burden to bring into the world "a being on whose happiness here and hereafter may mainly depend on one." Concerns about moral training filled the diary Elizabeth Gaskell kept of her oldest daughter's first three years, in which she expressed "extreme anxiety in the formation of her little daughter's character." Upset when she would lose her temper, Gaskell asked God's help in "checking each angry word that might injure the precious soul thou has given to this little child." Mrs. Augustus Hare adored her son, but in endless battles against his self-will, she refused to let him have his way because of her concern with his salvation.[16]

Mothers were responsible for the intellectual as well as moral training of their little children, a less anxiety-provoking duty for which they often expressed enjoyment. Emma Darwin, advised by her aunt that "no governess can do what a mother can do for their souls," taught her children to read, and found it "a great pleasure and interest." The mathematician and astronomer Mary Somerville gave her children "instruction in such things as I was capable of teaching, and which were suited to their age." Elizabeth Gaskell, who gave regular lessons to her daughter, decided, then the child was three, to send her to a nearby Infant School, in order "to perfect her habits of obedience." Afraid of becoming a lazy mother, "forgetting that on _me_ lies the heaviest responsibility," Gaskell vowed to fetch her daughter as often as possible from school herself, so that on the walk home she could weed out any false ideas the daughter might have picked up. She also continued lessons at home.[17]

Mothers also recounted pleasure in entertaining their children with games, excursions, and other amusements. Mrs. Frances Trollope, for example, delighted in putting on family theatricals and parties and taking her children to museums and plays. Almost all the mothers examined for this study manifested strong attachment for and involvement with their children. When John Stuart mill, in an early draft of his Autobiography, referred to "that rarity in England, a really warm-hearted mother,"[18] he was surely generalizing only from his own experience. In the last half of the nineteenth century, with the increase in middle-class wealth and social aspirations, there was much criticism of negligent mothers,[19] but that was not common in the earlier period.

Nevertheless, the time early-Victorian mothers spent with their children was at their discretion and choice and, because of the ever-present live-in nursery maid, the mothers were able to have time to pursue their own interests and pleasures. To show how busy she was with her children, in a letter to her aunt Elizabeth Gaskell detailed her daily schedule, which still included, despite her full nursery, blocks of uninterrupted adult time. When her nursery maid was sick, Gaskell complained that "we have had the children in the night," a responsibility she -- and most of the mothers -- usually did not assume. Nor did Gaskell bathe her children except when her daughter developed an aversion to her bath, and so Gaskell for a week washed her herself to make sure the water was the right temperature.[20] Other mothers had similar experiences caring for their children out of choice, not necessity, and also preserving time for themselves.

Moreover, when the mother was sick there was not a crisis of child care. Emma Darwin, for example, was too ill before the birth of her second child to take notice of her son, but presumably the child was not neglected, despite maternal inattention. Darwin later commented that her life was "entirely filled by the cares of husband children,"[21] but, as evidenced from her letters, it was her dependent husband more than her many children who demanded constant mothering.

The social constraints on Victorian women meant that many mothers used their freedom from child care in trivial social activities, although also often in charity work. The more self-directed and talented women, however, were able to combine concentrated work and active mothering. In middle age, Elizabeth Gaskell, warning an aspiring woman writer that the pleasure of exercising a talent should not be at the sacrifice of maternal duty, said that she could not have written when she had little children. But in fact she did. Her first novel, Mary Barton, was written when she was pregnant with her fifth child. In a more honest letter to her artist friend Eliza Fox, two years after the publication of Mary Barton, she maintained that women need "the refuge of the hidden world of art to shelter themselves in when too much pressed upon by daily small Lilliputian arrows of piddling cares." It is hard, she said, to blend "home duties and the development of the Individual . . . [but] I have no doubt that the cultivation of each tends to keep the other in a healthy state."[22]

The balance that Gaskell achieved between "home duties and the development of the Individual" was enjoyed by other early Victorian mothers, such as Mary Howitt, Mrs. Augustus Hare, Mrs. Oliphant, Mrs. Henry Wood, Mary Somerville, Elizabeth Holmes, Isabella Beeton and Jane Brookfield. They worked in the home for the most part as writers, but on specific time schedules protected from domestic interruption. Mary Somerville did complain about distractions, but from guests paying unwelcome calls, not from her children.[23]

Working mothers encountered social disapproval, as voiced even by Elizabeth Gaskell, if their work interfered with their domestic duties. Mary Howitt was defensive about the amount of time she spent writing, but explained to her sister that she was not out of her line of duty. Her work brought in money the family needed, and so "is it not a cause of thankfulness, dearest sister, and have I not reason to feel that in thus writing I am fulfilling my duty?" Early-Victorian mothers were not, however, inhibited by the physiological arguments against working mothers, particularly the law of conservation of energy, that were used to try to keep late-Victorian mothers passive and inert. Mary Howitt did frighten Mrs. Oliphant by saying that so many of her babies had died because of defective heart valves caused by her mental over-work,[24] but that type of opinion was not common before 1850.

In middle-class families the children's nursery was usually separate, although not isolated from, adult rooms. This provided a free, relatively unrestricted space for children as well as adult living undisturbed by children's activity. There was, therefore, the possibility of a greater intimacy between a wife and husband than when the couple is always _en famille_. The practice of children taking their meals in the nursery has been retrospectively commonly portrayed as cold and unnatural, and middle-class families that did share meals, such as the Isaac Taylors of Ongar and the parental family of Elizabeth Holmes, prided themselves on their familial closeness.[25] Nevertheless, separate dining meant that parents were not restricted to the plainer foods and simpler conversations of childhood, nor children constricted by adult regulations. When families did gather together, it was a special treat. Mary Howitt reported her pleasure of visiting her children during the nursery breakfast. In the Gaskell household the children would join their parents in the evening, and, as GAskell reported, her daughter would dance "with delight when she hears the bell which is the signal for her come in after dinner."[26]

The advice books emphasized the importance of the privacy of the husband and wife. Jane West, in her _Letters to Young Ladies_, warned that "the instructor . . . who requires a mother to be constant companion to her children, will render her such a wife as will drive most husbands from her fireside." Mrs. Eliza Warren apparently followed that advice. She said that, despite her devotion to her children, she "never allowed them to interfere with my time when my husband came home. They were early made to understand that mamma then could not be with them; and I would suggest to every woman never to allow her children to usurp the time and loving attention due to the husband." Mothers, home during the day, were able to maintain intimacy with both their children and their husbands, even as fathers became more removed from their children's daily lives. Mothers often shielded their husbands from domestic worries, as did Mrs. Warren, who had the rule that her husband was never to be bothered by the children's problems in the evenings. Unable to share her anxieties about her children with her husband, Elizabeth Gaskell poured them out to a friend, but said that if she could talk with her husband about her concerns, "it would be SUCH A RELIEF often."[27]

The freedom mothers gained by having nursery maids take over much of the physical child care was often at the cost of anxiety about the influence of the servants on the children. Included in the personal writings were references to illness and injury caused by nursery maid's carelessness,[28] and, even more frequently, to psychological and moral harm caused by servants filling children's heads with frightening or immoral ideas.[29] There was also the problem of the mother's jealousy of the child's preferring the nurse to the mother,[30] although this was not as common as later in the century when the nanny more completely replaced the mother. In spite of that, mothers felt comfortable enough about the nursery maids to leave their children with them not only during part of the day, but also for extended periods while the mother travelled.

Some mothers accepted very long separations from their children, especially when they went to the colonies and left their children in England. Caroline Norton was five years old when her parents went to South Africa, leaving her with an aunt for three years. William

Thackeray's mother sent her five-year old son from India to England to stay with relatives and did not join him until four years later. Isabella Beeton's mother, occupied with children from her second marriage, allowed her children from her first marriage to be raised by the children's grandmother. Anthony Trollope was twelve when his mother went to America, but she did stay there for four years. Augustus Hare's natural mother, who had a large number of children, agreed to a complete separation from her son and allowed him to be adopted by her widowed childless sister-in-law.

Most mothers during this time, however, were not separated from the children for such long periods. Their first lengthy separation was usually when their sons, and less frequently their daughters, at about age ten went to boarding school. (Later in the century children were sent at a younger age.[31]) Mothers repeatedly voiced concern about their children going away,[31] not because of the separation but because the schools were seen as nurseries of vice and brutality. Even when Emma Darwin's firstborn son was still a baby she fretted about the "awful ordeal at school and college which all men go through."[32] Nevertheless[33] she and the other mothers complied with social expectation,[33] and they were probably relieved, as Catherine Gladstone and Mary Howitt[34] both admitted, when the children returned to school after holidays.[34]

The possibility of a permanent separation in the form of maternal death loomed over all early-Victorian mothers. Several of the mothers cited earlier died in childbirth, and all had sisters or close friends who died either in childbirth or from diseases like tuberculosis to which women, worn out by frequent childbearing, were especially vulnerable. Elizabeth Gaskell, whose own mother had died at her birth, was especially anxious that she might also leave her children motherless. Her concern, however, was primarily for their emotional rather than physical well-being, for she, like the other mothers, was assured there would be available caretakers. When Catherine Gladstone, therefore, considered that she might die in childbirth, she felt confident that her husband could take care of the children since he would not have the responsibility of physical child care.[35]

Another form of separation came with the death of children, surely the most painful part of Victorian motherhood. Most Victorian mothers experienced the death of at least one child, and the grief and pain were deep and often long-lasting. Moreover, whenever a child got sick, the mother commonly expressed fears of losing the child,[36] fears which if voiced today could be interpreted as repressed hostility but which were very realistic in light of Victorian child mortality. Many of the early-Victorian mothers, however, had a strong Evangelical faith in divine providence that assuaged their grief. As Mary Somerville wrote after the death of her oldest daughter, "even in the bitterness of my soul I acknowledge the wisdom and goodness of God, and endeavor to be resigned to His will." Elizabeth Holmes could not "for many days . . . think or speak of [her dead son] without tears," but she was comforted that he was with God, and "would not, if he could, return to me." In the same way Mary Howitt said that, because her son was with Christ, "were the power to recall the dear boy given us, we would not do it."[37]

She earnestly anticipated reunion with her dead children in heaven and, like other Victorian mothers, became interested in spiritualism in the hope of communicating with them while she was still on earth.

In addition to their faith, the fact that mothers typically had so many children helped ease the pain of loss. As Emma Darwin wrote to her sister-in-law after the death of Darwin's third child, "with our two other dear little things you need not fear that our sorrow will last long." Frances Trollope's biographer Helen Heineman has suggested that after the death of a son Mrs. Trollope drew back from her others, in fear of too much emotional dependence. If so, then that could explain her ability, which amazed her son Anthony, of continuing steadily to write novels while sitting at the bedside of one after the other of her dying children. Other mothers did not commonly manifest this emotional distance. Despite religious faith and the consolation of other children, the death of a child remained the source of deepest grief. As Mrs. Oliphant said, it was "like the sun going out from the sky -- life remained, the daylight continued, but all was different."[38]

In conclusion, if the biological considerations of uncontrolled pregnancies and high maternal and child mortality are left out of account, then the conditions of middle-class motherhood in early-Victorian England seem enviable. Women could enjoy the new intimacy with their children through breastfeeding, primary instruction, and other responsibilities of professionalized motherhood while maintaining their own personal freedom. They did not have to choose, as have later mothers, among child neglect, maternal self-abnegation, or the guilt and frustration of a compromise. The Victorian solution was based on a class system which we would not want to see perpetuated, but it does offer a model that with imaginative institutional and familial change can perhaps be duplicated.

Loyola University
November 1986

Notes

1. Ann Dally, Inventing Motherhood: The Consequences of an Ideal (New York: 1983); Patricia Branca, Silent Sisterhood: Middle-Class Women in the Victorian Home (London: 1975); Priscilla Robertson, "Home as a Nest: Middle Class Childhood in Nineteenth-Century Europe," The History of Childhood, ed. Lloyd deMause (New York: 1974); Elisabeth Badinter, Mother Love, Myth and Reality: Motherhood in Modern History (New York: Macmillan, 1981).

2. For a bibliography of the early-Victorian guides for mothers, see Barbara Kanner, "The Women of England in a Century of Social Change, 1815-1914: A Select Bibliography, Part II," The Widening Sphere, ed. Martha Vicinus (Bloomington: Indiana University Press, 1977), 226-29; and Branca, 112-13.

3. E. g., Linda Pollock, Forgotten Children: Parent-Child Relations Between 1500-1900 (New York: Cambridge University Press, 1983).

4. Branca, 74.

5. Barbara Schnorrenberg provided me with invaluable bibliographical help in identifying sources to use for this study, for which I am most grateful.

6. Helene Deutsch, The Psychology of Women: A Psychoanalytic Interpretation. Vol. 2: Motherhood (New York: Grunear Stratton, 1945); Therese Benedek, "Motherhood and Nurturing," Parenthood: Its Psychology and Psychopathology (Boston: Little Brown, & Co., 1970); Judith Kestenberg, "The Three Faces of Feminity," Psychoanalytic Review 67 (1980):313-35; E. S. Stern, "The Media Complex: Mother's Homicidal Wishes to Her Child," Journal of Mental Science 94 (1948):321-31; Sylvia Brody and Sidney Axelrod, Mothers, Fathers, and Children: Explorations in the Formation of Character in the First Seven Years (New York: International University Press, 1978).

7. Jonathan Gathorne-Hardy, The Unnatural History of the Nanny (New York: Dial Press, 1973); Theresa McBride, "'As the Twig Is Bent': The Victorian Nanny," The Victorian Family, ed. Anthony Wohl (New York: St. Martin's Press, 1978).

8. For example, see Catherine Gladstone's experience, recounted in Joyce Marlow, The Oak and the Ivy: An Intimate Biography of William and Catherine Gladstone (New York: Doubleday, 1977), 30. Also John Hawkins Milter, "'Temple and Sewer': Childbirth, Prudery, and Victoria Regina," The Victorian Family, ed. Anthony Wohl, 26-36.

9. The Letters of Elizabeth Gaskell, eds. J. A. V. Chapple and Arthur Pollard (Cambridge, Mass.: Harvard University Press, 1967), 823-24.

10. Quoted in Marlow, 40.

11. Niles Newton, "Interrelationship Between Sexual Responsiveness, Birth, and Breast-Feeding" Contemporary Sexual Behavior: Critical Issues in the 1970s, edited by Joseph Zubin and John Money (Baltimore, Johns Hopkins University Press, 1973), 78-94; Havelock Ellis, "Analysis of the Sexual Impulse," Studies in the Psychology of Sex, 3d ed. (New York: Random House, 1936), 1:18 19.

12. Deutsch, 290.

13. Isabella Beeton, Book of Household Management (London: S. D. Beeton, 1861), 1034; Branca, 103. For references to the pleasures of breastfeeding, see especially The Letters of Elizabeth Gaskell, passim; and Mary Howitt, An Autobiography, ed. Margaret Howitt, 2 vols. (London: Isbister, 1889).

14. Mrs. Eliza Warren, How I Managed My Children from Infancy to Marriage (London: Houlston & Wright, 1865), 11.

15. Mrs. John Sandford, Woman in Her Social and Domestic Character, 1831 (New York: Leavitt & Allen, 1854), 171. See also Mrs. Ellis, The Mothers of England: Their Influence and Responsibility (New York: J. & H. G. Langley, 1844), 17, and Deborah Gorham, The Victorian Girl and the Feminine Ideal (Bloomington: Indiana University Press, 1982), 65-83.

16. Marlow, 30; Elizabeth Gaskell, "My Diary": The Early Years of My Daughter Marianne (London: Clement Shorter 1923), 5 and 22; Diary of Mrs. Augustus Hare, in Augustus Hare, Memorials of a Quiet Life (London: Strahan & Co., 1872), 177. See also Lucy Cohen, Lady de Rothschild and Her Daughters, 1831-1931 (London: John Murray, 1935), 71.

17. Emma Darwin, A Century of Family Letters, 1792-1896, ed. Henrietta Litchefield (New York: D. Appleton & Co., 1915) 2:98, 100; Mary Somerville, Personal Recollections from Early Life to Old Age, ed. Martha Somerville (Boston: Roberts Brothers, 1885), 127; Gaskell, "My Diary", 34, 39.

18. Helen Heineman, Mrs. Trollope: The Triumphant Feminine in the Nineteenth Century (Athens, Ohio: Ohio University Press, 1979), 26; John Stuart mill, Autobiography, ed. Jack Stillinger (Boston: Houghton Mifflin, 1969), 33.

19. E. g., Eliza Lynn Linton, "Modern Mothers," Saturday Review, February 29, 1860, 268-69, and "The Modern Revolt," Macmillan's Magazine, December 1870, 142-49; Victoria Magazine, "An Appeal to Fashionable Mothers," 10 (1868), 537-38.

20. Letters of Elizabeth Gaskell, 16, 46, 823-24.

21. Darwin, 2:51, 92, 99.

22. Letters of Elizabeth Gaskell, 693-96, 106.

23. Somerville, 164.

24. Howitt, 249-50; Mrs. M. O. W. Oliphant, Autobiography (London: William Blackwood and Sons, 1899), 36.

25. Ann Taylor Gilbert, Album, ed. Christina Duff Stewart (New York: Garland Publishing, 1978), 522; Elizabeth Erma Holmes, Scenes in our Parish, by a "Country Parson's" Daughter (New York: Stanford and Swords, 1851), ix.

26. Howitt, 1:291; Gaskell, "My Diary", 19.

27. Jane West, Letters to a Young Lady (London: Hurst, Rees, & Orme, 1806), quoted in Maxine L. Margolis, Mothers and Such: Views of American Women and Why They Changed (Berkeley: University of California Press, 1984), 23; Warren, 41-42, 55; Letters of Elizabeth Gaskell, 45.

28. Eg. Annie Lee, Laurels & Rosemary: The Life of William and Mary Howitt (New York: Oxford University Press, 1955), 256; Warren, 25-26.

29. Howitt, 1:69; Jane Panton, Leaves from a Life (London: Eveleigh Nash, 1908), 3; Gaskell, "My Diary", 27.

30. Gaskell, "My Diary", 16, 33.

31. Eg. Hare, 2:258; Lady Jeune, Pages from the Diary of an Oxford Lady, 1843-1862 (Oxford: Basil Blackwell, 1932), 36-37, 110; Marlow, 61.

32. Darwin, 2:59.

33. Boarding schools were seen as especially important for social advancement, and to free sons from softening maternal influence. See Issac Taylor, Home Education, 5th ed. (London: Bell & Daldy, 1851), 157; and J. R. de S. Honey, Tom Brown's Universe: The Development of the Victorian Public School (London: Millington, 1977).

34. Quoted in Honey, 207; Howitt, 1:324.

35. Gaskell, "My Diary", 5, and Letters, 46; Marlow, 30.

36. Eg. Hare, 155, Jeune, 47-48; Darwin, 2:163.

37. Somerville, 153; Holmes, xxix; Howitt, 1:204.

38. Darwin, 2:78; Heineman, 37; Anthony Trollope, Autobiography (Berkeley: University of California Press, 1947), 24-25; Oliphant, 33.

Bertha von Suttner, Gender, and the
Representation of War

Anne O. Dzamba

In 1977 I came across Bertha von Suttner's Lay Down Your Arms in a
second-hand bookstore. Trained as I was in traditional history and
only vaguely aware of peace and women's studies, I found my curiosity
mixed with a twinge of guilt as if, by purchasing the novel, I were
indulging in a frivolous whim. I was initially attracted to the work
by Alice Asbury Abbott's introduction.[1] She described von Suttner as
the first woman since Corinna to speak publicly at the Capitol in Rome,
as the author whose book was comparable in influence to that of Uncle
Tom's Cabin, and as the defender of the claims of the individual and
the family against those of the militarized state.[2] These allusions--
to the Corinne of Mme. de Staël's novel, to Harriet Beecher Stowe, to
women and children--all seemed to connect von Suttner not only to
pacifism but also to some sort of feminism, at least in the mind of the
translator. Abbott also praised the strength of von Suttner's
reasoning, her application of an evolutionary viewpoint to social
problems, her acute realism, and her anticlericalism. What sort of
novel could this be? Though once popular, why was it now buried in the
nineteenth century? I proceeded to read the story, and though it
turned out that my particular version was abridged, I was and remained
impressed.

Die Waffen Nieder! describes the life and milieu of an Austrian
countess whose two marriages, fortune, and most of whose family were
destroyed by European conflicts between the years 1859 and 1870. These
years were significant because they marked the wars of Italian and
German unification, not only at the expense of the Austrians and the
French but also at great cost to human life. The fictional countess
narrates the story with the help of her diaries, the "red books." This
is the same method von Suttner, consulting her own extensive diaries,
used to write the book. First published in 1889, reprinted thirty-one
times in Germany alone before 1914, produced as a film, and in 1972
reissued in the Garland Library of War and Peace, the novel is regarded
as a classic work in the struggle to achieve peace, though the reasons
given for this status vary and verge on the ambiguous and ambivalent.[3]

Twentieth-century commentators consider Lay Down Your Arms devoid
of great literary qualities and rarely have explored its expressive
power. According to biographer Beatrix Kempf, the work, no different
from her other novels, was "certainly no masterpiece,"[4] Two factors
explained its success: its appearance at the right historical moment
and its universal comprehensibility, a quality that Kempf does not
elaborate upon. Another biographer, Hertha Pauli, considered it a
powerful, personal statement, the "cry of the heart" of a notable
woman.[5] Philip Wiener, while noting its "aesthetic shortcomings,"
preferred to study it as a political novel in comparison with the
writings of social or political scientists.[6] Roger Chickering, in his
meticulous study of the peace movement in imperial Germany,

61

acknowledges the novel's great effect and success "as the principal ideological document of the German peace movement," while at the same time making it sound somewhat ridiculous: its artistic value not very high "by even the most compassionate standards;" its prevailing tone, melodrama; its dialogue, declamatory and tedious; its analysis, not compelling.[7] Either the novel was considered too flagrantly sentimental or too woodenly argumentative, and it is sometimes difficult to avoid the impression of damnation with great praise.

Whether this novel is also a classic of feminism or of a particular type of feminist pacifism is yet another question. Sandi Cooper, in a study of European women in peace movements, has said the "the methods and ideas in favour of peace, in. . . Suttner's estimation, had nothing to do with sex."[8] Nevertheless, Suttner often appeared before women's groups, belonged to women's rights organizations, found friendship with women's rights activists, and wrote about women's rights issues. Consequently, feminist scholars may wish to look again in her direction. What is needed, I think, to overcome such fragmentation is a more encompassing and less condescending view of her public and private life, the dozen or so novels she wrote, the political journalism, and the Memoirs. Such a discussion might begin with Bertha von Suttner's vision of the past and future of gender relations in four works: Das Maschinenzeitalter (1888), Lay Down Your Arms (1889), Martha's Kinder (1902), and When Thoughts Will Soar (1912). This vision, I will argue, is an essential and necessary part of her program for peace.

Das Maschinenzeitalter, or The Machine Age, is a work of cultural criticism. Its narrator is positioned in the future and looks backward at attitudes and institutions of the nineteenth century. The chapter specifically devoted to women exposed the rationalizations of 19th century writers in support of the inequality of the sexes as intellectually dishonest. In the 19th century, she wrote, women were relegated to a class very different from that of men. Consider the language itself wherein the word "man" was used both generically and to mean "male" but where there was as yet no word for female person. Consider too, the widespread opinion that progress had been perfectly achieved once women were no longer exploited as beasts of burden or slaves as in the ancient past but had become companions to men. Such companions were in actual fact still subordinates, treated like children, not fully human. Noting that, unlike the prehistoric period, brute strength was no longer regarded as the highest human attribute, she shrewdly observed that other reasons now had to be found to sustain the idea of sex inequality. Since theological grounds alone were no longer entirely convincing in the 19th century, scientific and philosophical reinforcements had to be introduced. Thus women were found to be "naturally" inferior in intellect, more emotional than reasonable, and, of course, uneducable.

Suttner scornfully attacked arguments from the writings of Schopenhauer, Eduard Reich and others. First, the arguments were illogical; their assumptions dictated their conclusions. The reasoning was circular; for example, "because" philosophy in unnatural to female minds, there are no female philosophers. Or, again, "because" women have no inclination to thought, if a woman is a thinker, then she cannot really be a woman. Secondly, these authors neglected the influence of culture as an explanation for differences that occur among individuals and groups. Rather than considering historical, political, and social circumstances, these authors fancied abstractions such as "the Eternal Feminine" to carry the weight of their arguments. Moreover, the same men who denounced the intellectual inferiority of women, hailed their excellence of character, holding that women were too good to be equal to men. The latter opinions were powerful, Suttner wrote mischievously, because they were rooted in emotions.

Characteristically, the method Suttner employed to ridicule arguments for inequality consisted of reversing the gender. For instance, women who are supposed to be "the fair sex" are much demeaned by that "compliment." Suppose we said of a man that he was "a beauty of the first rank" or that "a garland of splendidly blooming men decorated the ballroom?" Both sexes would be degraded by such a manner of speaking. Suttner dwelt extensively on the tyranny of "toilette" in the 19th century and the sad fact that to please men was the one duty and only chance of happiness for most women. In another example of her rhetorical strategy, Suttner signaled out contemporary criticism of women medical students. If dissecting corpses was thought to brutalize the student, should not male as well as female students suffer in this way? Or are only women to exercise love and compassion and men only cruelty and inhumanity?

Bertha von Suttner observed that the best way to keep people in chains is to keep them ignorant and that this was the main reason the upper classes and the clergy opposed mass education. In a more progressive era, every individual would have equal claim to education, freedom and dignity without regard for race, class, or sex. Kindness, as well as justice and reason, would prevail. Crucial to this change, according to Suttner, would be a shift in the qualities assigned to women and men. Aggression and battle-readiness would no longer be considered supreme virtues in men--and the anomaly of a female field marshall would therefore be entirely irrelevant. In a more progressive time, compassion as well as intellect would be considered the province of both women and men. Both sexes would be held to the same standard, share the same qualities. Men would not become "feminine," nor women "masculine," but both would achieve a greater human dignity. Suttner's fervid optimism in this regard stemmed from her faith in sexual-cultural evolution which informed her discussion throughout and from her notion that whenever social relations between individuals are modified, the transformation of the social whole can be expected.

Suttner's writing in Das Maschinenzeitalter is witty, sarcastic, and well-informed. She had read not only the apologists of inequality but also John Stuart Mill, whom she quoted extensively, and female intellectuals as well, such as Mme. de Staël, Mathilda von Meysenburg, and Irma Troll-Borostyani. Her analysis was couched in the detached, formal style of the predominant (usually male) discourse of her day, but it is also leavened by apostrophes to her readers and by her astonished exclamations of personal outrage. Most outrageous of all, however, is that Suttner's voice in this book was anonymous. Das

Maschinenzeitalter was published under the pseudonym "Jemand" (Someone) because, as she says in her Memoirs, she was afraid that if the book were signed with a woman's name it would not reach the readers she desired: "for in scientific circles there is so much prejudice against the capacity of women as thinkers that a book signed with a women's name would simply remain unread by those for whom it was expressly designed."[9]

In her next work, Lay Down Your Arms (1889), Bertha von Suttner abandoned both the pseudonym and the scholarly tone. This time she embodied her ideas in fictional characters in novelistic form. She realized, as we learned from her Memoirs, that treatises "can only lay down abstract appeals to reason," and that she wanted to write not only what she thought but also how she felt about it and that this could best be accomplished in the form of an autobiographical novel.[10] Clearly, her assertion of personal experience in a more subjective, less imitative form was what some interpreters today might regard as a feminist act, subversive of patriarchal claims to universality. Therefore, if we grant that this novel by a woman was planned to express emotion, among other things, and did not just happen as the result of a chromosomal outburst, it is necessary to inquire how this particular "cry of the heart" was constructed and what made it powerful.

The outline of the story is a familiar one. The young and beautiful countess falls in love at first sight and marries a dashing young army officer. They have one son. The officer dies in his first battle (Magenta). After a suitable period of mourning, the somewhat chastened countess marries an older man, also in the military. He fights Austria's war with Denmark and also witnesses Austria's defeat at Königgrätz by the Prussians. Then the husband resigns his commission to work for peace. Ironically, the countess loses him, though he is now a civilian, to mob violence during the course of the Franco-Prussian War. They have one child, stillborn during wartime, and one living daughter. Certainly, personal tragedy is the impetus to political growth.

This novel centered foremost on education, both formal and informal, personal and societal, intellectual and emotional. There is an almost relentless reading of books accompanying every turn of the countess's life. Thus Martha in the novel resembles her creator:

"In all the time to which my thoughts go back, I have always, under all circumstances and in every direction, led two lives--my own and that of my reading. I mean the events that I lived through and those that came to me through description have simultaneously enriched my store of memories; to the persons known to me in daily intercourse there have been added the heroes of my authors; it is under the influence of a double experience that what I am has taken shape."[11]

64

Each turn of life, each period of reading propels her beyond the traditional curriculum that molded Austria's children into warriors and mothers of warriors. From the beginning, when describing the sensibility of young Martha, Suttner criticized the standard historical texts that reinforced the militarization of Austrian society:

"Speaking generally it is history which, as our youth are instructed, is the chief source of the admiration of war. Thence it is stamped on the childish mind that the Lord of armies is constantly decreeing battles, that these are, as it were, the vehicle upon which the destiny of nations is carried on through the ages; that they are the fulfillment of an inevitable law of nature and must always occur from time to time like storms at sea or earthquakes; that terror and woe are indeed connected with them, but the latter is fully counterpoised for the commonwealth by the importance of the results, for the individual by the blaze of glory which may be won in them....All this came out clear and unanimous in all schoolbooks."[12]

Because she was a female in a patriarchal society, the countess conceived of women's equality only as a means to become a Joan of Arc, a Semiramis, or a Catherine II and to participate in war as fully as her brothers. Such schoolbook history contrasted sharply with the new history written by Thomas Buckle (1821-1862), a figure who is mentioned significantly in many of Suttner's works. Buckle viewed the past in terms of developmental laws and general historical principles and argued that the violence of war represented only a preliminary and not a final stage in the development of civilization.[13] Clearly, Suttner understood that our concepts of past history are largely constitutive of present possibility.[14]

In the second place, Suttner's countess frequently challenged tenets taught by the clergy, particularly the notion that God is an accomplice of war. Aunt Marie is the voice in the novel of pious but always contradictory commonplaces; such as, that one must accept war and death in war as God-ordained while at the same time praying mightily for God to spare one's own relatives on the battlefield. The countess, bolstered by German biblical criticism and French skepticism, eventually breaks free of religious cant. Much later in the text, the countess and her pacifist husband expose the clerical casuistry of a Prussian military chaplain in a scene for which the plot is the merest pretext but which forms the necessary climax to the anticlerical theme.

The author's sensitivity to the power of rhetoric in society and to the uses of rhetoric in promoting the acceptability of war is also a significant characteristic of the novel in which the radical questioning of linguistic conventions plays a great part. Suttner has been acknowledged as the first woman political journalist in the German language. Certainly, in the novel, she was a student of the press and, in the voice of the countess, commented extensively on its coverage of the wars of 1859, 1864, 1866 and 1870. For instance, when in 1866 the Austrian press demanded that Berlin be leveled to the ground, she observed "'To pillage,' 'To level to the ground,' 'To put to the sword' -- these expressions do not represent the opinions of the conscience of the time but stick to people who learned them at school."[15] And after having toured Königgrätz, the despairing countess declared, "Words, words, nothing more--contemptous words, bombastic words, threatening words, spoken, written, and printed--these have caused this field to be filled with dead."[16]

Prefiguring more modern Austrian critics of language, Suttner's countess condemns the clichés passing for wisdom that gain their force largely through repetition than sense. Her father's defense of war, for instance, included the arguments that wars were the decree of God, that wars have always existed, that the earth without war would become overpopulated, that perpetual peace would weaken the species, that war develops character, and that humanity will always have disagreements and therefore be at war. When opposed in discussion the old general, she says (using a military metaphor) uses each argument "as a breastwork when he sees the preceding one fall around him; and while he retreats from the ruins of one he entrenches himself in the old earth works around another."[17] When completely cornered, the countess's father suddenly complains of deafness. If he can't have the discourse his way, then there is no discourse. In such passages, Suttner anticipates modern feminists' concern with the ways in which alternate views, and women's voices especially, fail to be heard.

Perhaps the most controversial aspect of Die Waffen Nieder at the time was Suttner's treatment of gender in relation to war. The book nearly failed to find a publisher partly for this reason and provoked criticism subsequent to publication because of it.[18] Her mention of sex roles is frequent. As stated previously, the countess expressed her concern for the socialization to war of both male and female children. She was critical too of her female relatives' indifference to politics and their love of military glamour. This is in keeping with Suttner's disapproval of aspects of the construction of "femininity" in the 19th century. The countess also noted that her male acquaintances changed the conversation from serious to light matters whenever she drew near, that they would never acknowledge her right to think about or to analyze war or diplomacy, and that they had no idea that her diaries contained not appropriately frivolous gossip but comments on the leading social theorists of her day.

What was most offensive, however, was the fact that Martha's husband was a peace activist. Because the military life was a primary occupation of the male of the aristocratic class and because the military ethos profoundly influenced the diplomacy of pre-war Europe, Suttner not only pleaded the case of women and children but also directly confronted the problem of male violence and questioned concepts of male heroism and male identity. Countess Martha met Frederick von Tilling, an army officer of the Prussian nobility, at a family dinner party and was immediately attracted by his unconventionality of mind. After courtship and marriage, Tilling continued his military career for a time because he had no other income. He explained that it was the youth not the man who had joined the army in the first place and that, though he might not enjoy it, he

66

might still serve honorably. By the end of his serve at Königgrätz, he found it impossible to serve at all. The Königgrätz chapters include a series of letters from Tilling to his wife. Using materials from her archival research, Suttner organized the war scenes around concrete episodes: the horseman riding with his intestines on the saddle; the execution of alleged spies together with their young children; the statue of the Blessed Virgin impassively watching the village burn to the ground. These scenes make an effective contrast to official propaganda as well as move the hear. Count Tilling explains his decision to quit as a kind of apostacy:

> "...in a word, my former vague, half-smothered feeling changed into a clear conviction, a conviction which makes it from this time impossible to do service to the war god....The mysterious, supernatural, awe inspiring feeling which the appearance of this deity generally awakes in men and which in former times obscured my sense also, has now passed away from me. The liturgy of the bulletins and the ritual of heroic phraseology no longer appear to me as a divine revelation; the mighty organ-voice of the cannon, the incense-smoke of the powder have no more charm for me."[19]

Subsequently, the couple jointly become advocates for peace, a partnership very much the reflection of Suttner's own married life. The career of Frederick von Tilling, in contrast to the other men in the book, would seem to be a fulfillment of Suttner's vision of androgyny, as set forth in Das Maschinenzeitalter. Both men and women are now held to the highest standard of kindness and justice and both husband and wife share convictions which, if they became universal, would lead to a reorientation of female and male personality and, according to Suttner, the end of violence.

Although Bertha von Suttner's project failed to end war, might Lay Down Your Arms still be compared with Uncle Tom's Cabin? Both novels were perplexingly popular, unlike more canonical works. Both were seemingly straightforward stores with many realistic details. Both were rich in idealism and sentiment. Harriet Beecher Stowe's novel, however, was Christian in concept; Bertha von Suttner's markedly secular. Stowe's novel, according to Jane Tompkins, was a reenactment of the Christian drama of redemption; its characters were figures in an allegory.[20] Suttner, on the other hand, fashioned a secular mythology with the help of Buckle, Darwin, Büchner, and Strauss; her characters, apart from the protagonists, were deliberate stereotypes. Both novelists planned to arouse their audiences' participation in the myths. Stowe's plot needed only to follow the Christian drama. Suttner's rested on contemporary historical events and on a symmetry contrasting the claims of the personal and the political, the concrete and the abstract, the Austrian and the Prussian, the female and the male, life and death. Both books also depended upon a transformation of gender relations without which the social and moral transformation the novelists desired could not take place. For Stowe, the centrality of motherhood and domesticity was essential to the power of Christian love to change society. Her new society would therefore be controlled by women and not by men. For Bertha von Suttner, both women and men might serve progressive forces, but men would have to shed their habits of aggression and women would have to become more politically knowledgeable and responsible.

The sequel to Lay Down Your Arms is Martha's Kinder. The story takes peace and gender reform into the second generation. Countess Martha von Tilling's son Rudolf is mired in conflict between responsibility to his family and class and his yearning to serve humanity. Ultimately, he repudiates his entail and his military rank and, following in the footsteps of Fredrick von Tilling, he joins the peace movement. Rudolf, unlike Fredrick, has had no specifically military experience. Consequently, Suttner had a more difficult task in explaining his metamorphosis. Thus she presents him endlessly groping for words in his own mind and in the texts of his public speeches. In a tragicomic sequence, he uses the rhetoric of violence, to his later chagrin and regret, in speaking against violence: i.e., delivering blows against and slaying the dragons of militarism. In a more dramatic scene, Rudolf visits a café in suburban Vienna where, to his horror and anger, he witnesses the victory celebration of an anti-Semitic Christian Socialist party candidate and his violence-prone petit bourgeois friends.

By far the more powerfully imagined and written story is that of Rudolf's younger sister Sylvia. In the beginning she is preoccupied with courtship and a wedding celebration which is presented as a piece of enchantment, not unrealistic, if Suttner's Memoirs of her aristocratic youth are to be believed. Very quickly, however, Sylvia's marriage sours. Her sensual temperament requires a consort of sensitivity and intelligence. Her husband, Capt. Delnitsky, is handsome but brutal, anti-intellectual and unfaithful. Sylvia decides to obtain a divorce and makes a determined, poignant case against the double standard of sexual morality. The moment when Sylvia confesses her unhappiness to her mother is the stormy moment in the novel when the two themes of peace activism and women's rights confront one another. Martha has reserved her energies mainly for keeping the memory and the peace cause of her husband alive.[21] Now Sylvia protests to her mother that, in her devotion to peace, she has overlooked a moral and social injustice comparable, if not worse than, anything her mother has campaigned against. Sylvia angrily shouts, "I rebel."[22] Meanwhile her equally angry husband exclaims that the peace movement is totally harmless, but the question of women's rights--that was taking on serious dimensions![23] The worried Martha cannot but grant the validity of Sylvia's complaint.

Sylvia's and Rudolf's issues in this novel are linked together by the self-conscious reflections of Martha in the form of letters or diary entries. While she continues to press themes raised in earlier works and, as before, is best at criticizing her own class and her own liberal politics and political allies, she now recognizes a greater complexity and intractability in social affairs and is especially concerned with a more immediate attainment of women's rights. In the end, she sticks to her theory of change based upon non-violent androgynous social evolution, which, she believed, may enable even aristocrats and patriarchs to accept the destruction of their own privileges, though she despairs of her ability fully to articulate her vision.

Bertha von Suttner's last novel, When Thoughts Will Soar: A Romance of the Immediate Future was published in 1912, in spite of and perhaps because of her premonitions of war and revolution. It found little acclaim. Suttner, as was well known, had played an important role in the decision of dynamite manufacturer Alfred Nobel to establish a prize for peace. Her final novel used advanced technology, in this case air flight, as its leading motif. Modern technological capability should not be permitted to outrun moral progress. Humanity, in other words, was "to learn to fly morally."

The leading character, Franka Garlett, is the daughter of an impoverished intellectual. After his death she is alone in the world, her mother having died many years before. At the very outset she rejects a dubious offer of "protection" from a wealthy profligate. Luckily her mother's family comes to her rescue and she finds herself with a magnificent inheritance and aristocratic relatives. Epitomizing reactionary politics, these relatives caution her against the evils of socialism, feminism, and pacifism. She in turn resolves to strike an independent course, rejects impending marriage, and bravely sets off on a lecture tour with a message for the young women of the world. Elsewhere Suttner had stated that first of all it was necessary for women to become better informed; that in itself was revolutionary. Hence Franka's first speeches stressed education:

"Place and voice in the direction of public affairs?

That certainly is already on the programme of the Movement, but the most important thing is a knowledge and understanding of the universal laws that govern nature and the world; then only can she judge and cooperate where social arrangements are to be decided."[24]

As her fame spreads, Franka is invited to a special gathering of notables subsidized by an American millionaire (modeled on Andrew Carnegie): they are what we today call futurists. Franka confounds the conference with lectures that place women directly in the public arena. As one listener observed

"Indeed you went beyond your accustomed domain, the education of women for an intellectual participation in the questions of the day; you entered the domain of actual feminism--you pleaded for practical cooperation of women in government and lawmaking."[25]

Or, in the words of the erstwhile progressive German prince, whose offer of marriage she has just rejected

"And suddenly yesterday you began to join all the demands of the Women's Rights party--female votes, members of Parliament...perhaps I am reactionary, but I shudder at the mere though of seeing women--delicate, lovely women--dragged about in the dusty battlefield."[26]

And Franka replies, "Do you mean Parliaments? Parliaments need not be dusty and need not be battlefields, but places for work." To the end,

Bertha von Suttner was insistent that equal rights for women were essential but that they would make no sense at all "Unless we have sufficient imagination to conceive of simultaneously altered forms of society" and that the achievement of that community depended upon a sea-change in gender relations.[27]

Bertha von Suttner's liberal humanism was enriched and made more complex by her feminism. She began to deconstruct sexual identity and to imagine a world in which power was neither genderized nor violent. Like Betty Reardon in Sexism and the War System (1985), she emphasized the social and learned causes of war and considered women's and peace issues inextricable. Like Virginia Woolf in the classic Three Guineas (1938), she stressed the education of women but always on condition that men's education also be modified. Prevailing scholarly views would suggest that Suttner had a cause but "was no rebel" because she did not challenge the established order of society, only the assumption that war was part of that order.[28] On the contrary, to classify Suttner as a pacifist of the type that was confident peace could be achieved without altering the existing political and social order is to overlook and underestimate the utopianism of her life-long advocacy of women's rights.

West Chester University
November 1986

Notes

[1] Bertha von Suttner, Ground Arms! Translated by Alice Asbury Abbott (Chicago: McClurg, 1892). Abridged. I located no information on Abbott.

[2] Suttner reported that her appearance in Rome, while applauded, also occasioned some ridicule in the press. Memoirs 1:365-66. Leo Tolstoy wrote to Suttner that he though the novel might have as much impact as Stowe's work; later commentators assumed so. Memoirs 1:343.

[3] Bertha von Suttner, Lay Down Your Arms: The Autobiography of Martha von Tilling, 2d ed., rev., trans. T. Holmes, 1894, with an introduction by Irwin Abrams (New York: Garland, 1972). The film, produced by Nordisk, Copenhagen, was canceled due to the outbreak of the world war.

[4] Beatrix Kempf, Woman for Peace: The Life of Bertha von Suttner (Park Ridge, New Jersey: Noyes Press, 1973), 24.

[5] Hertha Pauli, Cry of the Hear (New York: 1957).

[6] Phillip B. Wiener, "Bertha von Suttner and the Political Novel," in Siegbert S. Prawer, R. Hinton Thomas, and Leonard Foster, eds., Essays in German Language, Culture, and Society (London: University of London Institute of Germanic Studies, 1969), 160-76.

[7] Roger Chickering, Imperial Germany and a World Without War (Princeton: Princeton University Press, 1975), 89-94.

[8] Sandi E. Cooper, "Women's Participation in European Peace Movements: The Struggle to Prevent World War I," in Ruth Roach Peirson, ed., Women and Peace: Theoretical, Historical, and Practical Perspectives (London: Croom Helm, 1987), 66.

[9] Bertha von Suttner, Memoirs: The Records of an Eventful Life (New York: Garland, 1972), 1:276, 289-93.

[10] BvS, Memoirs, 1:294.

[11] Memoirs, 1:99.

[12] BvS, LDYA (Holmes), 3.

[13] Buckle criticized contemporary historians for their naive lack of theory. He believed that human actions were governed neither by chance nor by God, but were the result of understandable laws (including statistical laws). He was, in a word, a positivist of the mid-nineteenth century. He also believed that while physical conditions were important variables in history, the progress of European civilization was increasingly marked by the decline of the arbitrary, unmediated influence of the external, material world. It was, therefore, especially important to study the laws of internal human mental processes.

[14] Lynette McGrath, "A History of Peace," Lancaster Independent Press, 18 No. 10 (Feb., 1987): 11.

[15] BvS, Ground Arms! (Abbott), 129.

[16] Ibid., 209.

[17] Ibid., 119-20, 123.

[18] BvS, Memoirs, 1:294-302.

[19] BvS, LDYA (Holmes), 224.

[20] Jane P. Tompkins, "Sentimental Power: Uncle Tom's Cabin and the Politics of Literary History," Glyph 8 (Baltimore: Johns Hopkins University Press, 1986), 79-102.

[21] BvS wrote on one occasion to Auguste Fickert that she did not have the energy to work personally for her women's rights group but that she would and could proclaim her sympathy for her goals. Brigitte Hamann, Bertha von Suttner, Ein Leben für den Frieden (München: Piper, 1987), 453.

[22] Bertha von Suttner, Martha's Kinder: Eine Fortsetzung zu Die Waffen Nieder! (Dresden: E. Pierson, 1903), 272-73, 337.

[23] Ibid., 280.

[24] Bertha von Suttner, When Thoughts Will Soar: A Romance of the Immediate Future, trans. Nathan Haskell Dole (Boston: Houghton Mifflin, 1914), 113-34.

[25] Ibid., 260.

[26] Ibid., 269.

[27] Ibid., 247.

[28] Irwin Abrams, "Bertha von Suttner," in Harold Josephson, ed., Biographical Dictionary of Modern Peace Leaders (Westport, Conn.: Greenwood Press, 1985), 923.

Other Works Consulted

Abrams, Irwin B. "Bertha von Suttner and the Nobel Peace Prize," in Journal of Central European Affairs, 22 (Oct., 1962), 286-307.

Key, Ellen. Florence Nightingale und Bertha von Suttner: Zwei Frauen im Kriege wider den Krieg. Zurich, 1919.

Laurence, Richard R. 'The Viennese Press and the Peace Movement: 1899-1914," Michigan Academician 13:2 (1980), 155-63.

Playne, Caroline. Bertha von Suttner and the Struggle to Avert War. London: Allen Unwin, 1936.

Reardon, Betty. Sexism and the War System. New York: Teachers College Press, Columbia University, 1985.

Schnedl-Bubeniček, Hanna. "Pazifistinnen. Ein Resümee zu theoretischen Ausführungen und literarischen Darstellungen Bertha von Suttners und Rosa Mayreders," in Friedensbewegungen: Bedingungen und Wirkungen. Gernot Heiss und Heinrich Lutz, eds., Wien, 1984.

Stockwell, Rebecca, "Bertha von Suttner and Rosika Schwimmer: Pacifists in the Dual Monarchy," in Seven Studies in Medieval English History and Other Historical Essays. Richard H. Bowers, ed. Jackson, Mississippi, 1983.

Suttner, Bertha von. Miscellaneous pieces at the Swarthmore College Peace Collection, Swarthmore, Pa: "Marianne Hainisch als Pazifistin"; "Die Frauen und der Völkerfriede"; "Bertha von Suttner's letzter Brief an die deutschen Frauen."

_____. "Universal Peace from a Woman's Standpoint," North American Review. CLXIX (July, 1899), 50-61.

Part II

The Joseph J. Mathews Address

Presented at the European History Section Luncheon

November 13, 1987

New Orleans, Louisiana

Toynbee and the Historical Profession

William H. McNeill

Within the profession, Toynbee was surely the most controversial historian of our century, with A.J.P. Taylor a distant runner up. Taylor's book about Hitler and World War II provoked a good deal of professional thunder, but Toynbee's enormous popularity in the late 1940s and early 1950s made him an especially tempting target; and the profession responded by challenging both the accuracy of his facts and his entire conception of the course and meaning of history. Today he is almost forgotten in this country and in Europe; only in Japan does his reputation endure, sustaining the existence of a Toynbee Society that publishes three periodicals, holds meetings regularly, and in other ways seeks to perpetuate his angle of vision on human life and history twelve whole years after his death.

Memory is so short among us that perhaps I should begin by rehearsing the simple facts of Toynbee's rise and fall in the English-speaking world. His fame went up like a rocket in March, 1947 with the publication of a one volume condensation of the first six volumes of A Study of History. This provided Time Magazine with the occasion to hail Toynbee as a guide for Americans through the confusion created by their new rivalry with Russia; and a large part of Toynbee's popularity in this country depended on the way he was touted by Time editors for the next ten years or so. Toynbee had indeed made much of 'challenge and response' as the pattern of civilizational growth; and it certainly seemed to many Americans in 1947 that the country faced a new and entirely unexpected challenge in the form of Communist advances in Europe and China.

Nonetheless, Toynbee was always a reluctant Cold Warrior and never lent himself wholeheartedly to the cause that Henry Luce, the publisher of Time, had wished upon him. By 1954 Toynbee made his reservations against British and American self-righteousness explicit by publishing a little book, The World and the West, in which he denounced westerners for past aggression against the other peoples of the earth. This damaged his reputation in Great Britain, for it came at a time when the British empire was in full retreat, and most Englishmen felt that their contribution to the progress of civilization as rulers and managers in Asia and Africa, deserved a kinder judgment than Toynbee was prepared to allow. Americans rather agreed that European empires were wicked; but when, in the 1960s, Toynbee started to criticize United States government actions in Vietnam, the Middle East and elsewhere, only a few dissidents agreed with him, so that he alienated most of his American admirers, if they had not already grown tired of him.

This political trajectory defined the rise and fall of Arnold J. Toynbee as a public figure in the United States and Britain, first sustaining and then destroying his popular following. But a second current also contributed to the rise and fall of his reputation. Most of us have forgotten, or never knew, that the volumes of his great book, A Study of History, were warmly praised by academics when they first appeared, both in literary reviews and in professional journals. The breadth of his learning and the scope of his vision dazzled nearly everyone; and I know of only one reviewer of the first three volumes who suggested, almost sotto voce, and after paying warm tribute to Toynbee's achievement, that perhaps the history of the entire world was too much for any one mind to grasp.

This, of course, all occurred before Toynbee suddenly became famous in 1947. In spite of the praise his volumes received, professional historians paid little attention to his work since, after all, experts did not expect to learn anything important from the pages of a world history. But once Time Magazine made his name into a household word in Britain as well as in America, ordinary historians suddenly found it necessary to have an opinion about this new star in the firmament. Naturally, they turned to the places in his book where he treated whatever they knew best, and it was not difficult for experts to find things left out, lopsided judgments, and even positive errors. Finding such defects, most historians started to give free reign to the streak of jealousy that runs in us all, and started to criticize Toynbee for making mistakes. Initially, criticism often took the form of praising the work as a whole, except for the passages dealing with the subject the critic happened to know most about. In the late 1940s, the Dutch historian, Pieter Geyl, took this line in a debate with Toynbee on the BBC, and he continued thereafter to be the most prominent and persistent critic of Toynbee's detailed accuracy.

Academic dismissal of Toynbee's importance took a different tone and direction in the next decade. Instead of admiring the whole while criticizing the parts, academics began to denounce the entire structure of the work and deny the value of Toynbee's approach to history. The high point of this intensified attack was a savage article by Hugh Trevor-Roper, published in Encounter in 1957. Trevor-Roper chose to burlesque Toynbee, accusing him of being not a historian but a prophet who ought, even if he had not yet gotten round to it, to want to found a new era, A.T. (Anno Toynbeeana) to supplant the more familiar A.D. with which historians had hitherto had to put up. Dubbing Toynbee a prophet allowed Trevor-Roper, and all who concurred in his dismissive wit, to refuse to consider Toynbee's ideas seriously at all. Being a prophet, and a false one at that, historians need not bother reading his ten volumes and could simply forget about him. This swiftly became the dominant professional attitude and remains so to this day.

The cutting edge of most historical research and debate in the post World War II era confirmed this posture, for it was poles removed from the ecumenical overarching vision that Toynbee had sought to cultivate. Historians specialized and then specialized some more, creating a multiplicity of sub-disciplines; and in their haste to develop new techniques and open new areas of research, lost interest in how their discoveries could be fitted together into history as a whole--or even into separate national histories treated as wholes.

It would be unfair for me not to point out that Toynbee exposed himself to Trevor-Roper's attack by his frequent invocation of "Spiritual Reality" as a factor in human affairs. This arose out of key moments in Toynbee's private experience which he interpreted as encounters with a transcendental Being that comforted him at times of extreme personal stress. Toynbee's view of this "Spiritual Reality" approximated to the God of traditional Christianity for a while in the early years of World War II, but eventually diverged, and took on Buddhist overtones in his old age. This may well have helped to assure the extraordinary upsurge of Toynbee's influence in Japan in the 1970s. It also made Trevor-Roper's burlesque just close enough to the truth to be damning in the eyes of persons who did not share Toynbee's mystical experiences, and distrusted anything smacking of the abnormal or unreasonable as a source of truth.

Academic dismissal of Toynbee's significance as a historian therefore more or less coincided with Toynbee's public criticism of American policies towards the Arab and Vietnamese peoples, and thus confirmed and reinforced the popular disenchantment with his pronouncements that became definite in this country after about 1965.

Is it time now, in 1987, to reconsider? I think so, for the dismissal he suffered was, in its way, as lopsided and extreme as his earlier apotheosis had been. We are getting to be far enough removed from the years of his extraordinary rise and fall to be able to assume a more neutral, more detached, and more genuinely historical attitude towards what he had to say, and how he said it. I have, accordingly, begun work on a biography, which will, probably, appear on the centenary of his birth, in April 1989. I hope it will help to bring professional opinion around to a juster appreciation of his accomplishment, both in its greatness and its limits.

Biography is a new venture for me, and I undertook the task, initially, at the invitation of Toynbee's surviving son. The invitation was attractive because my own youthful encounter with Toynbee's vision of history did much to shape my mind. It follows that if I can do something to rescue his reputation in professional circles, I will be helping my own cause, and the cause of macrohistory generally as a branch of historical study. So I freely admit that I have an axe to grind.

I also find myself walking a difficult line between praise and blame. A just balance is always hard. It is doubly hard for me in writing about someone who once illumined my darkness with a dazzling light, showing that history embraced the whole world instead of being confined to ancient, medieval and modern European and Western history, as I had been educated to suppose. In retrospect, indeed, I find it all but incredible how my teachers left out so much. Everyone knew that China, for instance, had a long history; but all the same China, along with all the rest of the non-European world entered history with the arrival of Europeans on its shores. China's separate history was, well, separate--the domain of language experts, of Orientalists, or perhaps of comparative religionists. Historians simply eschewed such exotica as irrelevant to their subject.

I understand in retrospect how such an ethnocentric view of the appropriate subject matter of historical study had arisen, for if what really and truly mattered in human history was the rise of liberty as embodied in European constitutional forms of government, then by definition all the peoples and regions of earth who had not contributed to the development of such governments were excluded from meaningful history, and entered the mainstream only when they collided with European governments in recent centuries and entered, as beginners, upon the difficult process of becoming worthy of constitutional liberty too. There was, therefore, a perfectly good reason behind the way my teachers distributed their attention and professional labors; but they had forgotten it themselves, and perhaps no longer really believed it.

As a graduate student in 1940 I was apprentice to that tradition of learning, entirely ignorant of why it was shaped the way it was, and ignorant, as well, of how naively limited it had become. Casually picking three green bound volumes off the shelf one day in 1940, non-committally titled A Study of History, therefore inaugurated an extraordinary experience for me. For my reading of Toynbee's pages opened new vistas--extraordinary new vistas--of the rightful realm of historical study. He showed me that all the world has a history, or rather histories; and, what was equally exciting, that those histories had intelligible shapes that all conformed to roughly the same pattern. I have never been the same since; and I still feel that a book that had such power for a young fellow nearly half a century ago deserves to be remembered as something more than the work of a crackpot and should not be assigned to an Orwellian memory hole, as our profession has tended to do.

Yet the filial piety that I feel for Toynbee runs headlong into my consciousness of all the points on which I have come to differ from him. My view of history is not his any longer, and the segmentation of the historical record into separate civilizations, which was the way he ordered the confusion of the world's past, seems to me imperfect as best, and positively misleading inasmuch as it denies the power of contacts across civilizational boundaries to stimulate new departures and drive the wheels of historical change. I believe such contacts were the main drive wheels of change throughout history--before as well as after the emergence of the earliest civilizations; and that such contacts and rivalries remain the main disturbers of the status quo-- whether it be our rivalry with the Soviets since 1945, or our more recent perplexity in trying to compete economically with Japan.

I face another difficulty in treating Toynbee fairly, for like Trevor-Roper I do not share Toynbee's transcendentalism. It is tempting to explain it all away by arguing that the Toynbee was self-deceived in supposing that the extraordinary states of consciousness he experienced in moments of extreme personal distress were encounters with a transcendent "Spiritual Reality." Unbelievers and scoffers have often behaved in just that fashion and as Trevor-Roper did in 1957. But I am also aware than human history shows how important the mystical tradition has been, not only among Christians, but among devotees of every other major religion of the

80

world. Can anyone justly scoff at what he has not experienced himself? Can one dismiss what many millions have reverenced and aspired to as mere delusion? Perhaps one can and should. But for a biographer of a man who had such experiences, and who was shaped, or rather reshaped, by them, to do so would be presumptuous indeed, even if I cannot pretend to enter into the mystic realm with real sympathy or conviction. To be sure, my Toynbee, the man whose vision of the past entranced me when I was young, had not yet revised his view of human history to take account of his encounters with transcendent Being. That began in volumes 4-6 of A Study in History, which appeared in 1939, and achieved full and uninhibited expression in the concluding four volumes that came out in 1954.

So today, in trying to write his biography I find myself removed from his initial viewpoint by all those discoveries, insights and judgments that constitute my adult professional life; and then doubly isolated by my failure to share his mystical experiences and his access to transcendental truths that resulted. The temptation, under these circumstances, is to explain things awa, and to diminish Toynbee's achievement by criticizing all the ways he differed from my own points of view. I am far from sure that I have resisted this temptation as thoroughly as I could wish. It is, after all, self-centered folly to suppose that he ought to agree with me and deserves censure when he does not. Failure to recognize the circumstances and precedents within which Toynbee worked, and failure to recognize the things he did differently and put together in new ways is failure to be a historian. And I do aspire to deserve that label. Suffice it to say, therefore, that I have tried to present the evolution of his views with as much detachment and precision as I can; and have tried to account for the rise and fall of his reputation in the United States, in Japan and elsewhere with as much insight as I could.

The result, I hope, is a portrait that will perhaps make others besides myself think that Toynbee was an important figure in the development of our profession and deserves continued attention, even if, or just because, our views of the human condition and of the patterning of history differ from his, in greater or less degree. Pending the appearance of my book, and the fuller account of his life and thought that it will offer, let me merely say here that we ought, as historians, to be interested in his career on two levels. He was, after all, the only member of our profession in this century who achieved the status of wise man and policy advisor to men of affairs--a status that since World War II has normally been reserved for economists. The rise of the economics profession to this eminence in public estimation would be an interesting inquiry--a reflection, I believe, of the practical success economists had in inventing the science of macroeconomics during World War II. Toynbee's version of macrohistory therefore deserves to be compared with Keynesian and post-Keynesian macroeconomics as a medium of public enlightenment and guidance in questions of public policy. He in effect entered into competition with the economists of 1947, thanks to the way Henry Luce chose to treat Toynbee and his book. The circumstances and personalities, the modes of communication and public anxieties that entered into Toynbee's public career in this country (and in other countries) therefore deserves our professional attention. The fact that he was a historian might even be expected to give such inquiry a special resonance for us, since historians' wisdom is usually confined to captive classroom audiences, or diffused, palely, through books that are read mainly by other historians.

On a second level, Toynbee ought to interest us even more, for he addressed the question of what the study of history is and ought to be far more explicitly and with much greater originality than is usual among us. He began, indeed, with a radical rejection of the sort of patriotic, national history his mother had taught him. (She was a historian too, of a precise, even pedantic and fiercely patriotic stripe.) He first knitted Greek and Roman history, taught to him as separate subjects in school, into a seamless whole extending from about 900 B.C., when something he came to call Hellenic civilization began to emerge until about 500 A.D. when the emergence of a new Byzantine style of civilization announced the demise of the classical world. Next, Toynbee wrestled with the question of how to fit the history of what he called "the East" into the pattern of rise and fall that he saw on either side of Hellenic civilization. For the Hellenic adventure of 900 B.C. to 500 A.D. had been preceded by an earlier Minoan-Mycenaean cycle of Aegean civilization, and was followed, of course, by the rise of Western civilization--a civilization whose impending fall was a matter of common discussion in Edwardian England even before World War I. Eventually, with help from Spengler and from his direct observation of the breakdown of civilized restraints among Greeks and Turks who were warring in Anatolia in 1920-22, Toynbee concluded that the "East" had to be subdivided into a series of separate civilizations, each analogous to the Hellenic civilization whose lineaments had become clear to him before 1920.

To flesh out this vision required years of voracious reading--exploring Moslem, Indian, Chinese, Japanese, and Amerindian histories, with excursions into anthropology, comparative religion, psychology and other related disciplines. The end result was A Study of History, the book on which his professional reputation centrally rests. If one approaches it not as truth revealed from on high, as some of Toynbee's admirers once tended to do, but instead views it as a milestone in the development of historical scholarship in our century, then, I think, Toynbee's enduring professional significance ought to become apparent. From my standpoint, its central significance is still the same that its first volumes had for me back in 1940. The simple fact is that Toynbee's book, for the first time, made all parts of the earth and all branches of humanity historicable. Nothing and no one was, in principle, left out. His information, of course, was limited to what the state of scholarship allowed him to know. Africa, for instance, had yet to be explored by historians; and aboriginal Australia, remained, as it remains today, beyond the reach of our discipline. In general, hunting and gathering peoples attracted little of Toynbee's attention; but the great literate traditions (and among Ameridians, protoliterate and merely monumental traditions) did enter Toynbee's purview, and he saw them all, in principle, as equivalent to one another and therefore of equal value and importance.

82

This broadening of view, and its escape from previous ethnocentrism, seems to me an enormous step forward. We are heirs of all the human past, not just of the Christian or European past; and our history deserves to be--indeed must be, if it is to be true--the history of all of humankind in all its branches, everywhere in the world. No other history is adequate to the circumstances and realities of the 20th and still more of the 21st century. Toynbee, more than any other single person, was its pioneer. His enduring importance for our profession rests on that simple fact. We neglect it, if we persist in neglecting it, at our peril, for historians who teach and practice a merely specialized history are falling short of our basic professional responsibility, which is to make the world make sense--I am tempted to add, whether it does make sense or not.

No one before Toynbee attained to anything more than a programmatic sketch of world history. The general progress of scholarship, together with Toynbee's synthetic imagination, powerful memory and insatiable curiosity, especially in matters political and religious, allowed him to flesh out his scheme of civilizational rise and fall more richly and exactly than had been possible in any earlier age. His book therefore deserves admiration and professional esteem, despite all the errors that he committed and despite the ultimate inadequacy of the scheme he adopted for giving form and meaning to his history. Every scheme proves inadequate sooner or later--even Newton's. Successors always find errors in the work of their predecessors. But only a few intellectual pioneers break through older paradigms as dramatically as Toynbee managed to do. Such figures set an agenda for the future which others may pursue. But there is no assurance that full professional exploration and exploitation of the new possibilities will actually take place. So far, few historians have found Toynbee's challenge worth pursuing. If that attitude persists, his importance for our discipline will shrink to marginality.

On the other hand, if world history does come to life in our schools and colleges, as many thoughtful persons now believe ought to happen, then Toynbee's standing among historians is bound to grow. Which way things will go remains to be seen. In the meanwhile I commend him to you as a genuinely great historian and poet of the human condition. Let me leave you with the thought that as Herodotus was to Homer, so Toynbee is to Milton. These equations strike me as genuinely and rather surprisingly accurate. In each case a prose writer elaborated upon and altered the world view of his poetic forerunner. In each case the historian reached out to embrace the entire knowable world in his account of the great and wonderful deeds of his fellow human beings. All four set out to make the world intelligible, and all four failed to convince those who came after them, or all of their contemporaries for that matter.

Anyone who seeks to reduce the complexity of the world to a coherent vision is bound to fail. But then, heroes, too, are bound to fail, and have always done so every since Gilgamesh and Hector defined the meaning of heroism for us. But we do not withhold our admiration from heroes because they fail; and we ought not to withhold our admiration for such a hero of the lamp as Arnold Joseph Toynbee just because we cannot now subscribe to all the details or even to the general framework of his history. He was heroic; he did open vast new vistas to historians. We ought to reverence such boldness and even try to emulate him in viewing the world as one intelligible, or almost intelligible, whole.

Williams College
November 1987

Selected Papers from the 1987 Annual Meeting

The Austrian Military Response to the French Revolution
and Napoleon: The Problem of Popular Participation in War

Gunther E. Rothenberg

The Wars of the French Revolution and Napoleon shook the European
state system and raised basic questions about its methods of conducting
war. The emergence of a revolutionary regime in France, served by vast
armies mobilizing all the physical and emotional resources of the
"nation in arms" posed a major challenge to the other powers. Although
these new armies were by no means uniformly successful, and while
revolutionary ardor did not survive for long after 1794, their vast
numbers, reaching some 650,000 by 1793, continued to fuel French
expansion. Fighting with considerable enthusiasm under young and
energetic commanders, these armies continued to wage mobile, offensive,
and ruthless warfare, disregarding the constraints of limited manpower
and resources which had limited conflicts earlier in the eighteenth
century. In 1799, these forces came under the control of Napoleon who
used them in his own pursuit of power, using their numbers and fighting
capabilities to establish, if briefly, a new Carolingian Empire from
the Tagus to the Vistula.[1]

The evident superiority of the French forced their adversaries to
look for effective military responses. The problem was not just
Napoleon's military genius, important as it was, nor the new fighting
methods of the French, or for that matter new weapons or strategic
innovations. During the wars from 1792 to 1815 there appeared no new
weapons, except for shrapnel projectiles and rocket artillery, both
used by the British, and while there were some operational and
administrative advances, there were none that had not been extensively
discussed and to some degree practiced by theorists and commanders
before the Revolution.[2] Indeed, some keen contemporary observers
perceived that the key elements of the new, more energetic and decisive
style of war were political, the result of major changes in the
relationships between armies and societies. "The tremendous effects of
the French Revolution abroad," Clausewitz wrote, "were not caused so
much by new military methods and concepts as by radical changes in
policies and administration, by the new character of government, the
altered conditions of the French people." As a result, the "people
became a participant in war; instead of governments and armies as
heretofore, the whole weight of the nation was thrown into the
balance."[3]

And here exactly was the main problem. Although taken together
the various powers opposing the Revolution and Napoleon clearly were
capable of matching, even surpassing, French manpower and resources,
they did not wish, and perhaps were unable, to make the socio-political
changes necessarily required by popular participation in war. Among
the major powers, England, of course, never even contemplated fielding
a popular-based mass army; Prussia belatedly did so in a limited

fashion after 1808, while Russia, a society in which serfdom was fundamental and fear of rebellion pervasive, met the challenge from the west in its own traditional way.[4] Austria, finally, was a special case. Between 1792 and 1814, its army carried the main burden of fighting on land both in numbers engaged and in time at war, and though repeatedly defeated, this army displayed astonishing staying power. An English military historian, Cyril Falls, described the Habsburg army as the most formidable force the French had to face in the last years of the eighteenth and the first few years of the nineteenth centuries, while Albert Sorel concluded that Austria "always was one idea and one army behind, [but] she always had an idea and an army."[5] Yet, this organization made no fundamental changes, but remained in its essentials, and above all in its recruitment practices, basically an eighteenth century institution, solidly based on the military system established by Maria Theresa and Joseph II.

The reasons for this conservative posture are clear, deriving both from the character of the rulers and the multinational character and diverse institutions of this empire. The rulers, first and foremost of whom was the Emperor Francis who ascended the throne in 1792, were cautious conservatives, nervous and suspicious of all innovations. Like almost all Austrian rulers since the days of the Thirty Years' War he distrusted outstanding soldiers and was unwilling to grant them too much authority. For that reason, he never fully trusted his brother, the Archduke Charles, the monarchy's foremost general, and always was careful to circumscribe his power.[6] For that matter, Charles also distrusted fundamental change which, so he believed, would endanger the established order. The archduke always believed that popular participation in war was undesirable. The monarchy, he held, could neither afford to rouse the latent national spirits nor mobilize its resources to the utmost. Discussing options open to the government in 1804, Charles concluded that Austria could indeed raise an enormous army if, "like France in 1793, the entire state became a vast encampment where every able-bodied man would be a soldier;" but, he warned, this not only would ruin the economy "but also destroy the established order."[7]

Therefore, neither the archduke nor any other leading soldier ever was prepared to make radical changes in the relationship between the army and society; and especially, they had little faith in relying on popular participation in war. They realized as Colonel Karl Leiberich Baron Mack, who later led an Austrian field army to disaster at Ulm in 1805 but who in the 1790s was regarded as an up and coming officer, put it, "the lack of unity, conflicting jurisdictions, and large distances make the Austrian military system far more complex than the Prussian."[8]

What Mack meant was that the "Austrian Monarchy," a convenient misnomer for the territories collected by an ambitious dynasty represented the most ethnically and culturally diverse group of peoples in Europe, stretching from the Lower Rhine to Galicia and from Bohemia to northern Italy. From Vienna the Habsburgs ruled over these lands by virtue of separate titles and their military posture was constrained by the lack of a uniform authority. manpower for the army was collected on the basis of different arrangements in the various lands, and neither men nor money could always be counted on.[9]

Although by 1792, the Habsburgs possessed a regular standing army numbering, at least on paper, about 300,000 men, it was not a national army. The officer corps, aristocratic and international, had professional and personal loyalties to the monarch. While the highest command positions were reserved for members of the dynasty and the great families, the lower grades included many sons of the small nobility and even the bourgeoisie, educated in the military academies or in foreign armies. Promotion from the ranks was possible, though infrequent. Overall, the officers varied in quality, but their devotion to the dynasty and their bravery never were in doubt.[10]

The rank and file was procured by selective conscription and voluntary enlistment. Although in 1771, Joseph II had introduced a systematic census, a Conscription, in the Austrian lands, the service obligations applied only to the hereditary alpine possessions, except the Tyrol, and to Galicia. Hungary, the Austrian Netherlands, and the Italian duchies were excluded. Also exempt everywhere were nobles, officials, and revenue producing elements, including whole areas and towns. In practice, conscription was implemented only for the lowest classes, so that with an overwhelming rural population the ranks were filled with the poorest peasants and agricultural laborers. Serving for life or until invalided out, they made steady soldiers, tough and inured to hardship. In Italy, the Tyrol, and the Netherlands men were obtained by free recruitment. Hungary was a special case. Here the "ruling nation," that is the magnates, nobles, and clergy represented in the Diet had accepted the principle of a standing army, but had retained control over recruitment and supply. Hungarian units were filled by the local authorities according to quotas fixed by the Diet, and usually the Hungarian contribution to the army was small compared to the hereditary provinces and even in times of crisis the Habsburgs had to negotiate and cajole for manpower and supply rather than to command.[11] Of course, the southern regions of Hungary and Croatia were a special case. Here, on the so-called Military Borders, established originally as a defense against Turkish incursions, military service was truly universal and the mostly South Slav Grenzer contingents provided between one fourth and one third of troops in the Habsburg army.[12]

Finally, the military establishment retained two relics of the late medieval organization. In the Tyrol, the free peasants and townspeople constituted militia sharpshooter units, to be used only in defense of the country, and in Hungary proper, that is excluding the Military Borders and Transylvania, the traditional noble levy, the insurrectio still existed. During this period the noble levy was called to arms on four occasions - in 1797, 1800, 1805 and 1809. On the first three occasions it did not attain combat readiness before the war ended, but in 1809 it saw action during the Battle of Raab, allegedly performing poorly.[13] Repeated Hungarian plans to modernize the levy and make it a more competent force ran into opposition from

Vienna, where it was believed, not without cause, that such a force could become the base for a national Hungarian army under the control of the Diet.[14]

The Habsburg army then was a heterogeneous force and control of formations speaking German, Czech, French, Flemish, Serbo-Croat, Magyar, Italian, Rumanian, or Polish could, as one officer noted, cause "singular confusion."[15] But this was not the most serious problem. Writing in 1794, a young officer questioned whether an army of "Hungarians, Croats, Transylvanians, Italians, Bohemians, Moravians, Poles, Wallachs, Slavonians, Austrians, Styrians, Tyroleans, Carnioleans, and gypsies could march under one flag and fight for a cause of which it knew nothing."[16] Indeed, nationalism, though still in a seminal state, except perhaps among the Magyars, was a constant worry to the military authorities and this fear above all tended to prevent reliance on popular participation.

Moreover, such fears were not without foundation. Hungary, of course, had been in open rebellion several times since it had come into the Habsburg realm and always remained restive, and even the Military Borders, in part maintained as a safeguard against Magyar aspirations, on occasion were considered as potential trouble spots.[17] The Hofkriegsrat, the highest administrative military agency, often worried about the influence of the Orthodox Church on the allegiance of the Serb and Rumanian Grenzer.[18] Galicia was another potential trouble spot. In 1778, Fieldmarshal Lacy, then the leading soldier of the Monarchy, argued against the idea of raising "national" regiments in Galicia, where, he wrote, a "national spirit is taking general hold, especially among the common people," and continued that this would be inimical to discipline.[19] In 1790, finally, there was a noble revolt in Hungary and a nationalist tinged uprising in the Austrian Netherlands. Although both were put down rather quickly, they served, together with the spectacle of the popular National Guard providing much of the armed force for the Revolution in France, to further solidify opposition to popular participation in war in the minds of the Habsburg decision makers.

Instead, a solution to the problems of a national army was sought in greater internal unity within the regular establishment, in the words of the Walloon Fieldmarshal Prince de Ligne, to create "a national army, albeit one made up of several nations."[20] Moreover, since the mid-eighteenth century efforts had been made to improve conditions of the rank and file and to appeal to a sense of soldierly honor rather than fear of punishments to have soldiers perform their duties.[21] Efforts in this direction continued throughout the period. When, following the defeat of the First Coalition and the Treaty of Campo Formio in October 1798, the Hofkommission Alvintzy deliberated on measures to improve the army, Colonel Anton Baron Zach submitted a memorandum arguing that the troops had lacked cohesion and spirit. A multinational empire, he continued, could not hope to produce a national army like the French, but closer relations between officers and men might result in raising an army esprit de corps while reducing the number of exemptions to conscriptions would contribute to having a wider popular representation in the ranks.[22] Similarily, when after the debacle of 1805, Archduke Charles was entrusted with a general overhaul of the army, he introduced a new Dienst-Reglement animated by the same spirit. The soldier, the regulations stated, had to be disciplined, but should never be treated as a convict. "Love of his monarch and an honest life, . . . obedience, loyalty, and resolution, these are the true soldierly virtues."[23]

But this was a far way from endorsing a people's war. The spectre of subversive nationalism remained at all times and prevented Austria from making full use of its population potential. Already in 1793-94, when a large part of the army still was held in the East to assert Austrian claims in Poland, an attempt to use armed peasants against French incursions along the Upper Rhine had aroused misgivings in Vienna. Lacy, retired but still very influential, worried about "waking the sleeping beast," and argued that in any case "such a mass of people, lacking organization, discipline, and proper officers will be an impediment rather than an advantage."[24]

Here Lacy raised another objection against popular participation in war--the alleged superiority of highly trained troops. To soldiers schooled in the rigid and formalistic fighting methods of the eighteenth century only such troops, performing precise battle evolutions, mattered; and Austrian senior officers, including the Archduke Charles, never understood that the élan of men, who for the first time in modern European history fought for a state in which they had a stake, however nominal, could not be matched by rigidly disciplined troops fighting in close order. In 1795, in his first book, On War against the New Franks, Charles asked how a "well-disciplined, balanced, and disciplined army had been defeated by raw troops?" His answer was conventional: lack of cooperation between the Austrian commanders and poor strategy had been the causes of defeat.[25]

Events the following year proved him right. Placed in command in Germany, he temporarily ended feuding among the generals and restored troop morale, and managed by clever maneuvers to drive the invading French back across the Rhine. His reputation made, he was sent in 1797 to restore the crumbing front in Styria. Here he found that the desperate Austrian authorities had hastily called out levies in Styria and volunteers in Vienna, but convinced that these efforts would do no good, he immediately ordered all units raised disbanded at once.[26]

The issue of augmenting the army with citizen levies, militias, or Landsturm, emerged again after the war had terminated in the Peace of Campo Formio of October 1798. When such matters came before the Hofkommission Alvintzy, Charles immediately informed his brother, the Emperor Francis, that "popular risings, arming the people, rapidly gathering untrained volunteers and such, can never provide reliable troops"[27] Other senior officers in his entourage expressed similar feelings. In a memorandum submitted to the commission, General Mayer von Heldenfels stated that any attempt to supplement the regular army with popular forces was a serious mistake. No hastily mobilized "land militia, Landsturm, volunteers, Cerniden, insurrectio, or fencibles - in fact any armed force not properly trained - has a chance against the enemy, . . . even if they are commanded by a Xenophon, Alexander, Turenne, Eugene, Montecuccoli, Condé, Frederick or Bonaparte."[28]

In any case, the work of the commission ended with the renewal of war in 1799. When, following the defeats at Hohenlinden and Marengo, Charles was appointed president of the Hofkriegsrat as well as war minister and charged with a reform of the military establishment, he did nothing to change the basic nature of the army and spent most of his time on administrative reforms. He acknowledged that the French had achieved numerical superiority and greater strategic mobility by exploiting the potential of a national army, but denied that this was a viable option for Austria. At most, he was prepared to make military service more attractive by replacing the lifelong enlistments by ten years in the infantry, twelve in the cavalry, and fourteen in the artillery, and to continue his efforts to humanize treatment of the rank and file. But even these modest proposals ran into opposition by conservatives who feared that discharged soldiers might constitute the core of radical rebellions against the established order, and though eventually enacted in 1804, were not implemented until 1807.[29]

By this time, following yet another defeat, Charles, who had opposed the war and had been relegated to a minor command, was restored to his former position and once again there was an opportunity to overhaul the military system of the Austrian monarchy. To be sure, even now there still was opposition; even the emperor did not support him fully. But Charles, despite his real military talents, remained an eighteenth century soldier, unable to accept the new concepts of the Vernichtungskrieg. His 1806 treatise on higher strategy described war as the "greatest evil a state can experience" and though not lacking in personal courage, he lacked the will for victory at any price.[30] For that matter his new infantry manual, issued in 1807, adhered to the formal linear order of battle and retained, even elaborated, "all the refinements and artifices of Frederician drill."[31] Clearly, there was no room in the archduke's thinking for popular forces; on the contrary, he always considered the regular army as the ultimate guarantor of the monarchy to be preserved above all.

No wonder therefore that when, beginning in 1806, plans for raising a national militia were advocated by several progressive writers and Archdukes John and Francis d'Este, he was opposed. Such forces, he maintained, were a little combat value, even dangerous, because, as he wrote to his friend, Duke Albert of Sachsen-Teschen, "they give the appearance that we have large masses of combatants and thus a false sense of security."[32] Such sentiments were shared by senior generals as well as the emperor, though in the late spring of 1808 two related developments compelled them to change their stand. One was the shock of Napoleon removing the Bourbon dynasty in Spain, the other was that the monarchy no longer could sustain the costs of a large regular establishment. Even Charles now conceded that a militia had become unavoidable, though only to "augment the inadequacy of military resources remaining after fifteen years of fighting and fifteen years of misfortunes."[33] The patent establishing the Landwehr was issued on 8 June 1808. Service was to be obligatory for all males between the ages of 18 and 45 in the hereditary lands and Bohemia, though there were broad exemptions. Also, the patent did not apply to Galicia where Polish sentiment was suspect, and in Hungary the Diet refused to accept the patent, though it promised to call out the insurrectio when needed.[34]

The Landwehr has become part of the Austrian patriotic legend of the War of 1809, the Anno Neun. And yet, performance fell short of expectations. Instead of the 250,000 men expected, only some 80,000 actually were mustered and when the French actually invaded Austria, most units melted away, while others performed poorly. To be sure, there were honorable exceptions. Volunteer Landwehr battalions fought well on occasion, while others did their duty when integrated with regular brigades at Aspern and Wagram. Overall, however, it was not a great popular rising.[35]

For that matter, the entire war was somewhat of a fiasco. Persuaded to support a preemptive war, Charles who previously had favored an accommodation with Napoleon, lost heart before hostilities opened. After a rather slow advance into Bavaria, he unexpectedly found that Napoleon, who was supposed to be occupied in Spain, had appeared to take command on the Danube and promptly defeated the archduke in a series of battles. Retreating rapidly towards Vienna, Charles appealed to his brother to make peace in order to save the army. No reliance, he urged, should be placed on the Landwehr or insurrectio, but the regulars should be saved because they might be "needed to deal with eventualities in the interior of the monarchy."[36]

Nonetheless, fighting with unexpected tenacity, the archduke scored the first major victory over Napoleon at Aspern on 21-22 May, though, ever cautious, he refused to press his success and it remained a tactical rather than a strategic victory.[37] Thereafter, hoping to use his advantage to arrive at a negotiated armistice, Charles did little to improve his posture and on 5-6 June, in a battle marred by faulty dispositions, he was defeated at Wagram, though he did manage to extract the bulk of his army.[38] But this was the end. Military zeal and patriotic ardor evaporated; no attempt was made to rally remaining resources, and Charles was abruptly dismissed.[39]

In October 1809, Austria had to sign the Treaty of Schönbrunn which deprived her of much territory, including a major part of the Military Borders, imposed heavy indemnities, and limited her army to 150,000 men. Control over the army returned to the Hofkriegsrat, with Fieldmarshal Lieutenant Radetzky as Chief of the Quartermaster General Staff.[40] In December 1809, he submitted a combat capability estimate to the emperor. The army, he claimed, no longer was in a position to fight; and, delivering his verdict on the past seventeen years, he declared that the basic reason for the repeated defeats was that the army "had never been popular among the masses, while the higher classes too had little interest in a strong army."[41]

But Vienna had no inclination and no capacity for changing these conditions. For the moment the direction of Austrian state affairs fell into the hands of Prince Metternich, no supporter of participation, political or military, who hoped that Austria's fortune's might yet recover if the French were seriously weakened. Meanwhile the Hofkriegsrat, albeit with considerable difficulty, managed to keep the regulars together as a framework of a larger force to be raised when circumstances permitted.

The opportunity came in 1813 when Napoleon's power had been seriously shaken by the loss of his army in Russia. Beginning with a partial mobilization in the spring, by early summer Metternich felt strong enough to offer armed mediation between the French and their adversaries, backing up this position with an army of observation, almost 200,000 strong in Bohemia, and a second, if smaller, force in Italy.[42] And when Austria actually entered the coalition against Napoleon, the very size of her army, 480,000 men and 300,000 combatants, gave her a major voice in allied decisions. This army of 1813-14 was primarily regular forces, with reactivated Landwehr and volunteers brigaded with regulars. Compared with Prussia, Austria did not mobilize as great a percentage of her total population, but her resources were stretched to the utmost so that in 1813 many soldiers lacked overcoats and even boots. Yet, when the occasion demanded, they fought with spirit and tenacity, restoring the monarchy's position as a great power.[43]

The Habsburg army achieved its mission, adopting only minor modifications in its fighting techniques and recruitment system. Retaining its character as an old fashioned dynastic army, it met the challenges of the French Revolution and Napoleon. Though repeatedly defeated, it always rose to fight again, defying both the judgment of contemporary observers and later scholars that informed and motivated citizen armies always were superior to regular dynastic forces.

Purdue University
November 1987

Notes

[1]Gunther E. Rothenberg, "The Origins, Causes, and Extension of the Wars of the French Revolution and Napoleon," Journal of Interdisciplinary History, 18 (Spring 1988):784-89.

[2]Gunther E. Rothenberg, The Art of Warfare in the Age of Napoleon (London: B.T. Batsford Ltd., 1977), 11-30.

[3]Carl von Clausewitz, On War, transl. and eds. Michael Howard and Peter Paret (Princeton: Princeton University Press, 1986), 592, 609-10.

[4]Geoffrey Best, War and Society in Revolutionary Europe, 1770-1870 (New York-Oxford: Oxford University Press, 1986), 184-86.

[5]Cyril Falls, The Art of War from Napoleon to the Present Day (New York-Oxford: Oxford University Press, 1961), 34; Albert Sorel, L'Europe et la révolution française (Paris: Plon-Nourrit, 1884), 1:455.

[6]Manfried Rauchensteiner, Kaiser Franz und Erzherzog Carl. Dynastie und Heerwesen in Österreich 1796-1809 (Munich: Oldenbourg Verlag: 1972), 69, 77, 88.

[7]Memo. of 5 March 1804 printed in Oskar Criste, Erzherzog Carl von Oesterreich (Vienna-Leipzig: Braumuller, 1912), 2:455.

[8]Cited in Gunther E. Rothenberg, Napoleon's Great Adversaries. The Archduke Charles and the Austrian Army 1792-1814 (London: B. T. Batsford Ltd., 1982), 16.

[9]Ibid., 14-16.

[10]Ibid., 20-23.

[11]Béla K. Király, Hungary in the Late Eighteenth Century: The Decline of Enlightened Despotism (New York: Columbia University Press, 1969), 7-8, 103-7.

[12]Gunther E. Rothenberg, The Military Border in Croatia 1740-1881. A Study of an Imperial Institution (Chicago: University of Chicago Press, 1966), 79-93.

[13]Josef Freiherr Hormayer zu Hortenburg, Das Heer von Innerösterreich unter den Befehlen des Erzherzogs Johann im Kriege 1809 in Italien, Tirol, und Ungarn (Leipzig: Brockhaus, 1817), 197-203.

[14]Jenö Gyalókai, "A mágyar nemési insurrectio reformtervei 1797-töl 1809-ig," Szadadok, 59 (Spring 1925):126-59.

[15]Jacopo de Cognazzo, Freymüthiger Beytrag zur Geschichte des oesterreichischen Militairdienstes (Frankfurt-Leipzig: no publ., 1789), 18.

[16]August Ellrich ed., Humoristische und Historische Skizzen aus den Jahren der Revolutionskriege. Aus den hinterlassenen Papieren eines verstorbenen Soldaten (Meissen: Goebsche Buchhandlung, 1844), 251-53.

[17]Rothenberg, Military Border, 31-32, 57-60.

[18] Ibid., 102-5.

[19] Edith Kotasek, Feldmarschall Graf Lacy. Ein Leben für Österreichs Heer (Horn: Verlag Ferdinand Berger, 1956), 123-24.

[20] Christopher Duffy, The Army of Maria Theresa. The Armed Forces of Imperial Austria 1740-1780 (New York: Hippocrene Books, 1977), 16-17.

[21] Ibid., 61-62.

[22] Anton von Zach, "Eine Denkschrift Zach's aus dem Johre 1798," Mitteilungen des k.u.k. Kriegsarchivs, 3d ser., 2 (1903), 166-67, 172-73, 190.

[23] Dienst-Reglement für die kaiserlich-königliche Infanterie 2 parts (Vienna: Hof und Staatsdruckerey, 1807-08), Part 1, 1, and part 2, para. 5.

[24] Kotasek, Lacy, 207.

[25] Alfred Freiherr von Waldstätten ed., Erzherzog Karl. Ausgewählte militärische Schriften (Berlin: Richard Wilhelmi, 1882), 4-11.

[26] Criste, Erzherzog Carl, I:496-97.

[27] Eduard Wertheimer, "Erzherzog Karl und die zweite Coalition bis zum Frieden von Luneville 1798-1801," Archiv für Österreichische Geschichte, 67 (1882):203.

[28] Austria, Kreigsarchiv Wien [hereafter cited as KA], Nachlass Mayer von Heldenfeld, B/857-80.

[29] Rothenberg, Napoleon's Great Adversaries, 66-71.

[30] Grundsätze der höheren Kriegskunst fur die Generäle der österreichischen Armee (Vienna: Hof-und Staatsdruckerey, 1806), 1-2.

[31] Eberhard Mayerhoffer von Vedropolje, Regensburg, vol. 1 of Kriegsarchiv, Krieg 1809, 4 vols. (Vienna: Seidel und Sohn, 1907-1910), 1, 102.

[32] Christe, Erzherzog Carl, 2:400-402.

[33] Cited in Helmuth Rössler, Österreichs Kampf um die deutsche Befreiung, 2 vols. (Hamburg: Hanseatische Verlagsanstalt, 1940), 1:319.

[34] Rothenberg, Napoleon's Great Adversaries, 119.

[35] Ibid., 137-39.

[36]In Mayerhoffer, Regensburg, 581-82.

[37]This is the conclusion of the archduke's latest biographers, Helmut Hertenberger and Franz Wiltschek, Erzherzog Karl. Der Sieger von Aspern (Vienna-Graz-Cologne: Styria, 1983), 256-58.

[38]Ibid., 264-80.

[39]Rothenberg, Napoleon's Great Adversaries, 169-71.

[40]Ibid., 172-74.

[41]"Eine Memoire Radetzky's das Heerwesen Österreichs beleuchtend aus dem Jahre 1809," Mitteilungen des k.u.k. Kriegsarchivs, 10 (1884):361-70.

[42]Rothenberg, Napoleon's Great Adversaries, 174-77.

[43]Ibid., 190-91.

Italy's Peculiar Institution: Internal Police Exile,
1861-1914

Richard Bach Jensen

The peculiar institution of "forced internal exile," domicilio coatto, was a system by which the Italian police were allowed to send suspected criminals to various small islands off the coast of the peninsula, to remote villages in the interior, and to the Italian colonies in Africa. At high points in the 1860s and the 1890s, domicilio coatto interned between 5,000 and 12,000 people. Most astounding about this system was its character as an instrument of arbitrary police power. Its victims had no recourse to the judicial system but were simply at the mercy of commissions composed of government bureaucrats and police officials. This was in a country which, until the coming of fascism, embraced the liberal ideals of elected parliamentary government and of basic, guaranteed civil liberties. Because of the existence of domicilio coatto, as well as of other weapons of police and military repression, some historians have found compelling evidence for a basic continuity--rather than a break-- between the supposedly liberal regime which governed Italy until 1922 and the fascist dictatorship which succeeded it.[1] The peculiarity of the continued existence of domicilio coatto alongside liberal, parliamentary institutions is accentuated by the fact that its myriad critics included almost every Italian government after the mid-1870s. Between 1897 and 1910 five different cabinets proposed laws abolishing or substantially modifying domicilio coatto. Yet none of these reforms ever became law, despite the fact that even a conservative prime minister had felt constrained in the 1890s to describe domicilio coatto as a "verminous plague" and "a real legal crime."

This article will look at two aspects of domicilio coatto in some depth. After briefly sketching its overall history, the article will examine the institution during its most controversial phase, the 1890s, when the Crispi and Di Rudinì governments at first used it as a tool for political repression but later tried to reform it. Secondly, the article will present some hypotheses as to why, despite the universal discredit into which it had fallen, it proved such a hardy institution, defying all attempts at reform.

The history of domicilio coatto prior to World War I can be roughly divided into four periods:

1.   1863-1876. This period saw the birth of forced internal exile as a response to the problem of brigandage in southern Italy. At one point during the savage guerrila warfare of the early sixties, as many as 12,000[2] people were being forceably detained away from their homes. Never again would so many be rounded up in this fashion. Even after brigandage was crushed, the arbitrary police power to exile was still

needed to deal with problems of thievery, the mafia, and general social discontent, especially in Sicily and to a lesser extent in Romagna.

2. 1876-1893. During this era, which coincided with the moderate Left's coming to power, attempts were made to restrict and discipline the incidence of domicilio coatto, as well as of ammonizione. Ammonizione, a police warning to "behave," could, if transgressed, serve as a stepping stone to domicilio coatto. In this period, up until 1882, there was a steep decline in the total number of coatti, or internees. Subsequently the figures began to rise, but in 1890 a new public security law led to another, although less precipitous, decline in the number of people sent to the exile colonies.

3. 1893-1900. In the 1890s domicilio coatto was greatly extended as Italy experienced a severe social, economic, and political crisis. Domicilio coatto was also greatly politicized as laws were passed making it possible to send anarchists, socialists, and other political suspects into exile. After reaching a peak in 1894, the number of those detained dropped sharply with the coming to power of the Di Rudinì government in 1896. In the spring of 1898 another crisis broke out followed by a rising rate of internment for the next two years.

4. 1900-1914. Once we enter the twentieth century and the so-called Giolittian Era, we find that fewer and fewer people--and almost no political suspects--were assigned to the internment islands. Repeated efforts were made to abolish domicilio coatto and to replace it with a judicially-mandated penalty for habitual criminals, but these attempts were all unsuccessful.

This rough sketch of domicilio coatto before 1914, with its irregular pattern of ups and downs, presents a significantly different perspective on the issue from that taken by many historians. Several authors tend to see the history of domicilio coatto as one of a situation worsening continually, with every new law on the subject exacerbating and further institutionalizing its repressive effects. These historians systematically overlook or misread the frequent attempts to restrict, control, and reform domicilio coatto.[3]

So much for a general overview and historiographical introduction to domicilio coatto. The decade of the 1890s witnessed the most use--and abuse--of that peculiar institution since the troubled period following unification. Like the 1860s, the precipitating cause for the great increase in domicilio coatto during the nineties was upheaval in southern Italy--Sicily to be exact--set against a background of general economic and social malaise. The 1890s had also seen the founding of the Italian socialist party as well as a spectacular series of bombings and assassination attempts carried out by anarchists. The prime minister at the time, a crotchety septuagenerian named Francesco Crispi, responded to these threats by pushing through parliament a law granting the government temporary authority to exile those suspected of planning to destroy or damage buildings and public transportation, of using or threatening to use explosives, or of other crimes typically associated with the anarchists. Instead of using this law just against the anarchists, however, Crispi rounded up hundreds of socialists and other political dissidents as well.

This blatant politicization of domicilio coatto together with the scandalous condition of some of the hastily formed internment camps was what really discredited the institution. In early 1895, rioting broke out in protest against the terrible living conditions at the colony of Port'Ercole off the coast of Tuscany. Official reports submitted by government inspectors noted such items as the insufficiency of food and the fact that the coatti's miserable sleeping pallets were full of insects. Coatti in sickbay were receiving only one meal a day and irregular visits from the doctor. The system of discipline in the colony had also broken down. Sometimes it was excessively severe and other times too lax. For minor infractions, a coatto might be thrown into a horrible punishment cell.

On the other hand, the inmates were allowed to sing socialist and anarchist songs if they liked, play cards and bring plates, bottles, and even pocket knifes into their rooms. The government inspector's conclusion was that "the penalty of domicilio coatto at Port'Ercole, as it is applied, is no longer just a punishment, nor can it lead to correction, for it will serve only to embitter the spirits of those against whom it was inflicted, who will return to freedom longing for revenge[4] and [becoming] more than ever the enemies of all social order."

There is plenty of other evidence as well that domicilio coatto was self-defeating if the authorities intended that it should deter or cure criminal or anti-social tendencies. We have the memoirs of one young Italian, Amedeo Boschi, as proof of this view. Boschi, a Tuscan artisan, was initially apprehended in 1893 on the apparently unfounded suspicion of involvement in a dynamite plot. Following the passage of the July 1894 laws he was rearrested and sent to domicilio coatto for two years. The trip to his place of confinement in an airless prison coach during the middle of summer turned out to be hellish and far worse than domicilio coatto itself.

On the other hand, at the various places where Boschi was interned--at Tremiti island, off Italy's Adriatic coast, and at Lipari and Pantelleria, off the northern and southern coasts of Sicily, respectively--he found a good life. In the domicilio coatto colonies he began to associate with anarchists; and indeed, he really became a convinced anarchist because of his experiences there. In most of the colonies the anarchists had their own community. In the Tremiti, for example, they met several times weekly for discussions, set up courses in foreign languages, and even produced a little newspaper combining political and humorous articles. During daylight hours the anarchists were relatively free to roam around the towns of their confinement. On Lipari island, Boschi and the others spent their time at a local inn talking, singing, and enjoying themselves. Through debates and discussion with the other coatti, Boschi was able to complete his education in the theoretical principles of anarchism.[5] At night the anarchists slept in makeshift dormitories or, at Lipari, in a castle. On occasion they were able to propagandize and even carry on love affairs with the local inhabitants. Moreover, found that the police treated him with respect, using the title of "Don" when addressing him.[6] Sporadic acts of violence or of repression by the authorities, however, occasionally marred this idyllic scene. Comparable to and contemporary with Boschi's experiences were those of the young socialist Vittorio Buttis, who was sent to the domicilio coatto colonies of Port'Ercole and Tremiti.[7] Buttis's account also depicts forced exile as a mild "punishment" punctuated a few times by outbursts of violence.

Other coatti, however, who did not have the support of fellow detainees with similar political ideas, often did not fare so well. They fell prey to idleness, alcoholism, gambling, and the coercion of the mafia-like organizations which sprang up within the colony and pitted the stronger and more unscrupulous coatti against the weak and defenseless.[8]

The revelations of the poor conditions in the domicilio coatto colonies and the riots at the Port'Ercole colony caused the Crispi government to appoint a blue-ribbon committee to study the whole question of domicilio coatto. This commission, chaired by Sen. Canonico, recommended making internal exile a predominately judicial penalty with the exclusion of all direct government influence. The commission's report represented the beginning of fifteen years of effort at the highest levels to reform the institution. While pressing political business prevented any changes from taking place during the remainder of Crispi's premiership, the succeeding cabinet under Di Rudini took up the task.

The Di Rudini government's interesting attempt at ameliorating and reforming domicilio coatto remains little known or understood. While it ultimately failed, this failure in itself helps clarify why domicilio coatto for so long remained resistant to basic reform. Di Rudini himself, an aristocratic landowner from Sicily, has not usually been considered much of a reformer, at least in regard to the internal exile system. In fact, both contemporaries and many later historians have portrayed him as a die-hard reactionary, just as committed to repression as his predecessor Crispi. For example, in January 1897, the political theorist Vilfredo Pareto wrote Napoleone Colajanni, an independent socialist, asking him if he had "seen that Rudini wants to send all those that don't think like him into domicilio coatto?"[9] Historians have alleged that he went even farther than Crispi by attempting to institutionalize the temporary laws of July 1894 and by refusing to free those people who had been sent into domicilio coatto under the previous administration.[10]

What is the truth of the matter? Considerable evidence suggests that Di Rudinì's general policy up until the crisis of 1898 was to release as many people from forced domicile as possible and through administrative and legal reform to end the system's worst abuses. Only a few days after he came to power, Di Rudinì ordered the conditional release of all those coatti without previous convictions and whom the police did not consider especially dangerous.[11] At the same time he set up a commission to examine the cases of the rest of the coatti to see if their sentences should be revised or if they should be conditionally freed for reasons of "humanity or of health."[12] On August 18, 1896, Di Rudinì issued a decree provisionally releasing coatti who had served half their assigned time and demonstrated good conduct. On 3 September the Interior Ministry ordered that even those coatti who had not completed half their term (the assignees under the 1894 Crispi law excluded) but who had shown good conduct, might ask to be sent to a town of their choice on the understanding that they would try to find work there. For the first two months, the latter would also receive a subsistence allowance from the State.[13] This policy in effect restored the old institution of confino, which antedated domicilio coatto in Italian law but had later fallen into disuse and which Rudinì justifiably thought "less inhumane" than forced domicile.[14]

On 4 June 1896, less than three months after he had come into office, Di Rudinì told parliament that two-thirds of those whom Crispi had sent into domicilio coatto for political reasons had been freed. Those who remained were not political prisoners at all, Di Rudinì claimed, since they had prison records.[15] As of 1 December 1896 the government had freed 1,569 coatti assigned according to the provisions of the public security law as well as 372 persons who had fallen victim to the July 1894 laws. Another 49 coatti had been transferred to towns of their choice on the mainland.[16] Since a total of 387 persons had been held under Crispi's anti-anarchist legislation it is clear that the government freed almost all of them. According to official statistics, the total number held in domicilio coatto declined 38 per cent between 31 December 1895 and 31 December 1897 (from 4,385 to 2,682).[17]

Besides releasing the detained, Di Rudinì ordered a general inspection of and inquest into the conditions of the various forced domicile colonies prior to making new recommendations on reforming the entire institution.[18] Di Rudinì had in his hands the report and proposed reform legislation of the Crispi-appointed commission on domicilio coatto. Although the Prime Minister declared himself generally in favor of the Canonico report, which advocated abolishing forced domicile as an administrative penalty, replacing it with a punishment inflicted by special courts, he wanted more time for study before making final recommendations. Rudinì admitted that he was "unenthusiastic" about this peculiarly Italian institution and recognized that "profound and radical modifications" were necessary.[19] At the same time, he did not believe that complete abolition was possible since "you will always have some persons dangerous due to their past record, their attitude, their temperament, their capacity and tendency to commit crime, against whom society must absolutely defend itself, even if there may be no certain and secure proof of their culpability in criminal acts."[20]

Private as well as public statements by the Prime Minister reveal his desire to reform domicilio coatto, a desire motivated by both personal distaste for the institution and utilitarian considerations. In a 30 August 1896 letter Di Rudinì urged Giovanni Codronchi, the "Civil Commissioner" (temporary head administrator) of Sicily, to parole as many coatti as possible. Confidentially, Di Rudinì explained his reasons:

> Above all, domicilio coatto is a verminous plague. The coatti don't reform themselves but become wicked. The fewer coatti there are the better it will be in the long run for public security.

> In the second place, the exemplariness of domicilio coatto is obtained by shipping [someone] to a [detention] colony. It is unimportant whether the entire penalty is expiated. In the third place a coatto who has expiated his entire penalty cannot be taken back quickly on simple suspicion, but the coatto freed conditionally can be picked up again when one wants.

> Fourth, we are not within the spending limits of the budget and [releasing the coatti] helps us remain within them.

> In the fifth place (regarding the politicals) it is prudent and just to free them conditionally now that maximum quiet exists [in the country]. This liberation is a logical sequel to the amnesty [of March 1896].

Another practical reason for releasing the coatti was the dangerous situation created by overcrowded facilities, as the riots at Port'Ercole in September 1895 had demonstrated. In fact soon after Di Rudinì came to office, the army commander temporarily supervising Sicily's public security reported that the condition of the colony of coatti at Lampedusa was dangerous due to excessive crowding.[22]

A particularly difficult question was that of releasing detained anarchists, an issue which brought into focus humanitarian as well as empirical considerations that influenced Di Rudinì's policies. Writing after Codronchi had made an inspection of the domicilio coatto colonies in the islands off Sicily, Di Rudinì told the Civil Commissioner that:

> . . . it is necessary to be generous in [granting] provisional release [liberazione condizionale] . . . of those who spoke with you. Free the blind Gavilli. Free him as soon as possible. The blind anarchist couldn't be dangerous. And even if he were, it would still be necessary to free him unless he had been convicted by the judicial authorities through due process. If the blind man needs assistance, assist him. If he needs to be helped in going abroad, help him. But for the love of heaven, we must not make

ourselves unintentional accomplices in the infamies committed by someone[23] who wanted to ingratiate himself with some foolish [folle] minister. These benighted police [sbirreschi] usages and methods, these and these alone endanger public order. Therefore, make as quickly as possible the widest proposals, and propose via telegraph the freeing of the blindman.[24]

Even when Di Rudinì discovered that the blindman, a Florentine professor, was "dangerous" and twice convicted by the courts, he still urged Codronchi to release the man, granting him assistance should Gavilli wish to emigrate.[25]

Another letter sent to the Civil Commissioner of Sicily in late August 1896 provides more evidence of Di Rudinì's liberal stance on domicilio coatto:

> I am of the opinion that when possible one ought to be very free in secretly releasing [the anarchists]. Woe to us if any talk is made of this because then the usual fearful ones, who don't understand anything, would say that we are the anarchists, as well as all the usual nonsense which they use to embroider similar accusations.

> The inquest on the coatti colonies was already made under Crispi. Now one knows only too well that domicilio coatto as constituted is a real legal crime.[26]

On the other hand, Di Rudinì still wanted the government to maintain domicilio coatto for common criminals.[27] Di Rudinì was in fact willing to resort to almost any methods to strike at the mafia and other underworld elements in Sicily.[28]

While Di Rudinì was taking various measures to lessen the abuses of domicilio coatto, he also planned to reform the entire institution on a permanent basis. On 1 December 1896, he introduced his proposed law to the senate, which passed a modified version in April 1897. There is no space here to discuss in detail this interesting and highly controversial piece of legislation. Suffice it to say that Di Rudinì wished to retain administrative control over the process while implanting various safeguards against potential abuses. The senate amended the bill in an important way by requiring that judges fill all the positions on the central commission in Rome that made the final decisions on assigning people to domicilio coatto.[29] This was a significant step toward making internal exile a judicial rather than a police and administrative penalty. The government grudgingly accepted the change, and the head of the senate committee, Sen. Majorana-Calatabiana, predicted that if the amended proposal became law, it would lead to the reduction of the total number of coatti from 2700 to less than 1000.[30] Despite these promising developments, a storm of protest broke out in the press and among the public. The critics of Di Rudinì's legislation, who were much less interested in discussing the merits of the reform than in abolishing domicilio coatto altogether, ultimately succeeded in blocking the bill's passage.[31]

This universal tide of opinion against domicilio coatto, "condemned" as Prime Minister Luzzatti would put it later, "by the experts, by Parliament and by public opinion as well as by long experience that its effects were the opposite of those hoped for,"[32] changed the way subsequent governments dealt with the question. In their reform proposals of 1900, 1904 and 1911, the Saracco, Giolitti and Luzzatti cabinets all indicated their willingness to abolish domicilio coatto, replacing the old system with court-determined penalties for habitual criminality. Yet despite this unanimity of opinion in public and in private, on the left and on the right, the reforms all failed to be enacted. Why was this?

Several possible reasons can be cited. Many contemporary observers, including Prime Minister Luzzatti, blamed the slow moving parliamentary process itself, which blocked or lost needed reforms due to the myriad vicissitudes of parliamentary life.[33] Indeed, none of these reforms was debated, let alone passed by either house of parliament. Certainly one reason parliament hesitated to act was that the abolition of domicilio coatto and its replacement by some other system of confining habitual criminals promised to cost tremendous sums. For example, the Saracco government's reform, presented by Justice Minister Gianturco in November 1900, provided for the deportation of habitual criminals to Assab in the Italian-controlled colony of Eritrea. The expenses of creating a suitable internment camp in Assab as well as shipping detainees all the way to Africa were considerable. The most elaborate and well-thought out reform plan was that proposed by Luzzatti in 1910. While his projected law did not call for deportation to Africa, it did foresee abandoning all the old domicilio coatto colonies except for one, and the creation of six new agricultural and/or industrial colonies in Sardinia, and perhaps in Basilicata and Calabria. Yet this scheme would have cost five million liras to set up, whereas the old system, which had provided far fewer facilities and much less supervision, only required an annual budget of a million liras.[34]

Luzzatti claimed in 1910, that one of the reasons for the failure of earlier reform legislation had been that it was not "sufficiently mature."[35] Several commentators criticized Luzzatti's own proposal for lack of a similar practicality and refinement. The psychiatrist Emanuele Mirabella, who had worked with the coatti of Favignana for eighteen years, wrote that most of the detainees were too "degenerate" to carry out the agricultural and industrial work envisioned in Luzzatti's plan. The director of the penal work colony of Castiadas, Sardinia, agreed with Mirabella on the unsuitability of the coatto as a workers, since he was a man "consumed by vice, proud of the rot of a life of filth, of usury, gambling, brawls, sexual corruption, alcoholism, crimes of every type; in short everything evil one could imagine."[36] The moderate socialist Matteotti also expressed grave doubts about the proposed law, criticizing various technical aspects. For example, he noted the failure to classify and group scientifically the habitual criminals, separating the tubercular from the mentally defective, the rebels and epileptics from the young offenders amenable to rehabilitation, and making other divisions as well.[37]

106

These criticisms and the lack of enthusiastic support for any of the reform plans suggest another and more fundamental reason for their ultimate failure. In the case of domicilio coatto reform, as in so many other instances in Italian history, the "better" plan became the enemy of the "good" one. All the proposed reforms may have had their defects, all may have offered no real hope of curing the country's habitual criminals, but they did have one important merit. By turning over jurisdiction to the courts, they would have ended Italy's infamy as the only country in Europe possessing such an arbitrary tool of police repression.

These intended reforms also appeared to lack any real political will behind them. No government gave them priority over other proposed laws being considered at the time. In 1910-11, for example, the importance of reforming domicilio coatto was lost in the growing debate over Luzzatti's proposal to widen the suffrage. Despite the universal discredit into which domicilio coatto had fallen, public opinion was not that interested in the question after 1900. Almost all the articles on the issue appeared in professional journals of law and criminology, not in the popular periodicals. What brought about this change?

First of all, the number of people assigned to internal exile dropped dramatically after 1900. By 1910 there were one-third fewer and by 1912 one-half fewer coatti than there had been in 1897. Moreover, these twentieth century coatti were almost all habitual criminals with fearsome records; few commentators complained after 1900 that the police were arbitrarily exiling people for petty misdeeds or for political actions.[38] In short, the hoary old monster of domicilio coatto had had its teeth pulled, and if still loathsome, it was no longer so frightening.

Shifts in criminological theory, particularly the growing influence of positivism, may also have undercut opposition to domicilio coatto. Lombroso had argued that deviance was the result of degenerate physical characteristics, that many individuals were born criminals, throwbacks to an earlier stage of primitive human development. Lombroso's disciples Ferri and Garofalo believed that the "role of justice" was not to punish offenders but to protect society against their degenerate actions."[39] These views increasingly influenced not only the thinking of the public-at-large but also the police and government.[40] By changing the focus of attention from the crime (which had been the concern of classical criminal theory) to the criminal, the precise determination of the guilt and innocence of each morally and rationally responsible individual became less important. What gained importance was "social defense," that is, removing the rotten core of born and habitual criminals from the bosom of society, and exiling it more or less permanently to some safe or distant location. the only exceptions would be for the few who might be susceptible to curative treatment.

After 1900 the influence of positivist thinking is very evident on both the reform proposals and on the critics' commentaries. Fear of "that nucleus of dangerous habitual delinquents" had led Luzzatti to introduce the principle of indeterminate sentencing into his proposal on domicilio coatto.[41] In other words, if the habitual criminal failed to mend his ways, he stayed in a penal work camp forever. The critics of Luzzatti's reform plan were also attuned to positivist concerns. What primarily worried them was whether the 1910 proposal would or would not lead to proper social defense or the reform of the criminals. They seemed little interested in whether a commission of bureaucrats and police or the courts imposed the penalties. While domicilio coatto certainly found no outright defenders among the positivists, internal exile did serve in its crude way some of the ends of social defense.[42] Such defense seemed increasingly necessary by 1909, given the growing crime wave and the "fearsome increase" in habitual criminality.[43]

Finally, the failure to reform domicilio coatto, the lack of government will to push it though parliament, may have reflected the authorities' uneasiness about the capacity of the Italian police to handle criminality without the use of this arbitrary weapon. After 1900, Prime Minister Giolitti had done much to increase the size, improve the organization and leadership, and bolster the technological and scientific expertise of the police. Yet these reforms had all been carried out cheaply with one eye constantly on the budget. On paper the size of the civilian police forced had doubled, but in practice it still proved difficult to fill the police rolls with competent personnel, given the miserably low salaries. Even with the mandated increases, Italy remained underpoliced in comparison to other European countries.[44]

In conclusion, domicilio coatto proved such a tough weed to uproot from Italian soil because of its amazing ability to adapt to changing circumstances. Chameleon-like, it changed from being a savage weapon employed against brigands, vagrants and mafiosi, to becoming a concentration camp for the anarchists and socialists. Later it jettisoned its political character, surviving and gaining new resilience as a crude but low cost way of controlling habitual criminals. Domicilio coatto also survived because governments that proposed reforms found themselves trapped between their own unwillingness to dispense with it altogether, albeit in the transmutted form of judicially-mandated labor camps, and a hostile public opinion which preferred no reform to partial reform. Thus, Italy preserved that detested old monster or, as one Italian senator described domicilio coatto, that "fatal necessity."[45]

Skidmore College
November 1987

AMMONIZIONE AND DOMICILIO COATTO, 1870-1914[1]

	Ammonizione		Domicilio Coatto	
	Number of Persons Assigned Annually	Total Under Detention as of Dec. 31	Number of Persons Assigned Annually	Total Under Detention as of Dec. 3
1868	35,000[6]			
69	35,000[6]			
1870	22,754[2]			
71	*17,633[2]			
72	28,158[2]		1,302[2]	
73	25,173[2]		1,071[2]	
74	25,455[2]		1,894[2]	
75	23,169[2]	189,719[3]	1,094[2]	
76	17,226[2]	**184,000[4]	662[2]	4,011
77	31,838[2]		1,467	3,765
78	24,945[2]	** 72,000[4]	852	3,113
79	23,610[2]		1,082	2,190
1880	23,417	115,819[5]	932	2,029
81	17,655	109,621[3]	863	1,671
82	14,085		829	1,456
83	9,778		944	1,607
84	8,568	40,000[4]	* 675	+1,914
85	7,333		976	(84-5) +2,200
86	8,421		1,243	(85-6) +2,493
87	6,981		1,597	(86-7) +2,795
88	6,961		1,373	(87-8) +2,720
89	5,627		1,884	(88-9) +2,927
1890	1,153		1,121	(89-90) +2,811
91	1,989		1,153	(90-1) +2,960
92	3,050		1,430	(91-2) +3,235
93	2,871		1,381	(92-3) +3,448
94	2,738		2,979	(93-4) +5,043
95	2,806		2,170	(94-5) +4,100
96	3,282		1,561	2,863
97	2,802		1,181	2,682
98	2,529		1,291	2,764
99	2,584	8,233[3]	1,502	3,379
1900	2,696		1,128	3,488
01	2,222		1,061	3,259
02	1,787		1,176	3,262
03	1,659		960	3,071
04	1,503		834	
05	1,587		883	
06	1,405		874	

[Table Continues on Next Page]

109

	Ammonizione		Domicilio Coatto	
	Number of Persons Assigned Annually	Total Under Detention as of Dec. 31	Number of Persons Assigned Annually	Total Under Detention as of Dec. 3
1908	1,777		1,054	
1910	1,513		657	1,770
1912	1,256		561	1,146
1914	1,299		738	1,464

[1]Except as indicated, these figures are from the Annuario Statistico Italiano, vol. 1900: 319, 353; vol. 1905-07: 369, 379; vol. 1911: 90, 93; vol. 1916: 126, 128.

[2]Luigi Lucchini, "Sull'ammonizione e sul domicilio coatto, secondo la vigente legislazione italiana," Annali di statistica, ser. 2, 25 (1881): 30-33 [ammonizione statistics]; 82 [domicilio coatto statistics].

[3]Annali di statistica, ser. 4, 99 (1902): 493-94.

[4]Carocci, Giampiero, Agostino Depretis (Turin, 1956), 214, n. 1; 573, n. 2.

[5]Direzione generale della statistica, Statistica giudiziaria penale (1880), xiv.

[6]Lucchini, AS (1881), 27. The figures for 1868 and 1869 are rough estimates based on Lucchini's figures of 60,974 ammoniti for the period 31 January 1868 - 31 October 1869, and 55,571 for 31 September 1869 - 31 December 1870.

*First semester
**January
+June 30

NOTES

[1]"Fascism will resume the institution [of domicilio coatto], giving it a new name, in order to use it still another time against political opponents. . . .These comparisons [between fascist mechanisms of repression and domicilio coatto, state of siege, and military tribunals], seem suitable to confirm--also under new profiles--the continuity in the sector of public order and public security between the liberal State and the fascist regime." Luciano Violante, "La repressione del dissenso politico nell' Italia liberale: stati

d'assedio e giustizia militare," Rivista di storia contemporanea, fasc. 4 (1976), 522-23: see also Ambra Boldetti, "La repressione in Italia: il caso del 1894," Rivista di storia contemporanea (Oct. 1977), 481, 514-15.

[2]Franco Molfese, Storia del brigantaggio dopo l'unità (Milan: Feltrinelli Editore 1964), 351.

[3]Violante. Several historians fail to note that the new public security law of 1889 on the whole ameliorated domicilio coatto, making its regulations more precise and raising the prerequisite number of contraventions or convictions necessary to commit someone to internal exile. The total number of coatti dropped somewhat and the annual number declined significantly after the law's passage. For the 1889 law's critics see Giorgio Candeloro, Storia dell'Italia moderna (Milan: 1960), 6:351; Leo Valiani, "L'Italia dal 1876 al 1915. 2: La lotta sociale e l'avvento della democrazia," Storia d'Italia (Turin: Unione tipografico-editrice torinese, 1965), 4:536; Mario Galizia, "La libertà di circolazione ed soggiorno," La tutela del cittadino 2: La pubblica sicurezza, ed. Paolo Barile, (Vicenza: N. Pozza, 1967), 503-6.

[4]Report of Inspector General Baldovino to the ministry of the interior, cited by Boldetti, 510-11.

[5]Amedeo Boschi, Ricordi del domicilio coatto (Turin: Seme anarchico, 1954), 43.

[6]Boschi, 44.

[7]Buttis, Memorie di vita di tempeste sociali (Chicago: n.p. 1940), 37-38.

[8]Boldetti. 511. For a good contemporary account of the seamy side of domicilio coatto see Jessie White Mario's "Il sistema penitenziario e il domicilio coatto in Italia," Nuova Antologia pt. 1-64 (1 July 1896):16-35.

[9]Lausanne, 17 Jan. 1987, cited in Vilfredo Pareto, Lettere a Maffeo Pantaleoni, 1890-1923 (Rome: Edizioni di Storia e Letteratura 1962), 3: 412.

[10]Umberto Levra, Il colpo di stato della borghesia. La crisi politica di fine secolo in Italia 1896-1900 (Milan: Feltrinelli 1975), 17; Candeloro, 7:20, asserts that Di Rudini refused to free the persons sent into domicilio coatto under Crispi's regime.

[11]The date of Di Rudini's order was 14 Mar. 1896. See Di Rudini's statement to the Chamber, 28 May 1896, Atti parlamentari (hereafter cited as "AP"), cum. vol. 553. Discussioni, 4: 4864.
The parliamentary records of the Chamber of Deputies and the Senate can be located both through indicating a cumulative volume number (see Provveditorato generale dello Stato. Pubblicazioni edite dallo Stato o col suo concorso (1861-1923), 1-24 or a date and a subseries volume number. For added clarity in locating materials, both the cum. vol. number and the subseries vol. number will be used throughout this manuscript.

[12]Di Rudinì, Chamber, 28 May 1896, AP. cum. vol. 553. Discussioni, 4: 4864.

[13]See Di Rudinì's report to the Senate recommending proposed changes in the domicilio coatto law, 1 Dec. 1896, Senate cum. vol. 549. Disegni di legge--Relazioni--Documenti vol. 3: doc. no. 223, 2-3.

[14]Di Rudinì to Codronchi, 6 Sept. 1896. Archivio Codronchi Biblioteca Comunale, Imola.

[15]Di Rudinì, Chamber, 4 June 1896, AP. cum. vol. 553. Discussioni, 4: 5187. Rudinì said that between twelve and twenty so-called "political" prisoners were still under detention.

[16]Di Rudinì's report, Senate, 1 Dec. 1896, AP. cum. vol. 549. Disegni di legge, vol. 3, doc. no. 223, p. 3.

[17]Annuario statistico italiano (1900), 353; Relazione dell' ufficio Centrale, 18 Jan. 1897, Senate, AP. cum. vol. 549. Disegni di legge, vol. 3: doc. no. 223-A, allegato B., p. 26; Giovanni Rosadi, Del domicilio coatto e dei delinquenti recidivi (Florence: n.p. 1900), 100.

[18]Di Rudinì, Chamber 20 May 1896, AP, cum. vol. 553. Discussioni, 4: 4457; Sineo, Chamber, 1 July 1896, AP. cum. vol. 555. Discussioni, 6: 6903.

[19]Di Rudinì, Chamber, 28 May 1896, AP, cum. vol. 553. Discussioni, 4: 4864.

[20]Ibid., 4:4864.

[21]Arch. Codronchi.

[22]Gen. Leone Pelloux to Ministero del Interno, Direzione Generale della Pubblica sicurezza, 12 Apr. 1896, Arch. Codronchi.

[23]I.e. the prefect who had recommended Gavilli to the Interior Minister [Crispi] for assignment to forced domicile.

[24]Di Rudinì to Codronchi, 5 Sept. 1896, Castellamare, Arch. Codronchi.

[25]Di Rudinì to Codronchi, 8 Sept. 1896, Arch. Codronchi.

[26]Di Rudinì to Codronchi, 31 Aug. 1896, Arch. Codronchi.

[27]See Interior Under Secretary Sineo's speech, Chamber 2 July 1896, AP. cum. vol. 555. Discussioni, 6:6981.

[28]Di Rudinì to Codronchi, letter marked "riservatissima", 12 Oct. 1896. Arch. Codronchi.

[29]On the other hand the local commissions which proposed candidates for domicilio coatto would have had a mixed membership of judges and administrative personnel.

[30]9 Apr. 1897, Senate, AP. cum. vol. 577. Discussioni, 1: 68.

[31]Perhaps the most famous article, or series of articles, to come out of the anti-domicilio coatto campaign appeared in the distinguished literary journal, Nuova antologia. The well known Jessie White Mario, a friend of Garibaldi and a participant herself in the risorgimento, criticized Italy's prison system as well as forced domicile in "Il sistema penitenziario e il domicilio coatto in Italia," Nuova antologia 64 (1 July 1896):16-35; 65 (16 Sept. 1896):313-335; 68 (16 Apr. 1897): 680-707; 70 (1 Aug. 1897):503-19; 71 (1 Sept. 1897):121-42.

[32]Report introducing the proposed law "On the abolition of domicilio coatto and on measures against dangerous habitual criminals," presented to the Chamber 29 Nov. 1910 by Interior Minister Luzzatti in concert with Justice Minister Fani and Treasury Minister Tedesco; reprinted in the Enciclopedia giuridica italiana, s.v., "Domicilio coatto," by Luigi Anfosso, 680. Cited hereafter as "Luzzatti in Anfosso".

[33]Enciclopedia giuridica italiana, s.v., "Domicilio coatto," by Luigi Anfosso, 679; cited hereafter as "Anfosso". Domenico Lo Presti, Ammonizione e domicilio coatto (Messina, 1905), 86.

[34]Luzzatti in Anfosso, 685.

[35]Augusto Ferraro, who had served as a district magistrate in the penal colony of Ponza for three years, thought the earlier proposals had failed to regulate "the most minute forms" of prisoner activity. Because of their failure to address these questions, the reforms would only have changed the name of domicilio coatto without changing its substance. Delinquenti abituali e le colonie penali, (Naples: 1910), 50-51.

[36]G. Prencipe, "Domicilio coatto (case di lavoro agrario)", Rivista di discipline carcerarie e correttive, pt. 1 (Apr. 1911), 154.

[37]Giacomo Matteotti, "Il progetto Luzzatti per la riforma degli art. 81-83 del cod. pen." Rivista di diritto e procedura penale, fasc. 4(1911), 301.

[38]Enciclopedia del diritto penale italiano, ed. Enrico Pessina, 4: La pena e il sistema penale del codice italiano (Milan: Societa editrice libraria 1910), 793-94. Suspicions remained, however, that on occasion domicilio coatto was still used for political persecution. "L'istituto della relegazione da sostituirsi al domicilio coatto," Rivista di discipline carcerarie, pt. 1(1910):415.

[39]Steven Hughes, "The Theory and Practice of Ozio in Italian Policing: Bologna and Beyond," Criminal Justice History, 6(1985):96.

[40]Hughes, 96.

[41]Luzzatti in Anfosso, 681.

[42]"In former times, the essential purpose of domicilio coatto was to get rid of . . . the worst delinquents from their hometowns and send them to isolated localities where they couldn't harm anyone, in this fashion restoring tranquillity to so many towns where the conditions of public security were alarming. . . . many times it turned out that public security returned as if by magic to many places from which a few feared offenders had been removed." Ferraro, 29.

[43]Luzzatti speaks of a "fearsome increase", Luzzatti in Anfosso, 681; Fiorenza Fiorentino, Ordine pubblico nell'Italia giolittiana, (Rome: Carecas 1978), 68.

[44]Fiorentino, 38-40, 72. Lo Presti, 56, states that in 1905 England, France and Austria had about 50 police per 10,000 population and Italy 17 per 10,000.

[45]Sen. Majorana, Committee report, 18 Jan. 1897, Senate, AP., Disegni di legge, vol. 3: doc. no. 223A, p. 7.

From Theory to Practice: The Reorientation in Mechanical Engineering

Education and Bourgeois Society in Germany, 1873-1914

C. W. R. Gispen

1. Introduction

In their controversial 1984 work, the Pecularities of German
History, David Blackbourn and Geoff Eley argue that the paradigm of
recent German history associated primarily with liberal scholars like
Jürgen Kocka, Hans-Ulrich Wehler, Hans-Jürgen Puhle and Ralf Dahrendorf
has lost its heuristic value.[1] They say there is nothing further to be
gained from concentrating on Germany's alleged Sonderweg or its
multiple deviations from the norm of Western historical development.
German peculiarities, contend Blackbourn and Eley, have been vastly
exaggerated, as shown by informed comparative analysis and by new
research documenting the bourgeois-capitalist nature of 19th-century
Germany. Explanations of Nazism and of other German problems rooted in
the incongruities of rapid economic development and retarded political
development, in failed social emancipation and insufficient liberalism,
in the feudalization of the bourgeoisie and the debacle of 1848, etc.,
have become a dead end--uncritically accepted canons and axioms that
blunt a more accurate understanding of the recent German past.
Specifically, interpretations that center on Germany's preindustrial
institutions such as the Junkers and the bureaucratic-absolutist
heritage tend to absolve capitalism from responsibility for the rise of
Nazism; in fact the very successes and the crises of the capitalist
system were the real culprits.[2]

This new-Left attempt to revise the "new orthodoxy," as more than
one reviewer has called the collective exponents of the
German-peculiarity thesis, has considerable appeal if for no other
reason than the bridge it throws across the 1945 divide and the "hour
zero."[3] It asks us to stop beating what from an Anglo-American
adversarial perspective increasingly looks like a dead horse (e.g., the
Junkers), and it rekindles the flame of a critical history rooted in
contemporary concerns. Such passion was also the original impulse for
the early exponents of the German Sonderweg interpretation, but it is
in danger of dying now that the conditions that gave rise to it have
largely disappeared or no longer inspire a younger generation of
engaged historians.

Unfortunately the evidence does not always support the revisionist
argument, which as polemic runs the risk of becoming as one-dimensional
as that of the more strident defenders of the "new orthodoxy." In
truth only the unique combination of a victorious capitalism and
certain preindustrial peculiarities explains the extraordinary degree
of social discontent and ferment at the root of Germany's political
problem. This is not a new insight. Thorstein Veblen, despite flaws
in his argument, grasped the central issue in 1915, when he pointed out

that Germany's particular "congeries of cultural elements does not constitute a stable compound."[4] In other words, the crux is not the critical role of either industrial capitalism or preindustrial tradition by itself, but their mixture. The case of the reorientation in mechanical engineering education in Imperial Germany serves to illustrate the lasting relevance of this observation.

2. The Background

When in the aftermath of the Napoleonic wars the various German states embarked on an ambitious program to revive their economies and to catch up with Britain and France, they focused on technical education as one of the best means of achieving their objective. Germany would overcome its economic backwardness and make up for the lack of wealth and natural resources with the intelligence of its artisan classes--with what economists nowadays call investment in human capital. The political climate in which these plans were executed during the period 1815-1848 was one of restoration and reaction. This dictated that the existing social hierarchy and political order were not to be disturbed by the consequences of industrialization and economic modernization. Technical education for the private sector, conceived as practical knowledge for the "vile mechanical arts," was therefore organized in strict isolation from the dominant neohumanist educational establishment--concretely, the classical Gymnasium, the university, and Bildung, which was a form of inner, spiritual nobility serving as one of the few accepted avenues for upward mobility and assimilation to the aristocracy of birth. In other words, the technical schools established in the first half of the 19th century to stimulate private industry and business were intentionally kept segregated from education for the higher social classes and professions, whose knowledge was said to be pure, nonutilitarian, and, as it dealt with immaterial values, an end in itself.[5] This, in brief, is the background of the bifurcation of the German educational system between roughly 1815 and the 1950s into a socially superior branch oriented toward the classics, the humanities, and somewhat later the pure natural sciences as well, and a lower realm of (higher) technical training and its various satellites. Variations of this pattern recur in a number of other societies, but nowhere was it as pronounced, and the distinction as invidious, as in Germany.

In addition to the unusually powerful stigma under which technical education labored in 19th-century Germany, the early timing of its birth was significant. In Germany technical schools were founded to encourage the development of modern industry and therefore came into existence well before the latter. This contrasts with developments in countries like Britain, France or the United States. In those societies technical education either emerged long after the onset of industrialization or developed in tandem with it.[6] As a consequence, practicing engineers and empirically-inclined engineering entrepreneurs emerged as the first dominant faction of their profession in the West, while in Germany the engineering educators assumed this role. The unique combination of professorial ascendancy in a field designed to remain practical-industrial and hence socially inferior, situated in a context characterized by the hegemony of Bildung and ideals of pure science, constituted a peculiarity with fateful consequences for the history of the German engineering profession.

The first socially articulate engineers in Germany were the engineering educators at the newly-established technical schools, the forerunners of the future technische Hochschulen. Not only did they, as educated men, quickly and quite naturally assume the leadership of the incipient engineering profession, but they also were able to determine the intellectual agenda of the new discipline without significant opposition from practicing engineers or engineering entrepreneurs. Acting on motives that were a mixture of social, professional and personal ambitions, the early engineering professors--men like Ferdinand Redtenbacher and Karl Karmarsch--and also the next generation of educators--the most illustrious of whom were Franz Grashof, long-time executive director of the Verein Deutscher Ingenieure and professor at the technical institute at Karlsruhe, and Franz Reuleaux of the technische Hochschule Berlin--did all they could to give evidence of the scientific standing of their discipline and to overcome its practical, artisan stigma. In the process the technical schools' original mission was largely forgotten.

Exogenous social factors, therefore, rather than any dynamics inherent in the field came to account for the direction in which the mechanical engineering sciences developed between the 1830s and the 1870s.[7] Educators tended to prescribe a classical secondary education and the absorption of as much Bildung as possible as the best preparation for future engineering students, disregarding the substantive dysfunctionality of such education for engineering or for an industrializing society. In their quest for social respectability and emancipation they got rid of most of the applied and practical courses, such as training in the workshops, that were part of the original organization of technical education. The engineering educators also were able to upgrade admission standards and the academic content of the curriculum at the polytechnical schools, which by the second half of the 1870s had gradually been converted into university-like institutions known as technische Hochschulen.

In their own courses and in the textbooks they wrote, the professors increasingly redefined technical training and engineering education as pure natural science and theory to make it strictly conform to the prevailing 19th-century ideal of natural science. One of the best ways to do this was to increase the scope of mathematics instruction and to dispense heavy doses of differential calculus and various other highly abstract subjects, such as Professor Reuleaux's Kinematics, a body of theoretical abstractions and deductions about different categories of mechanical principles that was supposed to make invention a deductive-logical process. Professor Grashof's teaching, in the words of a sympathetic contemporary, was "total abstraction that went almost too far and avoided all visual aids, . . . [demanding] a high degree of understanding and intelligence that frequently exceeded the average comprehension of the students."[8] Summing up this entire trend, a certain Professor Hörmann, who taught at Berlin's Industrial Institute in the mid-1870s, expressed the ambition "that it will be possible to reach the highest goal: namely, to gradually transform the field of mechanical engineering into a pure science." The fact that engineering and technology were by definition fields in which practical creation, economic-financial calculations, and the manipulation of nature for useful purposes played a central role was suppressed as much a possible.

A key aspect of this project of social emancipation was to change the path of preparatory training whereby students reached the higher technical institutes, especially in Prussia. The Prussian system as originally established by Peter Beuth in the 1820s and 1830s consisted of a higher institute in Berlin, the Industrial Academy, surrounded by a string of lower schools in the provinces, the so-called Provincial Trade Schools (PTS).[10] The PTS had a double function. On the one hand, they provided technical instruction for artisan sons and other young men who upon graduation returned to practical life. On the other hand, the PTS sent their top students on to the Industrial Academy in Berlin and, therefore, also functioned as preparatory education for higher technical training. Just as the professors at the higher technical institutes, the teachers at the PTS were more interested in the higher functions of their schools than in its more mundane but ultimately more important practical duties. Thus the PTS gradually evolved into modern high schools, though until the late 1870s they never quite lost their practical side--and their artisan stigma not at all. To the professors at the higher technical institutes, especially the Industrial Academy in Berlin, the PTS were an undesirable reminder of their own lowly ancestry and ties to the dirty world of "nuts, bolts and business." They did their best to eliminate the PTS altogether or to exclude their graduates from admission to higher technical education. Though these efforts were unsuccessful, the net effect of all the pressures on the PTS (which combined with a political movement to reduce the Latin component in German secondary education) was the schools' complete overhaul in 1878. The name was changed to Oberrealschulen, and as non-classical nine-year high schools they were integrated into the main educational establishment.[11]

The result of these developments was that around 1880 technical education in Prussia and to a lesser extent also in other German states was characterized by a small number of highly theoretical and emphatically scientific institutions. Non-academic engineering education and practical training for the artisan and lower-middle classes had been organized out of existence. The would-be technical universities could only be reached by long and expensive general secondary education (at least in principle, since numerous exceptions continued to exist in practice for a long time), and they concentrated on teaching highly arcane subjects, such as Kinematics and "theoretical machine science," whose value for actual engineering was at best highly dubious. All the lower dimensions had successfully been cast off. From a social perspective the mechanical engineering disciplines had made great strides in becoming professionalized. The engineers trained at these elite institutions and their professors stood poised to enter the enchanted circle of Germany's cultivated classes and higher professions.

3. Reorientation

Had it not been for the industrial revolution and the powerful dynamics of industrial capitalism, the professionalization project of the engineering educators would undoubtedly have succeeded.[12] The tide turned against them exactly when it seemed they might consolidate their gains of the previous half century. Since the 1850s, criticism of the academizing trend from engineering entrepreneurs and managerial engineers had been on the rise; but until the crash of 1873 and the deep recession 1874-1879 that followed it, such complaints carried little weight. Even those who articulated these objections to the tendencies of an unchecked "school culture" did not give the matter priority. All this changed suddenly. In their infancy in the 1850s, the engineering industries had reached a certain maturity by the 1870s and were then plunged into a devastating crisis. The economic depression became the signal for the profession's much grown managerial-entrepreneurial faction--what Monte Calvert in the American context has called mechanical engineering's "shop culture"--to start a rebellion against the tutelage of the professors.[13] This movement, which ended with the managerial segment acquiring decisive influence on the profession's fate, started as a search for scapegoats for the economic downturn.

The ones who received most of the blame were the engineering professors at the technische Hochschulen. As a certain engineer Heine, who had spent many years in the United States, expressed it in 1876, the "way we train [our personnel] for many branches of industry is completely wrong. He suffer from . . . being forced into a stereotyped mold of scientific education. This tendency is most pronounced in mechanical engineering."[14] The most devastating criticism came from Joseph Schlink, managing and technical director of the Friedrich Wilhelm Works in Mulheim on the Ruhr. "If one compare[d] the large number of technische Hochschulen in Germany and the incessant efforts to expand them, raise their standing, and increase their numbers with the very modest institutions abroad," argued Schlink in 1878, Germany ought to have been far ahead of her competitors in the world market, at least "in so far as theoretical schooling is the only measure of competitiveness. But since . . . our products are in part too expensive and in part . . . 'cheap but bad,' . . . our beautiful theoretical efforts seem to have had but little success." Angrily Schlink pointed out that "in German technology, the 'professor' plays much too large a role, practice in contrast not nearly enough of one." He spoke with contempt of the "extravagant Redtenbacher cult" at the technische Hochschule in Karlsruhe, and claimed that "every graduation ceremony brings us, the machinery manufacturers, a number of educated engineers in whom we can study the achievements of the polytechnical school. As a rule these young men must start over with the very simplest design details, and often it takes years before they qualify for more independent work on larger projects." Regardless, "our professors blithely amble on . . . Everywhere they play first fiddle. . . ."[16]

Contrary to what the professors believed, Schlink continued, engineering and engineering education was not about Bildung or about theory for its own sake. Nor was it a pure science in which business and financial questions did not intrude. Instead, engineering was first and foremost a money issue. In Schlink's words: "All industrial products have their only standard of value in money. The difference between cost of production and selling price--the profit--forms the only justified and the only possible foundation for operating an industrial business. The most perfect production process is an economic absurdity if it sustains a financial loss." The message for the technische Hochschulen was clear. They "must not train scholars, not future professors, but energetic industrialists who want to increase their wealth and thereby that of their country. Profits are the final goal and not training in sterile Katheder-wisdom." The way to reach this goal was for the schools to become much more practical and applied and, above all, more specialized.[16]

Schlink's agenda, that of engineering's shop culture as a whole, went into effect between 1875 and 1895, the period also known as the "Great Depression."[17] The "most rational training of the engineer for his occupation" as measured by functional criteria became the new watch word and the key to economic recovery.[18] The perceived technological lead of the United States played a major role in this reorientation. Beginning with the Philadelphia Centennial Exposition of 1876, a steady flow of German engineering professors with ties to the business side of their discipline came to the United States to analyze the causes of American engineering successes. They were inspired and impressed by the pragmatism of American engineering education--increasingly in institutes of technology but predominantly based on shop training, practical know-how rather than theoretical school knowledge, extensive laboratory work, observation and experimentation without regard for Bildung, and above all, extreme specialization. Having seen schools like M.I.T. and Rensselaer Polytechnic Institute and having spoken to Robert Henry Thurston and Alexander Lyman Holley, German teachers such as Hermann Ludewig of the Munich technische Hochschule, Hermann Wedding of the Berlin Mining Academy, as well as others who until then had been in the minority, began to preach the gospel of a different kind of engineering education in the late 1870s and early 1880s.[19]

The economic depression and the resulting willingness to try new solutions were largely responsible for the positive reception of such recommendations. As early as 1877, money became available to expand a small testing station in Berlin and to integrate it into the technische Hochschule, where it became the basis for a future, much larger applied research facility. In 1881, Professor Carl Bach in Stuttgart established a new materials-testing laboratory that soon assumed additional research and limited teaching responsibilities. Other technische Hochschulen gradually followed and changed their curriculum. In 1886, the technische Hochschule Stuttgart became the first to require evidence of a "practical year" before students would be admitted to the preliminary examinations. In 1893/94, Charlottenburg Professor Alois Riedler, by far the most influential exponent of the new direction, published an important series of articles on U.S. technical education. In 1895, he was able to commit the Verein Deutscher Ingenieure and soon afterward, the Prussian government to undertake an ambitious program of engineering laboratories and research institutes. The new laboratories not only exposed all students to extensive practical training but also permanently transformed mechanical engineering education. From a stepchild of the natural sciences it matured into an autonomous professional discipline with its own particular subject matter and methodology. The fundamental principles of its method were model building and scientific experimentation and measurement.[20]

At the same time, the mathematical orientation of the preceding decades came under attack from a movement of "Anti-mathematicians," in which Riedler also played a leading role. Others in this camp were Professors Adolf Ernst at Stuttgart, Aurel Stodola at Zurich, Georg Meyer at Berlin, and Gustav Herrmann at Aachen. As early as 1884 Herrmann launched at attack on the absurdity of using calculus and other unnecessarily difficult mathematical methods where they were not needed, pointing out how much easier it was to understand and solve certain problems if they were approached graphically. It was the beginning of a revolutionary increase in the use of graphic methods of instruction, indicator and vector diagrams, probability and statistical techniques--which dovetailed to the new emphasis on experimentation and observation. Closely related was a heavy emphasis on drafting design in the new mechanical engineering education. Once again Riedler was instrumental in bringing about the change. Students spent long hours in the drafting rooms of the technische Hochschulen, learning how to become practical designers and do the work of ordinary draftsmen to develop their powers of spatial conceptualization.[21] The result of all these changes, accompanied by a steady expansion of the technische Hochschulen and dramatic growth in their enrollments, was that by the second half of the 1890s mechanical engineering education was radically transformed. Large numbers of graduates were much more specialized, more practical, and, if they could find the right job, more quickly usable in industry than earlier generations of engineers. Judging by Germany's rapid technological progress, by its surging industrialization, and by its engineering triumphs in the quarter century before World War I, the new orientation was an unqualified success from an economic point of view.

4. Social and political consequences

What were the social and political ramifications of the reorientation, specifically with regard to the history of the engineering profession and its place in German society before 1914?[22] The outcome was a permanent setback to the social-status and emancipatory ambitions inherent in the engineers' professionalization project. On the eve of World War I the vast majority of engineers were an embittered and fragmented lot, marked by internecine warfare, deep frustration, and double-edged resentment of the big industrialists and of Germany's older, "cultivated" and professional elites.[23] The reason was not that the new trend in engineering education had interrupted the academization process of the technische Hochschulen. On the contrary, the organizational and formal aspects of competitive assimilation to the universities had gathered sufficient momentum that those who made up the profession's managerial faction would probably have been unable to stop it even if they had tried, which they did not. The change that resulted was one of substance and content only. Thus the technische Hochschulen after 1880 continued to evolve into evermore formidable institutions--a development that culminated in 1899 when William II granted them the right to confer academic degrees nominally equivalent to university degrees. The same Professor Riedler who had been one of the foremost critics of the older abstract-theoretical trend in engineering education played a key role in organizing this victory for the technische Hochschulen.[24]

Instead, the profession's crisis was a product of the elimination of non-academic engineering education in the 1870s and the timing of its reestablishment. These developments combined with rapid industrial growth and the fanatical emphasis on practical utility and on extreme specialization at the technische Hochschulen to lay the foundations for the explosive decade before 1914. The insistence on practicality in higher engineering education was partly a reaction against prior tendencies and partly a consequence of the disappearance of precisely such applied training when the Prussian PTS changed into general secondary schools. The remaining nine technische Hochschulen, whose admission standards kept on rising, were incapable of producing enough engineers for all the positions that needed technically trained personnel. The ones they did train were from the engineering industrialists' point of view, too expensive ⌐ overeducated for many of the increasingly specialized and semi-professional functions. In consequence, the technische Hochschulen in the decades between 1880 and 1914 improvised by admitting large numbers of auditors and other unofficial students to compensate for the lost opportunities for non-academic technical education. Sometimes half the student body consisted of such auditors, whose educational and social backgrounds were much more varied than those of the regularly enrolled students. Even so, these irregulars got jobs in industry and, just like the matriculating students, called themselves engineers, a practice condoned by the engineering entrepreneurs and employers suspicious of education-based claims to recognition, promotion, or salary increases. Needless to say, this situation made all engineers socially suspect in the eyes of the established professions.[25]

Despite the makeshift arrangements and skyrocketing enrollments at the technische Hochschulen, the relentless growth of industrial capitalism and the rising popularity of technical careers soon made it obvious that the existing facilities still could not meet the demand. Thus plans were developed and executed to increase the number of higher technical institutes. In 1904, the newly-established technische Hochschule Danzig and in 1910, the technische Hochschule Breslau opened their doors. However, the increasing number of technische Hochschulen only aggravated the basic problem. Despite its new fixation on practice and emphasis on specialization, Germany's system of technical education after 1880 was top heavy. Farsighted government officials and engineering industrialists had recognized this in the early 1880s, but for a variety of reasons nothing was done about it until after 1890. Finally in the early 1890s the Prussian government, prodded by engineering industrialists in control of the Verein Deutscher Ingenieure, made a start with introducing non-academic engineering schools. At first it moved slowly and hesitantly. As a consequence the new institutions, known as Machine Building Schools, did not begin to make their impact felt until the early and mid-1900s. Meanwhile, the gap had been filled by countless proprietary engineering schools that had sprung up to capitalize on the surging demand for technical personnel in the 1880s, and especially the 1890s. With their nominal admission standards the proprietary schools turned out large numbers of would-be engineers who lacked all the normal attributes of professionalism in the German context but who had been taught how to draft and do other practical and routinized engineering tasks.[26]

The cumulative effect of all these developments, which came together in the first decade of the 20th century, was a tremendous glut of engineers. After 1900 all the engineering and technical schools were turning out more graduates--both official and unofficial--than industry could place in appropriate positions. Because the economy kept growing rapidly, significant unemployment of engineers did not materialize, but the openings that became available were frequently of a very subordinate and menial nature. Engineering salaries fell to levels that compared unfavorably with the wages of skilled blue-collar workers. Relations between engineers and management quickly deteriorated, giving rise to unionization, engineering strikes and union busting. To escape such proletarianization and conflict with management, certain academically certified engineers turned away from industry and concentrated instead on an ill-fated attempt at opening up civil-service and administrative careers to graduates from the technische Hochschulen. Their failure and the hostility they encountered from the established professions goes a long way toward explaining the resentment these engineers developed for the traditionally educated elites and the inherited social order.[27]

Unquestionably, the primary cause of the engineering profession's crisis was oversupply and a long-term cyclical imbalance between the output of the educational system and the labor market. The problem was intensified by structural changes in the organization of engineering work--increasing specialization, differentiation, division of labor and bureaucratization--that interacted with the new direction at the technische Hochschulen. As one commentator on German engineering education had written with specific reference to Professor Riedler's role in this regard, his emphasis on the drill and details of "design . . . promoted fragmentation within the Mechanical Engineering Department and raised specialists already at the [technische] Hochschule--specialists who were also being supplied by the [non-academic engineering] schools. Thus in practice the distinction between the graduates of the higher institutes and the [non-academic] schools disappeared, which resulted in regrettable competition."[28]

The words "regrettable competition" fail to do justice to the constant sniping, bitter recriminations, and rampant hostility between academically certified and non-academic or non-certified engineers in the decade before World War I. Though the details of this conflict cannot be discussed here, one thing is clear. Many graduates of the technische Hochschulen, who took great pride in their academic degrees and their nine-year high-school diplomas, hoped to used these credentials to monopolize the better positions in industry. Yet their actual technical skills were not all that different from those of their non-academic colleagues. The heavy emphasis on practical training and early specialization at the technische Hochschulen had been achieved at the cost of students' reduced command of the fundamentals of mathematics, mechanics, physics and chemistry--i.e., precisely that intellectual versatility and depth that eventually would have qualified them for the most creative tasks, made for a more profound distinction from the vocational engineers, and thereby better sustained their claims of professional standing. The new orientation, in some ways an overreaction to the earlier theoretical tendencies, had gone too far in its emphasis on practice. As one contemporary critic put it in 1907, "the pendulum has swung too far in the other direction. . . The healthy development of the mechanical engineering curriculum as well as the interests of the engineering profession today demand greater emphasis on theoretical training at our technische Hochschulen."[29]

In the end, all segments of the profession were drawn into the conflict. Prestigious engineering professors like Riedler accused the engineering industrialists of willfully creating the engineers' career crisis by founding non-academic engineering schools for the sake of profits. The industrialists issued vehement denials, making counter accusations regarding the reactionary caste mentality and anti-capitalist gospel of Riedler and his followers, and they successfully defeated all monopolization attempts of the academically certified engineers.[30] Government engineers and private-sector engineers attacked each other, as did unionizers and professionalizers, and the engineering employers and employees.

In sum, the decades before 1914 witnessed a process of educational variegation, of fragmentation and conflicting patterns of simultaneous professionalization and deprofessionalization among engineers that set the stage for an enormous amount of socio-political ferment, anxiety, and utopian speculation.[31] Locked in internecine warfare, the engineers collectively made a three-way front against the old order of the educated establishment, the industrialist-capitalist order of monied interests, and the proletarian left. As such, they were a microcosm of the social fissures in German bourgeois society as a whole, as well as a prefiguration of the Weimar impasse and the Nazi revolution, whose rhetoric capitalized precisely on such multiple frustrations. Preindustrial elements and industrial-capitalist factors were inextricably intertwined in this dynamic scenario, as Veblen recognized long ago. Arguments that fail to take this into account are bound to remain incomplete or misleading.

University of Mississippi
November 1987

[1] David Blackbourn and Geoff Eley, The Peculiarities of German History: Bourgeois Society and Politics in Nineteenth-Century Germany (Oxford and New York: Oxford University Press, 1984).

[2] Geoff Eley, "What Produces Fascism: Preindustrial Traditions or a Crisis of a Capitalist State?", Politics and Society 12, 1 (1983): 53-82.

[3] For the term "new orthodoxy," see, e.g., Robert G. Moeller, "The Kaiserreich Recast? Continuity and Change in Modern German Historiography," Journal of Social History 17, 4 (1983): 658, and the literature cited there, 674, note 18.

[4] Thorstein Veblen, Imperial Germany and the Industrial Revolution (Ann Arbor: The University of Michigan Press, 1966 [1915]), 239.

[5] C. W. R. Gispen, "Technical Education and Social Status: The Emergence of the Mechanical Engineering Occupation in Germany, 1820-1890" (Ph.D. dissertation, University of California, Berkeley, 1981), ch. 1.

[6] See, e.g., James M. Edmonson, From Mécanicien to Ingenieur: Technical Education and the Machine Building Industry in Nineteenth-Century France (New York and London: Garland Publishing, Inc., 1987); C. Rod Day, "The Making of Mechanical Engineers in France: The Ecoles d'Arts et Métiers, 1803-1914," French Historical Studies 10 (Spring 1978): 439-60; Terry Shinn, "From 'corps' to 'profession': the Emergence and Definition of Industrial Engineering in Modern France," in The Organization of Science and Technology in France 1808-1914, ed. Robert Fox and George Weisz (Cambridge: Cambridge University Press, 1980), 182-203; John Hubbel Weiss, The Making of Technological Man: The Social Origins of French Engineering Education (Cambridge and London: The MIT Press, 1982); Gordon W. Roderick and Michael Stephens, Scientific and Technical Education in Nineteenth-Century England (Newton Abbot: David & Charles (Holdings) Limited, 1972); Monte A. Calvert, The Mechanical Engineer in America, 1830-1910: Professional Cultures in Conflict (Baltimore: The Johns Hopkins Press, 1967).

[7] See Gispen, "Technical Education and Social Status," chs. 1 and 3; and Wolfgang Konig, "Wissenschaft und Praxis: Schlüsselkategorien für die Entwicklung des deutschen technischen Ausbildungssystems," Mitteilungen der Technischen Universität Carolo-Wilhelmina zu Braunschweig 20, 2 (1985): 30-36. See also, Hans-Joachim Braun, "Methodenprobleme der Ingenieur-wissenschaft, 1850 bis 1900," Technikgeschichte 44, 1 (1977): 1-18.

[8] Professor Karl Keller, a colleague of Grashof's at Karlsruhe, quoted in Paul Wentzcke, Franz Grashof: Ein Führer der deutschen Ingenieure (Berlin: VDI-Verlag, 1926), 64-65.

[9] Quoted in Joseph Schlink, "Die Bestrebungen der technischen Lehranstalten und die Anforderungen des praktischen Lebens," Glaser's Annalen für Gewerbe und Bauwesen 2 (Jan. 1878): 10.

[10] For the origin and history of the Provincial Trade Schools, see Gispen, "Technical Education and Social Status," chs. 1, 3, 4, and Peter Lundgreen, Techniker in Preussen während der frühen Industrialisierung (Berlin: Colloquium Verlag, 1975), 41-132. Also: Wolfdietrich Jost, Gewerbliche Schulen und politische Macht: Zur Entwicklung des gewerblichen Schulwesens in Preussen in der Zeit von 1850-1880 (Weinheim and Basel; 1982).

[11] See Gispen, "Technical Education and Social Status," ch. 4, and Jost, Gewerbliche Schulen.

[12] The term "professionalization project" comes from Magali Sarfatti Larson, The Rise of Professionalism: A Sociological Analysis (Berkeley: University of California Press, 1977).

[13] Calvert, The Mechanical Engineer in America, 1830-1910.

[14] H. Heine, Professor Reuleaux und die deutsche Industrie: Eine Skizze auf Grundlage amerikanischer sowie deutscher Beobachtungen und Erfahrungen (Berlin: Polytechnische Buchhandlung A. Seydel, 1876), 36.

[15] Joseph Schlink, "Die Bestrebungen der technischen Lehrinstitute und die Anforderungen des praktischen Lebens." Glaser's Annalen für Gewerbe und Bauwesen 2, 13-14 (Jan. 1878): 7-11, 33-38, 225. On Schlink, see Hans-Joachim Braun, "Wirtschafts- und gesellschaftpolitische Anschauungen von Ingenieuren am Ende des 19. Jahrhunderts: Das Beispiel Joseph Schlink," Technikgeschichte 45 (1978): 215-28. See also König, "Wissenschaft und Praxis," passim, esp. 32.

[16] Schlink, "Die Bestrebungen," 11-12.

[17] Hans Rosenberg, Grosse Depression und Bismarckzeit: Wirtschaftsablauf, Gesellschaft und Politik in Mitteleuropa (Berlin: Walter de Gruyter & Co., 1967).

[18] Professor Hermann Ludewig, quoted in Wochenschrift des Vereins Deutscher Ingenieure 1879: 312.

[19] Gispen, "Technical Education," 497-508.

[20] Ibid.; also König, "Wissenschaft und Praxis, 33-35; Karl-Heinz Manegold, Universität, Technischen Hochschule und Industrie (Berlin: Duncker & Humblot, 1970), 144-56.

[21] Ibid.; see also Braun, "Methodenprobleme," and August Hertwig, Der geistige Wandel der technichen Hochschulen in den letzten 100 Jahren und ihre Zukunft. (Deutsches Museum, Abhandlungen und Berichte 18, 1 [1950]) (Munich and Düsseldorf: R. Oldenbourg and VDI-Verlag, 1950), 11-17.

126

[22]This topic is discussed from a different vantage point in the author's "Engineers in Wilhelmian Germany: Professionalization, Deprofessionalization, and the Development of Non-Academic Technical Education" forthcoming in German Professions 1850-1950, ed. Konrad Jarausch and Geoffrey Cocks, (New York: Oxford University Press, 1989).

[23]Such hostility for the "cultivated" elites was an important ingredient in the subsequent appeal and practice of National Socialism. See Wolfgang Sauer, "National Socialism: Totalitarianism or Fascism?" American Historical Review 73, 2 (1967): 422-24.

[24]See Karl-Heinz Manegold, Universität, Technische Hochschule und Industrie, 249-305; also Wolfgang König, "Die Ingenieure und der VDI als Grossverein in der wilhelminischen Gesellschaft 1900 bis 1918," in Technik, Ingenieure und Gesellschaft: Geschichte des Vereins Deutscher Ingenieure 1856-1981, ed. Karl-Heinz Ludwig and Wolfgang König (Düsseldorf: VDI-Verlag, 1981), 235-87; and Volker Hunecke, "Der 'Kampf ums Dasein' und die Reform der technischen Erziehung im Denken Alois Riedlers," in Wissenschaft und Gesellschaft: Beiträge zur Geschichte der Technischen Universität Berlin 1879-1979, 2 vols., ed. Reinhard Rürup (Berlin, Heidelberg, New York: Springer Verlag, 1979), 1: 301-14.

[25]These problems are discussed in considerable detail in Alois Riedler, "Die Entwicklung des maschinentechnischen Studiums," Zeitschrift des Verein Deutscher Ingenieure (VDIZ) 1908: 702-21.

[26]The Machine Building Schools are discussed by Gustav Grüner, Die Entwicklung der höheren technischen Fachschulen im Deutschen Sprachgebiet (Brunswick: Georg Westermann Verlag, 1967), 13-122.

[27]See the reference cited in note 22, also König, "Die Ingenieure und der VDI als Grossverein."

[28]Hertwig, Der geistige Wandel, 14.

[29]Engineer Friedrich Bendemann, quoted in VDIZ 1908: 703. See also, Hertwig, Der geistige Wandel, 14-15, and Gispen, "Technical Education," 507-10.

[30]Riedler, "Die Entwicklung des maschinentechnischen Studiums," passim.

[31]Much of this material can be found in two crucial periodicals, the Deutsche Industriebeamten-Zeitung (1904-1914), published by the militant engineering union, the Bund der technisch-industriellen Beamten, and the Zeitschrift des Verbandes Deutscher Diplom-Ingenieure (1909-1914), the publication of the fervent professionalizers among academically certified engineers.

127

Gertrud Bäumer and the Weimar Republic:
"New Jerusalem" or "Politics as Usual?"

Catherine E. Boyd

In November 1918, German middle-class women experienced a season of traumatic change and uncertainty. Grounded as they were in the traditional forms of Germany's imperial past, they were stunned by the sudden collapse of all the old certainties. In a world robbed of truth, they heard rumors of Germany's defeat on the battlefields of France, defeat in a war they had worked and suffered to sustain for over four years. Revolution, violent worker's rebellions, demands for the Kaiser's abdication--what could it all mean? What did it portend for them?

On November 9, the old Empire gave place to a newly proclaimed Socialist Republic. Two days later, the new government affirmed Germany's military defeat by signing the Armistice presented by the victorious Entente Powers. On November 12, the new government turned to face the future when it proclaimed its support for universal suffrage for both men and women.[1] On November 30, the order for elections to the National Constituent Assembly was promulgated. The order read in part as follows:

-1-

The members of the German National Constituent Assembly shall be elected in general, direct, and secret elections according to the basic laws of proportional representation. Every voter shall have one vote.

-2-

All German men and women who have reached the age of twenty before election day shall have the right to vote.[2]

In that moment of military defeat, governmental dislocation and the social/economic disruption attendant upon such transformations, "Women entered not into the Parliament, but into the National Constituent Assembly, where with their own hands they could help to shape the outlines of the new society."[3]

Middle-class women reacted with conflicting emotions. To be sure, there was a sense of exhilaration about the sudden rush of events, a sense of gain and new promise; but there was also a sense of disquiet, uncertainty. Was the promise valid? Had women truly entered into a new realm of freedom? Did this grant of the franchise represent belated recognition for the years of diligent work and patient persuasion? Was it specific payment of the grueling four years of homefront war-support service? Or, more disturbingly, was it only a revolutionary flourish by the new Socialist Provisional Government, an

129

arbitrary recognition of women's existence, which would have been made even had they not exerted themselves in behalf of the state?

Gertrud Bäumer could not but share the middle-class women's conflicting sense of suspicion and delight. Active within the ranks of the Bund deutscher Frauenverein (BdF) for the last twenty years, Bäumer was already a public figure when the franchise was granted. Since 1910, she has served as President of the BdF, a position she would not relinquish until 1919. Since 1914 and the beginning of World War I, she has served as head of the Nationaler Frauendienst, Germany's female war-support program. In addition to her active leadership of the middle-class women's movement, Baumer held a fairly prominent position in the male-dominated Liberal Progressive Party, known after November 1918 as the German Democratic Party (DDP).[4]

The fact that her reputation rested on her pragmatic organizational abilities did not exempt Baumer from a fundamental identification with the idealism of the women's movement. Throughout the second half of the 19th century, middle-class women had worked to carve out an independent place for themselves, to assert their humanity and dignity in the world of the German patriarchy. Conscious of the militant male-dominance of German society, middle-class women had advanced carefully toward goals they held to be most sacred. Proudly, they had learned to repeat Friedrich Schleiermacher's "Catechism of Reason for Noble Women," looking forward to the day when "limitations imposed on the basis of sex" would be removed.[5] Firmly, but graciously, Bäumer and her middle-class colleagues had rejected the sensational violence of the British suffragettes, believing that "Shouting will not suffice, but deeds of action and sacrifice will."[6] Finally, in their earnest desire to act and to sacrifice, German middle-class women had volunteered for homefront service to the Fatherland during four exacting years of war.

Now, in the turmoil of November 1918, was this their reward for deeds of action and sacrifice? They could not know. They could only trust. When Bäumer and her colleagues in the old women's movement found themselves suddenly endowed with promises of power and influence, they seized the opportunity to infuse the new government with as much of their own idealistic Weltanschauung as possible. What they could not know was that their suspicions were more valid than their hopes and ideals. The "new Jerusalem" they would seek to create would prove to be only a fantasy, a dream soon to be dispelled by the onslaught of "politics as usual." The only remnant of their brief exercise in power would be their promise of a unique female spirit--intellectual as well as spiritual, patriotic as well as domestic--devoted completely to the nation and to the home. The ideals of the middle-class women, which were imprinted so early and so dimly upon the soul of the Weimar Republic, would reemerge a decade later in distorted guise, defined anew in Nazi terms as "Kinder, Küche and Kirche."

In fact, the franchise for German women had been decreed by the Socialist Provisional Government on the basis of its understanding that German women would provide a solid block of electoral support for the new socialist regime. Not only did the Social Democratic Party (SPD) expect women to express their gratitude for the grant of the franchise, but also they thought they would remember that the SPD had been the only political party in the old Reichstag to support women's political rights. The socialists were soon to be disappointed in their expectations, but only time and the electoral returns would reveal the error of their logic.

In the meantime, SPD women joined their male colleagues in celebration of the new regime of socialist equality, rejoicing in their good fortune even as their middle-class counterparts despaired. Klara Bohm-Schuch described the situation for socialist women in an article for Vorwärts, the SPD newspaper:

> We socialist women have reached our ideal, the land of our dreams, overnight. The door to the golden land of freedom stands wide open before us and we are walking though it into the light of a new day.[7]

Conversely, the attitude of the middle-class women was captured best in an article written by Marianne Weber for the Frankfurter Zeitung:

> What we women have worked for decades to achieve--the political equality of our sex--has come upon us like a thief in the night, in the dark hour of destiny which we have lived through with our people. We women will not try to deny that we looked forward to this break-through into democracy in a different fashion. We had hoped to bring it about by our own strength. . . . It is unbearably painful that our political freedom should be born first out of the collapse of our national hopes and, secondly, through the shattering of our state's form of being. This gift of the revolution lies like a great burden upon our shoulders.[8]

But if the unsolicited right to political equality was a "burden upon. . . [their] shoulders," as Weber said, it was still a burden that must be lifted and exploited. Bäumer did not approve of the irregular manner of female enfranchisement any more than Weber, but she was not one to nourish despair. Women must take what was given them and seek to infuse it with their own strength:

> Such power or influence as women desire can come only through personal authority--not through a law. Power is always its own measure--not some artificial standard or norm. If the new position of women is to stand the test, it is not a question of a new law passed by the Parliament, it is a question of whether or not women themselves can establish an inner legality for themselves--an inner legality that will control their inner space and extend itself from within to affect the life outside.[9]

If Bäumer's words sound cold or aloof to us, if she seems to ignore the real disorientation and sadness of her middle-class colleagues, we need to understand the context in which she spoke. She

131

was as distraught about the events of November 1918 as her friend, Marianne Weber. Everything she had loved and sought to serve over the last four years of war had collapsed around her. The high ideals and principles of the old women's movement were apparently being undercut, cheapened by the socialist revolution. But if the times were uncertain, grieving was not in order. It was time to move ahead.

Bäumer understood the caustic wit and criticism of her male party colleagues. She must have agreed with young Ernst Cassirer's evaluation of the whole socialist experiment in government as "nothing but a swindle--a Schiebung."[10] Max Weber, Marianne's husband, was probably correct, in Bäumer's opinion, when he labeled the November Revolution a "bloody carnival," and was only a bit over-exuberant when he suggested that Karl Liebknecht, the Spartacist leader, was fit only for the insane asylum and Rosa Luxemburg for the zoo.[11] Criticism was fine; humor was healthy. Even despair had its place, provided that it not be protracted. Women had work to do if they were to shape a new society for Germany, one to their liking. They had been given the vote, not by the Kaiser within the old imperial regime, as they would have preferred, but by the new provisional government. Whatever the source, Bäumer knew that the opportunity must be seized. Out of "politics as usual," even revolutionary politics, perhaps something of real value could be extracted.

In truth, there was good reason to be excited about the political challenge. Bäumer knew that middle-class women were far from being novices in the political game. Since 1908, when the old laws excluding women, children, and apprentices from political assemblies had been repealed, middle-class women had made significant political connections. Most of the leaders of the BdF, including Bäumer, Helene Lange, Marianne Weber, Marie-Elisabeth Lüders, Marie Baum, Agnes von Zahn-Harnack and Dorothee von Velsen, had joined the liberal Progressive People's Party. When the party changed its name to the DDP late in 1918, its leadership had remained unchanged. In company with such liberal political luminaries as Max Weber, Friedrich Naumann, Hugo Preuss, Friedrich Meinecke, Walther Rathenau and Ernst Troeltsch, the women of the old middle-class movement would be able to enter into the election process in January 1919 with grace and only a lingering touch of apprehension.[12]

There was cause to be apprehensive of political campaigning during the winter of 1918/1919. Berlin, along with other major German cities, was torn by revolutionary violence. Spartacist and Freikorps units dominated the streets, often making it dangerous for candidates to fulfill their campaign schedules. Over and above the flash of revolution loomed the potential for violence from angry demobilized soldiers, who were beginning to filter back into the homeland. The enemy blockade of food, fuel, and medical supplies continued, and the ravages of the Spanish influenza epidemic seemed only a minor addition to the common burden of death and dissolution. Germany was not a stable arena for those who were committed to the socialist-democratic experiment--much less so for those of more tentative enthusiasm.[13]

Actually, once they were involved in the frantic, ever-accelerating pace of popular campaigning, the formerly genteel DDP candidates, male and female alike, began to warm to the task. The campaign took on something of a battle-front character as the opposing parties struggled to assert their ability and readiness to save Germany from destruction. Echoing recent wartime rhetoric, the DDP called upon potential voters of the middle-class to rally in defense of the nation: "We need you! Without you Germany will collapse and fall into the chaos of Socialism!"[14]

Bäumer could call up her own particular examples of the disruptive nature of Marxian socialism within the German women's movement. Reaching agreement on matters of concern to women was always difficult, but the process became impossible when socialist women insisted upon interjecting their own peculiar ideological positions:

This difficulty became more complex as the women's movement became more deeply involved in the variety of women's problems. How to maintain unity and clarity of purpose in such a mosaic of conflicting needs, opinions, and programs? And always, of course, the most difficult piece to fit into the mosaic was that of Marxism. With its conviction that economic issues were more important than spiritual and intellectual concerns, Marxism posed a direct threat to the established trend of the women's movement.[15]

The DDP campaign paid off more richly than anyone could have anticipated. Disoriented and unnerved by the revolutionary upheaval, German voters responded emotionally to the militant rhetoric of the DDP. Turn-out at the polling places was unusually high. In 37 election districts, 87.7% of the eligible males voted; but women in the same districts exceeded even the high male rate, turning out 89.4% of their number.[16] Of the total vote, 18.5% went to the DDP, making the new party third in size to the SPD and Catholic Center delegations in the Constituent Assembly.

Of the 75 DDP delegates, 6 were female. Among the number were Bäumer, Marianne Weber and Marie Baum. Marie-Elisabeth Lüders was not seated by the first candidates list but would enter the Assembly as a replacement later in the year. Also, although Helene Lange, the grande dame of the BdF, had declined to campaign for a spot on the national party list, she was present at Weimar as a honorary delegate for Hamburg. In the opining ceremonies, because she was the oldest delegate present, Lange was asked to address the Assembly.[17] Bäumer was as emotionally moved by the honors paid her lifetime friend and colleague, Lange, as she was to see the large number of female delegates from all political factions seated about the Assembly. Out of the total Assembly membership of 423, 41 were women.[18]

Bäumer was exhilerated by the prospects she saw before the women of Germany. Now, at last, the moment for significant change seemed to be at hand. Almost a decade later, Bäumer would recall her high hopes for the future in the wake of those 1919 elections. She remembered her own sense of idealistic determination:

Only two months before, Germany had been a land of ruins, doubtful and needing direction, torn between opposing views and aspirations. In the bitterness of the time, little hope was to be found.

But if it is the will of destiny that women should be called upon to take part in the life the nation at its hour of greatest distress and crisis, perhaps the call has a special significance. Such crises are, after all, not foreign to women. For if the war was a judgement against technical civilization and capitalism, perhaps the remedy will be found in impulse, in the soul, in the dreams of the youth. A sense of revulsion against the old--a need for a new sense of human worth, social organization--for social humanism is to be felt--the old German idealism in a new world of work and life. . . . Today, perhaps the spirit of the women's movement can have an impact upon all Germany.[19]

With her last speculation, ". . . perhaps the spirit of the women's movement can have an impact upon all of Germany," Baumer was proffering the highest, most valued commodity in her possession. glorying in the unexpected power of the moment, as a member of the third most popular political party in Germany, as leader of the most powerful women's organization, Baumer had reason to be exuberant. For the moment, she and her colleagues in the DDP celebrated their hope for the future, failing to consider if the election was as much of a "fluke" as the franchise for women.

Operating on the understanding that the party controlled a solid block of electoral support, the DDP agreed to enter into a coalition government with the Majority SPD and Catholic Center Party. From recent campaign experience, they expected their participation in a socialist-dominated government to reinvigorate charges of disloyalty to the values and interest of the middle-class and to give new life to the slanderous charges of a cosmopolitan "Jewish spirit" within the DDP's ideology. Two of the right-wing parties, the German People's Party (DVP) and the German National People's Party (DNVP), had made effective use of those charges during the election. But not, with the strength of the election behind them, the party leaders thought their power base was solid enough to run the risk. They must help to give Germany a government, write a constitution, and make an honorable peace with the victorious powers in Paris.[20]

While the male leaders of the parties struggled to work out a coalition, female delegates from the same factions began to establish their own agenda. Cooperation was no easier among the women then among the men. Socialist women, led by Clara Zeitz and Marie Juchacz, seemed determined to portray the women of the DDP as class enemies rather than government allies. Clara Zeitz warned that a coalition with the DDP would violate Marxist ideology and turn Socialist members of the government into "nothing but the tools or servants of the bourgeois Democrats, who are totally immersed in class goals."[21] Baumer responded angrily to the constant criticism of the SPD delegates. In her maiden speech in the National Assembly, she chided both male and female SPD delegates:

134

What are these maneuverings for party power and coalition all about? Does anyone remember that we are here in behalf of the German people? . . . In this time of need, how can the left-wing parties continue to court the nihilistic destruction of further revolution?[22]

Germany deserved better than the old "politics as usual." Socialist representatives of the proletariat must cooperate with the liberal representatives of the middle-class if the vision of the new Germany were ever to become real.

Where legislation involved the welfare of women and children, female delegates to the National Assembly were generally able to bury partisan interests in cooperative effort. For example, between March 21 and March 28, 1919, DDP and SPD female delegates worked together to change the anti-female stipulations of the "Order Concerning the Dismissal, Suspension, and Paying-off of Factory Workers during the Time of Economic Demobilization." The law originally called for those persons who did not require their jobs in order to live--specifically, female workers who were provided for at home--voluntarily to relinquish their jobs to returning veterans.[23] When the final legislation was approved on March 28, the impact of the combined activity of the SPD and DDP women was evident. The new Order referred only to employees and employers, without designation of gender. Dismissal of workers, male or female, was made dependent upon economic provision at home. The Office of Economic Demobilization was authorized to determine the need of each employee, male or female, before replacement.[24] Socialist women had secured the cooperation of middle-class women on a working-class issue for idealistic as well as pragmatic reasons. Idealistically, women in the "new Jerusalem" should not be denied the right to work on the basis of sex. Pragmatically, however, it was also true that middle-class women considered themselves responsible, at least in part, for the surplus of female labor in industry. During the war, the Frauendienst, working through the Women's Labor Center of the German War Office, had actively recruited those women.

But idealism did not always require the sharp impetus of pragmatism. For example, when the issue of the rights of illegitimate children to "the same opportunities for physical, mental, and moral development as legitimate children" came before the National Assembly, Bäumer and others of the DDP found themselves drawn into support of the SPD, despite the fact that their position contradicted their own convictions about the sanctity of the traditional family structure. Middle-class women felt morally bound to defend such a large group of innocent lives. Germany, at the end of the war, reported almost 2,500,000 illegitimate children. To the women of the SPD, they represented the children of the depressed proletariat. To Bäumer and the women of the old BdF, they were victims of the war. In either case, they must be protected. The combined efforts of SPD and DDP women were sufficient to outweigh the opposition of both Center and DNVP delegates. Illegitimate children were recognized to be in possession of full legal rights by Article 121 of the new Weimar

135

Constitution.[25] Perhaps it was only a small step on the way to the "new Jerusalem," but for some 2,500,000 illegitimate children, it must have seemed a generous advance toward humanity.

Unfortunately, the cooperation of the SPD delegation was not so readily available when the rights of the middle-class were specifically concerned, especially if the problem reminded the socialists of old class privileges. Such was the case of female professionals--teachers, lawyers, doctors, civil servants and social-welfare directors--who were systematically dismissed or demoted in rank during the period of demobilization. At the same time, and for the same reasons, restrictions were imposed upon the number of female students enrolled in German universities.[26] While women of the DDP and the Catholic Center reacted with alarm, women of the SPD ignored the whole issue. Class bias was clear. Frustrated as she was about losses in that very area of women's professional advancement where the old women's movement had established its reputation, Bäumer could not rally enough support in the Assembly to reverse the discriminatory treatment of university students. The problem soon ceased to an active one, for it did not take long for the universities to return to a "normal" 10% female enrollment. Assembly action was taken to remedy the arbitrary dismissal of professional females. In line with the legislation protecting female factory workers, dismissal or demotion could not be legally carried out if real economic dependence could be proven. This protection applied most clearly to female teachers, although it could be used to protect other professional women. Article 128 of the Weimar Constitution provided de jure protection for such middle-class women, but nothing short of constant vigilence would insure de facto enforcement of the law.

When it was possible, then, Bäumer and her DDP colleagues sought to implement the ideals of a better, more humane Germany. When necessary, as in the debate over illegitimate children, middle-class women were willing to vote against their own deeply-held convictions. But in one significant area of legislation, Bäumer and her colleagues refused to violate or even to question principle. And that one area, unfortunately, would leave women most vulnerable to the forces of "politics as usual" once the electoral balance began to turn against the democratic/socialist majority.

The problem arose over Article 109, Section I of the draft constitution. Women of the Socialist delegation rose in strong objection to the wording of the clause:

> All Germans are equal before the law. Men and women possess fundamentally the same civil rights and privileges.[27]

One word, "fundamentally," set off the parliamentary dispute. Socialist delegates, led by Zeitz and Juchacz, were determined to strike the word from Article 109. Should the word remain, they argued, the guarantee of equality before the law was worthless. Zeitz reminded members of the Assembly that it had been just such justifications as this--women's "fundamental" difference from men--that had been used

136

before 1918 to deprive women of the franchise. women had been warned that they must not "dirty themselves in politics."[28]

But middle-class women, responding to Bäumer's lead, maintained silence throughout the debate. Why? In the silence of the middle-class faction, perhaps we begin to perceive the fatal flaw in the idealistic Weltanschauung Bäumer shared with her DDP colleagues. To their way of thinking, women had not entered the Assembly in search of a new view of life; on the contrary, they wanted to impart to Germany, through its new republican structure, the spiritual essence of the middle-class movement itself. That essence, that ideal, did not include a call for absolute equality between men and women. Women were equal, but they were different. It was because of that difference, that otherness, that middle-class women had embraced the franchise in 1918. Women needed their own, special political representation, because "no more than one class can represent the interests of another class can one sex represent the interests of the other."[29]

When Bäumer finally did address the issue of Article 109, her principles were clearly those of "equal but different."

We are not afraid to put forth special effort in those areas normally considered to be "women's work." We do not see it as a shrinking of our role, but rather as a way women can give actual promise of their will to cooperate and work competently in all areas. I cannot pose as an expert on military affairs, for example, but I do have expertise in some areas, and I want to be useful there. The task of women is not to seek equality in all things, but to seek in those areas where they can.[30]

Article 109 became part of the Weimar Constitution as it was originally written. Bäumer seems not to have regretted her decision, nor did the women of the middle-class organizations take exception to her stated philosophy. Any thought that power might shift, that the small gains made already by women might go down before a backlash of male "politics as usual," seems not to have occurred to any of them.

Bäumer's political myopia is puzzling. She seems to have possessed an unerring instinct for internal power struggles, protecting he own position with the leadership of the DDP and, incidentally, within the BdF with great skill and finesse. In matters of larger import, however, she revealed surprising ignorance. She did not seem to understand how much political damage the DDP had suffered from its initial association with the socialist dominated coalition government. After the Democrats withdrew from the government in June 1919, in protest over the Versailles Peace Treaty, the steady loss of popular support they had experienced since February momentarily stopped. But they were unable to dissociate themselves entirely from socialist policies. When, in October 1919 the DDP reentered a coalition government with the SPD and Catholic Center, the slow hemorrage of middle-class electoral support resumed.[31]

Having endured a punishing year, the male leaders of the DDP expected to be defeated in the next election. They knew that their old right wing political opponents, the DVP and DNVP, would be able to tempt away a portion of their 1919 electoral support. However, they did not expect, nor were they expected, to lose by the magnitude they did. From 18.5% of the vote in 1919, the DDP dropped to only 8.2% of the vote of June 6, 1920. The loss was catastrophic.[32] For Bäumer and the female leaders of the middle-class, the 1920 election revealed, for the first time it seems, the anomaly of the 1919 election. Looking back upon events with the advantage of hindsight, we can see that middle-class women had ever possessed the solid political platform they had taken so much for granted. A combination of unusual circumstances had worked together during the first few months of the republic's existence to destabilize the electorate. Fear of a violent revolution, alarm over the ravages of continued food shortages, and dread of the upcoming peace negotiations had combined with the general sense of disorientation over the disappearance of the monarchy and the old conservative leadership to produce a false political alignment. Confused conservatives had joined frightened radicals to vote for liberal idealists of the DDP, whom they would never normally have considered supporting. Liberal middle-class women had taken the elections at face value. They were wrong: there had never truly been an opening for middle-class women to infuse the German nation with their idealistic "new Jerusalem." In truth, it had been nothing but "politics as usual," played out in a most unusual, revolutionary form.

Thus, less than one year after they had entered upon their political enterprise, Bäumer and the women of the middle-class liberal faction found themselves stripped of their popular support, rejected before they could fully flesh out their promise of a new Germany. With some resentment, they withdrew from their positions of former prominence, settling into the practice of unimpassioned politics. Violations of Articles 109 and 128 became common events to be ignored after 1920. Men of the left-wing parties gradually came to join their right-wing colleagues in open disdain for "Weiberkram"--women's junk.[33] In the immediate aftermath of the 1920 elections, Bäumer exploited her role in the DDP to claim a permanent appointment in the Ministry of Interior. Serving as director of Youth and Welfare Concerns, Bäumer was relegated to "Weiberkram" issues, but seems not to have resented the delegation. Women were, after all, equal but different. Her position in the Ministry enabled her to preserve and protect their different world.

Over the years, Bäumer and most of the DDP leadership gravitated toward the political right, but they were never able to move far enough or fast enough to overtake the conservative swing of the electorate. Little could Bäumer or her colleagues know that all too soon the growing conservatism of the electorate, its rejection of any form of liberal-democracy, would culminate in a shattering triumph of masculine power. In that new world of brutality, the very differences Bäumer had emphasized in her own definition of women and their proper role would turn against them--serving to exclude women from the real world of power and influence. Bäumer, herself, would be one of the first high government officials to be dismissed after Hitler's seizure of power in 1933. Women were "fundamentally" equal, the Nazis agreed, but "politics was too dirty" for their different nature.

So the time of reckoning came for Germany, for the middle-class women's movement and for Gertrud Bäumer. The fragile life-affirming dreams of German women gave place to the brutal death-wish of men, men of vengeance, men of war. Scholars working on this period of the Nazi Machtergreifung are often tempted to turn against the displaced leaders of the Weimar Republic, to demand answers of them. Feminist historians have recoiled upon Gertrud Bäumer with frustrated vehemence. How could she have failed to see what lay before German women? How could she not have known how short her hour of productive labor would be? Or, more poignantly, did she and others of the middle-class women's movement set the stage for the return of the agents of bloody repression with their arrogant antifeminist philosophy?[34] Bäumer appears to be so strong, so capable of leadership. As a woman of intelligence and energy, she had been able to direct the fortunes of the large BdF, lead German women of all social classes into a massive program of war-support service, and participate in the leadership of the DDP. She had promoted a vision of the future where German women would occupy positions of spiritual and intellectual distinction, capable of infusing the nation with their unique, almost-mystical feminine attributes. With so much authority and a record of such accomplishment behind her, how could she have failed to carry though on her promise of a "new Jerusalem" for Germany?

What most contemporary critics fail to realize is that the force of "politics as usual" was brought to bear against Bäumer's idealistic program very soon under the Republic. The election returns of mid-1920 revealed the flawed base of the DDP: Bäumer had been banking on an empty account. Real political power had never truly been available to middle-class women. But beyond the realities of "politics as usual," feminist critics are correct in pointing out the deeper problems that plagued Bäumer. Her vision of the "new Jerusalem" was illogical, a contradictory mix of ideas. She called upon German women to lead their people into a promised land of intellectual and spiritual excellence, even as they continued to occupy positions of "fundamental" inferiority. She charged them with the task of infusing society with their own unique feminine attributes, while remaining themselves confined to the traditional identifications of wife, mother, and protector of the home. Bäumer's rhetoric seems to belie reality.

In the wake of the Nazi seizure of power, Bäumer and others of the liberal middle-class women's movement were hard pressed to distinguish their ideological position from that of Germany's new masters. Contemporary feminist critics appear unwilling to seek a serious difference between the two. But the effort to distinguish must continue, for neither Bäumer nor the noble women of the middle-class women's movement deserve to be degraded into the ranks of the NSDAP. Perhaps Bäumer's conception of a "new Jerusalem" was flawed, unworkable. By promising the impossible, perhaps she helped to undermine the Weimar experiment. Judged within the context of her time, within the parameters of pre-Nazi idealism, liberal-humanism and social conservatism, we might view her as unconsciously culpable, perhaps tragic, but never intentionally destructive of her own finest dream.

James Madison University
November 1987

NOTES

[1]The acquisition of voting rights by German women placed them eighth on the list of European nations extending that political privilege to women. Finland had approved the suffrage for women in 1907, Norway in 1913, Denmark in 1915, Holland and Russia in 1917, and Sweden and Great Britain in the Spring of 1918. Richard Evans, The Feminist Movement in Germany, 1894-1933 (London: Sage Publications, 1976), 227-29; Arthur Marwick, The Deluge: British Society and the First World War (London: The Macmillan Press, Ltd., 1973), 105.

[2]"Nr. 6553. Verordung über die Wahlen zur verfassunggebenden deutschen Nationalversammlung," Reichsgesetzblatt. 2 (1918): 1345.

[3]Gertrud Bäumer, Die Frau im neuen Lebensraum (Berlin: F. A. Herbig, 1931), 76-78.

[4]Daniela Weiland, Geschichte der Frauenemanzipation in Deutschland und Oesterreich (Düsseldorf: ECON Taschenbuch Verlag, GmbH, 1983), 47-51.

[5]Friedrich Schleiermacher, "Katechismus der Vernunft für edle Frauen," Athenaeum: Eine Zeitschrift von August Wilhelm Schlegel und Friedrich Schlegel. Erstes Band. Zweites Stuck (Berlin: Friedrich Vieweg der älteren, 1798), 286-87.

[6]Helene Lange, "Frauenwahlrecht," Cosmopolis: Internationale Revue, 3 (August 1896): 551-52.

[7]Klara Bohm-Schuch, "Die Frauen und die Revolution," Vorwärts: Berliner Volksblatt. Zentralorgan der Sozialdemokratische Partei Deutschlands. 35. Jahrgang, Nr. 332a (3 December 1918), 1.

[8]Marianne Weber, "Die Frauen und die Demokratische Partei," Frankfurter Zeitung und Handelsblatt. 63, no. 840. Erstes Morgenblatt (8 December 1918): 1.

[9]Bäumer, Lebensraum, 92-93.

[10]Peter Gay, Weimar Culture: The Outsider as Insider (New York: Harper & Row, 1968), 10.

[11]Bruce B. Frye, Liberal Democrats in the Weimar Republic. The History of the Herman Democratic Party and the German State Party (Carbondale, Ill.: Illinois University Press, 1985), 41.

[12]Ibid., 2.

[13]Ibid., 67-68.

[14]Renate Bridenthal and Claudia Koonz, "Beyond Kinder, Küche, Kirche," When Biology Became Destiny: Women in Weimar and Nazi Germany. Renate Bridenthal, Anita Grossmann, and Marion Kaplan, eds. (New York: Monthly Review Press, 1984), 41.

[15]Gertrud Bäumer, "Der erste Wahlkampf," Die Frau, 26, Heft 5 (Feb. 1919): 135.

[16]Gabriele Bremme, Die politische Rolle der Frau in Deutschland. Eine Untersuchung über den Einfluss der Frauen bei Wahlen und ihre Teilnahme in Partei und Parlament (Göttingen: Vandenhoeck & Ruprecht, 1956), 231-32.

[17]Bäumer, Lebensraum, 75-76.

[18]Bremme, Politische Rolle, 121-22.

[19]Bäumer, Lebensraum, 78-79.

[20]Frye, Liberal Democrats, 69.

[21]Germany. Reichstag Verhandlungen deutschen Nationalversammlung. Band 326. Stenographische Bericht von der 1. Sitzung an 6. Februar 1919 bis zur 26. Sitzung am 12. März 1919. (Berlin: Druck und Verlag der Norddeutschen Buchdruckerei und Verlags-Anstalt, 1920), 232-33.

[22]Ibid., 271-76.

[23]Verhandlungen, Band 326, Anlagen, no. 215: 135-203.

[24]Germany. "Verordung über die Freimachung von Arbeitsstellen während der Zeit der Demobilization," Reichsgesetzblatt. 1919, Band I: 355-59.

[25]Germany, "Die Verfassung der Deutschen Reichs," Reichsgesetzblatt. 1919, Band II: 1106.

[26]Germany. Reichstag Verhandlungen deutschen Nationalversammlung. Band 329, Stenographische Bericht von der 71. Sitzung an 31. Juli 1919 bis zur 90. Sitzung am 3. Oktober 1919: 2709-12.

[27]Reichsgesetzblatt, Band II, 1404.

[28]Germany, Reichstag Verhandlungen Deutschen Nationalversammlung. Band 328, Stenographische Bericht von der 53. Sitzung an 10. Juni 1919 bis zur 70. Sitzung am 30. Juli 1919: 5160-63.

[29]Camilla Jellinek, Frauen unter Deutschem Recht (Mannheim: J. Bensheimer, 1928), 67-71.

[30]Verhandlungen, Band 328, 5271-72.

[31]Frye, Liberal Democrats, 224-25.

[32]Ibid., 224.

[33]Marie-Elisabeth Lüders, Fürchte dich Nicht: Persönliches und Politisches aus mehr als 80. Jahren, 1878-1962 (Köln und Opladen: Westdeutscher Verlag, 1963), 96-97.

[34]Recently, Claudia Koonz has been most outspoken in her criticism. Indeed, in Mothers in the Fatherland, Koonz stops just short of labeling Bäumer a Nazi. Koonz was slightly kinder to Bäumer in an earlier essay, "Beyond Kinder, Küche, Kirche," which she wrote with Renate Bridenthal for When Biology Became Destiny, but her evaluation remains one of suspicion and distrust. Claudia Koonz, Mothers in the Fatherland: Women, the Family and Nazi Politics (New York: St. Martin's Press, 1986), and Bridenthal and Koonz, Biology Became Destiny.

Entering the Corridors of Power:
English Women and the High Civil Service, 1925-1945*

Gail L. Savage

When Richard Crossman, Minister of Housing in the 1964 Labour Government formed by Harold Wilson, published his political diaries, he revealed to the public eye the inner workings of government at both the cabinet and the ministerial levels. Crossman's difficult and dynamic relationship with the Permanent Secretary of his department, Dame Evelyn Sharp, formed one of the important themes of his Diaries. Crossman expressed a marked ambivalence towards his strong-willed subordinate, describing her as hard-working, intelligent and patriotic but also arrogant and reckless. In sum, he judged her ". . . quite unique in Whitehall, not merely because she was a woman. . .", but also because of her expertise in her department's policy area--town and country planning.[1]

When Crossman encountered Dame Sharp she was at the end of her long and distinguished career. She had entered the English civil service in 1926 by competitive examination, the only successful woman candidate that year. Yet, Crossman to the contrary, Evelyn Sharp did not embark on this professional venture alone. Three women had entered the civil service as a consequence of the previous year's competition, the first open to women. Interwar competitions produced thirty-two women officers between 1925 and 1938. Promotion from the lower ranks and direct appointment were additional avenues by which women could enter the Administrative Class of the Home Civil Service, so that the number of women holding office in this elite group totaled almost fifty by the time World War II began. The analysis below examines the position of these women in the civil service. It focuses first on the impediments to a successful career they encountered because they were women, and then considers women in their official role as policy-makers.

Women began to enter the English civil service during the 1870s, serving at first only in clerical and menial positions. In the years that followed a few women won appointments as inspectors and investigators to deal with questions that specifically concerned women,[2] such as female education or the conditions of work for women workers. Although they held administrative posts, their positions were carefully kept separate from the ordinary civil service hierarchy. Matters rested so until World War I when the exigencies of wartime led to a much more widespread employment of women at all levels of the civil service. Although many, if not most, of these women lost their positions to returning veterans after the war, the 1919 Sex Disqualification (Removal) Act firmly established the principle of women's right to employment in public service. House of Commons resolutions implementing this legislation provided that women could apply for posts in the Administrative Class. Hitherto virtually the exclusive property of men, this small elite group headed the civil service and served as expert advisers to ministers. Women could compete with men on an equal basis when competitive examinations began again in 1925, special post-war examinations to accommodate returning servicemen having temporarily replaced the usual procedure.[3]

As Graph I demonstrates, open competition examination constituted the most important avenue of entry to the Administrative Class, providing 78.45 percent of new recruits between 1925 and 1938. Women represented only a tiny minority of new entrants to the Administrative Class, 7.555 percent of the whole and 7.51 percent of the open competition recruits. Women formed an even smaller proportion of those who attempted the examination--only 154 (3.56 percent) out of 4,320 candidates. (See Table 2) Men appear to have been somewhat more successful than women in the examination, but the greater degree of male success turns out to be a function of the fact that the examination was used to fill many positions still closed to women, such as those in the Indian Civil Service. Of the male candidates, 22.52 percent received appointments as opposed to 18.18 percent of the female candidates. But only about one-third (300) of the men who obtained positions entered the Administrative Class of the Home Civil Service, 7.92 percent of the male candidates. In contrast, all but one of the women appointed to the civil service entered the Administrative Class, 17.53 percent of the women candidates.

Immediately following World War I senior civil servants greeted the apparently inevitable prospect of sexual integration with a distinct lack of enthusiasm. In 1920, Sir James Masterman-Smith, Permanent Secretary of the Ministry of Labour, circulated a printed statement in his department announcing that "whether we like it or not we have got to think in terms of men and women." Masterman-Smith tried to rally his department in support of this innovation with a declaration that the Ministry of Labour must live up to the public commitments of the government and show a lead to other departments in this matter.[4] Similar sentiments were expressed at the Ministry of Health, which was itself formed in part out of the same impetus for post-war social reform that opened the civil service to women. At a discussion of the organization of the new Ministry's Administrative staff, Sir John Anderson, Health's first Deputy Secretary, warned of the strong pressure for the hiring of women, especially in the Ministry of Health, which was considered an "especially suitable" department for their employment.[5] In 1921, Francis Floud, a high-ranking Ministry of Agriculture official who became Permanent Secretary of the Ministry the next year, asserted his belief in the principle of sexual equality, including the elimination of special posts for women and of limits on the number of posts open to women.[6]

Despite some expressions of good will, many positions within the civil service remained closed to women. Breaking down the barriers that barred women from holding these posts proved a very gradual and tedious process, by no means completed during the interwar period. The defense ministries and those that dealt with colonial policy did not accept women recruits at all, even those who passed the open competition examination. Departments that did accept women officers

144

GRAPH I: Administrative Class Recruitment, 1925 to 1938

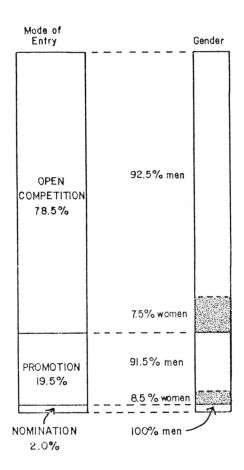

Mode of Entry

Gender

OPEN COMPETITION 78.5%

92.5% men

7.5% women

PROMOTION 19.5%

91.5% men

8.5% women

NOMINATION 2.0%

100% men

SOURCE: Civil Service Commission Annual Reports, 1925-38

TABLE 2   SUCCESSFUL CANDIDATES IN THE ADMINISTRATIVE GROUP EXAMINATION
1929-1938

	MEN			WOMEN		
	total candidates	appointed #	%	total candidates	appointed #	%
1929	337	111	32.93	10	1	
1930	348	112	32.18	9	3	
1931	386	72	18.65	15	--	
1932	373	70	18.76	6	--	
1933	385	91	23.63	6	--	
1934	450	86	19.11	13	1	
1935	432	82	18.98	4	2	
1936	522	106	20.30	18	5	
1937	467	108	23.12	29	8	
1938	466	100	21.45	44	8	
Total	4166	938	22.51	154	28	18.18

Source: Civil Service Commission Annual Reports, 1929-1938.

146

continued to reserve posts and tasks for men only. For instance, even though two women entered the Administrative Class of the Ministry of Agriculture prior to World War II, the department continued to designate positions by sex. The Ministry responded slowly to pressure to rectify this situation and, in the process, revealed the rationale used to justify their previous practice. Their arguments betray a reluctance to employ women on tasks which might bring them into contact with issues of a sexual nature.

In 1936 a sub-committee of the Ministry of Agriculture's Whitely Council[7] recommended opening more of the Ministry's posts to women. The sub-committee agreed, however, that a few posts remain reserved for men. Women still could not be appointed as veterinarians and livestock inspectors.[8] In defending this arrangement to the Treasury, the department most commonly gave "environment of work" as the reason for the exclusion of women. For instance, women could not join the Livestock Inspectorate because: "One of the principal duties of these officers is to advise on questions of breeding and however capable and willing a woman may be to do so, many farmers and herdsmen would refuse to discuss such matters with women." Moreover, the Ministry argued, women did not have the physical strength to undertake some of the duties of these officers--such as ear-marking of cattle.[9] This delicacy about sexual matters served to justify the exclusion of women from even clerical positions in the Livestock Branch of the Ministry's London Office. When the Ministry moved to discontinue sexual segregation in the Livestock Branch, Charles Nathan warned: "no distinction will in future be drawn in regard to discussion and correspondence on matters affecting the breeding of livestock, which up to now have been dealt with by the male staff (including the typing of certain categories of memoranda and letters)."[10]

The reluctance of the Ministry of Agriculture to allow female staff to do work which might involve issues of sexuality did not represent an eccentricity restricted to that department. In 1939 the Treasury surveyed government departments to determine the desirability of increasing the number of posts open to women. This inquiry elicited a similar rationale for the exclusion of women from the legal departments. The King's Proctor's Office, which prosecuted allegations of collusion in divorce suits, believed that is work was unsuitable for a mixed staff. The Director of Public Prosecutions argued that the type of cases tried, "e.g. Murder, Abortion, Buggery, Incest, Carnal Knowledge of Children, indecent assaults on boys and girls, gross indecency. . . Rape and Bestiality." made the work in the office "unpleasant" and unsuitable for women. The reply from the Lord Advocate's Chambers put their case even more strongly. In an office which dealt with "unnatural crimes and indecent offenses," it would be "quite intolerable" to employ female staff. Indeed, any woman who, despite being warned "of the nature of much of the work and of the pronounced repugnance felt by the Crown Counsel and the senior staff to being associated in its performance with a woman. . .," still wished employment in the office, would by that very fact call into question "her suitability for a post of responsibility and confidentiality."[11]

The Ministry of Agriculture proved itself to be much less intransigent by contrast. An inquiry from the Institute of Professional Civil Servants in 1938 moved the Ministry to consider opening inspector positions to women only to encounter opposition from the Official Veterinary Association. This group urged the continued exclusion of women from these posts on the grounds that they could not carry out certain of the duties, such as port inspection, that might be expected of them.

Agricultural officials had difficulty accepting this position, one that they had previously agreed with, after one or two women had obtained appointments and had performed satisfactorily. Charles Nathan summed up the department's view:

> There is, of course, a good deal of force in the argument that, to put it no higher, a woman or rather most women are not very suitable to control a collection of hard bitten drovers at a landing place, or to secure obedience and cooperation of a tough gang of butchers. . . though there doubtless are women who can successfully tackle such jobs. At the same time this argument is less potent than it once was now that the staff runs into hundreds. Only a limited number of staff will in the nature of things be called upon to do portal work and, even if some otherwise competent women may not shine as butcher gangers it must not be supposed that every male inspector is a star turn at everything.

Not exactly a ringing endorsement of sexual equality, but this view led the Ministry, unable to reach an agreement with the veterinarians, to act unilaterally, allowing women to take on these posts.

The veterinarians, for their part, stressed that, if women did enter the inspectorate, they should do so on an equal footing with men. On this basis Agriculture officials successfully resisted Treasury attempts to set lower salary rates for women inspectors, arguing that veterinarians would never accept such a differential.[12] This constituted a major victory for Agriculture. During the interwar decades the Treasury had systematically imposed pay differentiation where it did not already exist. Only the British Medical Association had successfully resisted such differentiation.[13] This series of episodes illustrates the slow erosion of prejudice in a department comparatively sympathetic to the claims of women.

Once in the Home Civil Service, female Administrative Class officers progressed through the ranks much more slowly than their male colleagues. Graph 3 shows the proportion of civil service officers who attained a measure of success in their career (defined by reaching at least the rank of Assistant Secretary--the lowest rank at which officials began to shape policy). The graph demonstrates that well over half the 394 men who entered the Administrative Class of the civil service by competitive examination between 1925 and 1938 achieved this status after the war. In contrast, less than one-third of the women enjoyed the same degree of success. This finding is rendered even more

148

GRAPH 3: Professional Success and Gender

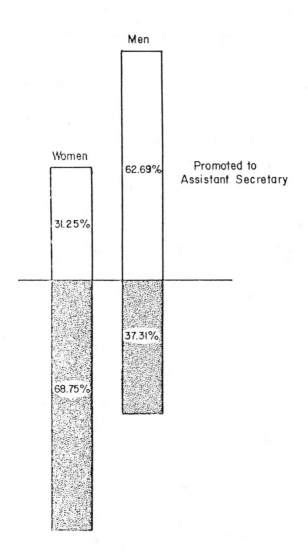

striking by the intervening war, which interrupted the careers of so many men while presumably enhancing the opportunities available to women.

The experience of Elizabeth Whyte at the Ministry of Labour illustrates the handicaps women in the Administrative Class endured in their struggle to ascend the career ladder. In 1927 Whyte came up for promotion from Assistant Principal, the civil service's entry rank, to Principal. She had reached the appropriate stage in her career to take the next step up and her case came to the promotion board very well recommended. The panel itself agreed that she was "uniformly competent" but observed that two women already held the rank of Principal in the Ministry.[14]

Whyte's superior, Humbert Wolfe, argued vigorously on her behalf and, in so doing, revealed the reasons given by those who opposed her promotion. These were, in addition to the presence of two women at the Principal rank, the unsuitability of women for some tasks, and the alleged decline in quality of women's performance after age 40--Whyte was 39 in 1927. To the first objection Wolfe replied that the prior promotion of women should not weigh against the principle of merit promotion. To the second he cited various cases in which women had carried out difficult tasks satisfactorily. But even Whyte's champion could not refute the third objection. He weakly observed: "I do not deny that in a certain proportion of cases, for reasons into which I need not enter, the period from 45 onwards is a difficult one for women officers. . .", but, he added, her difficulties need not interfere with work. Wolfe ended his defense of Whyte more strongly by arguing that "the only ground advanced against Miss Whyte was that of sex, and that, in my view if we fail to promote her on that ground, we shall be guilty of committing a grave miscarriage of justice."[15]

Wolfe's efforts did not sufficiently impress the promotion board. They included Whyte's name on their short list but elected to promote a colleague of hers--a man described as "not specially outstanding" but "well up to the average we expect." Wolfe case the only dissenting vote when the board made this decision.[16] The Permanent Secretary, H. J. Wilson, agreed to the appropriateness of the promotion board's decision, adding that Whyte had not really been passed over because she was on a separate promotion list.[17]

At the end of the next year, Elizabeth Whyte's name again came before the promotion board. Again Wolfe vigorously supported her candidacy. He wrote, "I cannot too highly recommend Miss Whyte, she has shown. . . grasp, imagination and vigor."[18] This time the promotion board endorsed her advancement. Elizabeth Whyte eventually rose to the rank of Assistant Secretary in the Ministry of Labour and later served in the Treasury.

In 1929 Wolf again supported a woman's candidacy for promotion. Beryl Millicent le Poer Power[19] brought to the Ministry of Labour a broad range of experience. She had organized speakers for the National Union of Women's Suffrage prior to the First World War and had first

150

entered the civil service as an investigator for the Board of Trade and the Ministry of Labour under the Trade Board's Act. With Wolfe's endorsement she became a Principal in 1929, reaching the rank of Assistant Secretary before her retirement in 1951.

Women advanced more slowly than men in the ordinary course of affairs, but marriage would bring their careers to a close. The marriage bar constituted a major obstacle to women's advancement within the civil service. The Treasury had always made resignation upon marriage a condition of the employment of women. The 1919 Sex Disqualification (Removal) Act prohibited the disqualification of women on the ground of either sex or marital status, but the Treasury used the law's provision for regulations by Order in Council to govern the admission and the conditions of service of women in the civil service to maintain the marriage bar.[20] This policy led Virginia Woolf to observe caustically, "In Whitehall, as in heaven, there is neither marrying nor giving in marriage."[21]

A study of resignations conducted by the Treasury for the years 1923 to 1926 clearly showed that many more women than men terminated their careers in government service before retirement and that the bulk of the women who left the civil service prior to retirement left upon marriage. The proportion of female staff who left the civil service before retirement age (15.6 percent) greatly exceeded the proportion of men (6.0 percent) who did so. Of the 2,346 women who left the civil service in those years, approximately half (1,449) left upon marriage.[22]

The attrition caused by the marriage bar had a profound impact at higher as well as at lower ranks. A study of the marriage bar conducted by the Treasury in 1945 identified twelve of thirty-five women who entered the Administrative Class by competitive examination between 1925 and 1939 who later resigned on marriage, although eight of these continued to serve in a temporary capacity during the war.[23] Six of the women who entered the civil service before the Second World War and pursued their careers after the war managed to attain promotion above the rank of Assistant Secretary. Only one of these, Alix Kilroy, married. Kilroy, who rose to the rank of Under Secretary in the Board of Trade before her resignation in 1955, married in 1946 at the age of 43 just as the Treasury dropped the marriage bar. The two women granted exceptions to the marriage bar prior to World War II, Alice Jennings at the Ministry of Labour and Elsie Tostevin at the Post Office, continued their careers during the war. Both attained the rank of Assistant Secretary by 1945. Of the two major impediments to a successful career, discrimination in promotion and the marriage bar, the latter posed the more formidable challenge to women in the Administrative Class.

Qualifying for an exception to the marriage bar proved a difficult enterprise subject to the vagaries of departmental interpretation of the grounds for granting such requests. Alice Jennings was the first Administrative Class woman to clear this hurdle. Her application argued that her department, the Ministry of Labour, could ill-afford to lose an officer with her experience and training. Her superiors, however, had some doubts about the legitimacy of making such a claim for a general administrator. The Treasury responded to Labour's request for guidance on this question by suggesting that the department consider "the value of the officer to the public service throughout his or her career," but bear in mind that the officer should be a "special case" who would achieve more than "the normal career of the Class." Since her superiors regarded Jennings as a better than average officer, they decided to support her application. The Treasury subsequently approved it.[24]

Women with technical or professional qualifications in general found it easier to make a case for themselves than administrative officers. Nevertheless, some departments showed themselves to be much less receptive to such requests than others. The case of Dr. Carol Sims, Medical Officer at the Ministry of Health, illustrates the resistance to lowering the marriage bar that persisted in some quarters. Although Sims had good qualifications and much experience, she did not enjoy the confidence of her superiors. She first applied for permission to marry in 1934. Her department refused to support her at that time because, in the words of a Treasury observer, they "regarded [her] as somewhat common and ill-bred, and hence the Ministry consider that by refusing her application they may be able to dispense with her services." The Treasury did not approve of this line of reasoning, especially as Dr. Sims apparently had determined to "stay, single, unless she can stay married." Carol Sims did outlast her superiors, and Treasury officials finally had the satisfaction of endorsing the department's 1946 request to retain Dr. Sims' services upon her marriage, although they could not resist pointing out they would have happily done so twelve years before. In 1946 Carol Sims was fifty-one years old.[25]

Not all women similarly refused stubbornly stayed in government service. A member of the Tax Inspectorate whose 1931 application was refused by her department, Inland Revenue, simply resigned upon her marriage and went to work for a private firm of accountants where she specialized in tax avoidance. Writing in 1946, a Treasury official commented, "enforced resignation from the Civil Service on marriage does not ensure that the women concerned will devote themselves wholly to domestic pursuits. It merely means that someone other than the State has the benefit of their training and experience."[26]

During the interwar decades, feminists took a keen interest in the position of women in the civil service. Women's groups led the fight to open the civil service to women on equal terms with men immediately after the First World War.[27] This issue could unite both the "egalitarian" feminists who had dominated the women's movement prior to 1918, and the "new" feminists who emerged to lead the women's movement after the victory of suffrage.[28] If the elimination of all legal distinctions between men and women necessitated their equal access to a civil service career, so did the view that only the participation of women in government could insure that their needs and interests influenced public policy.

152

Alison Neilans, a prominent figure in the social purity movement, articulated the latter perspective in her overview of the progress women had made in sexual standards and conduct. In the 1930s she looked back on the impact of women on local government and concluded: "Gradually the purely masculine conception of life was permeated with the feminine point of view, as women came more and more into public life."[29] Such a view rests on two assumptions: one, that women have particular and definable interests; and, two, that women once in a position of power will use that power to further or to protect the interests of women. Furthermore, this implies that the hope of any social group (whether defined by sex, ethnicity, race, national origin, social class, or religion) to achieve and to maintain equality depends upon their obtaining access to a society's instruments of power. This argument, although a commonplace one, has gone largely untested.

The careers of Administrative Class women thus claim special attention because the Administrative Class could play a key role in shaping policy. The social and political significance of this civil service elite rests in large measure on the power it wields. The privileged position of civil servants within the political arena raises the question of whether opening the civil service to women had any impact on the way the civil service employed its power. Did women in the civil service display a sensitivity to issues that had particular significance for women? The analysis below considers this question in light of a discussion of government policy towards prostitution carried on in the Ministry of Labour during the Second World War.

Because of the slowness with which women gained promotions, very few women were in a position to participate in forming policy until World War II. The demands of the war effort opened up broader opportunities for women such as had happened during World War I. On the other hand, the heightened atmosphere of wartime also intensified[30] long-standing, unresolved controversies about the status of women. For example, during the war years the Ministry of Labour had to deal with the delicate and contentious problem of wartime prostitution. The Ministry came under pressure from two different groups to do something about London prostitutes. Social reform organizations which had long taken an interest in the issue of prostitution wanted to use the war effort to integrate prostitutes back into society by employing them in war work. Officers in the American Army were more concerned to protect the innocent GI of rural origin from the predations and seductions of sophisticated temptresses.

Formulating a response to this issue for the Ministry of Labour fell to two women officers--Mrs. A. M. Riesner, formerly Alice Jennings, and Miss M. G. Smieton. Leaving a question about women in the hands of women accorded with the civil service tradition of a division of labor defined by sex. Nevertheless, women had finally attained a position to take a direct hand in formulating policy, rather than regulating already-defined policy as inspectors or criticizing it from outside the government.

Mrs. Riesner, under her maiden name of Jennings, had become an Assistant Principal in the Ministry of Labour in 1935. She was promoted to Principal in 1938, the same year she was distinguished by being the first Administrative Class woman to be allowed to retain her post after her marriage. Mary Smieton entered the Public Records Office by competitive examination in 1925, transferred to the Ministry of Labour in 1929 and received a promotion to Principal in 1935. She eventually rose to the rank of Deputy Secretary of the Ministry of Education, and subsequently served as Permanent Secretary of the Ministry of Education, one of only two women who entered the Home Civil Service Administrative Class during the interwar years to achieve that rank.

In October, 1941, Mary Smieton met with Alison Neilans, Secretary of the Association for Moral and Social Hygiene. This group succeeded Josephine Butler's Lady's National Association in 1915. Alison Neilans carried on Josephine Butler's struggle against the double standard and prostitution doing double-duty as Secretary and as editor of its official periodical, Shield, until her death in 1942.[31] During the meeting Neilans explained her views on prostitution to Smieton, suggesting that prostitutes be housed in hostels and be employed in some industry, possibly munitions. Neilans failed to persuade Smieton of her point-of-view. In her record of the meeting, Smieton observed: "Miss Neilans regards the whole matter with great sympathy for prostitutes. It struck me that her attitude was based to some extent on sentiment."[32] Smieton would not have to formulate a more comprehensive response for another year.

Two meetings held towards the end of 1942 illustrate the delicacy and complexity of the problem prostitution posed for the Ministry of Labour. In October, 1942, representatives of the U.S. Army visited the Home Office to meet with representatives of the Metropolitan Police and the Home Office to discuss the matter. The Army officers expressed their concern at the fate of inexperienced country boys on the streets of London with too much money in their pockets. The policy explained that they were handicapped in what they could do by the fact that immorality was not also illegality. The English suggested that the Americans instruct their troops in the danger of city life, keep back part of their pay, and impose a curfew. The Americans replied that they already did the first and were considering the second and the third. They also admitted that they needed more MPs. The meeting ended on this inconclusive note.[33]

A little over a month later, Mrs. Riesner met with the Social Implications of VD Committee, a subcommittee of the British Social Hygiene Council.[34] This group expressed more concern about the future of the prostitutes than the fate of their clients. They suggested opening training centers attached to some kind of residential accommodation staffed by psychologists and psychiatrists as well as by instructors for occupational training. Members of the committee expressed their admiration for the success of Russian Prophylactoria in redeeming "industrial misfits."[35] Mrs. Riesner undertook the task of formulating the Ministry of Labour's response to the push and pull of these contrary pressures.

154

Mrs. Riesner expressed her views in a memorandum composed early in 1943. She recommended against using the Ministry's powers to mix all types of "industrial misfits" in one institution. She argued that the case for doing something about prostitution rested on health grounds, and that, therefore, the Ministry of Health--not the Ministry of Labour--should shoulder the responsibility for taking action. Riesner did concede that should any action be taken the Ministry of Labour could give advice about suitable training.[36]

Only a week after this the Permanent Secretary of the Home Office, Sir Alexander Maxwell, wrote the Permanent Secretary of the Ministry of Labour, Sir Thomas Phillips, asking why prostitutes were not directed into some form of National Service. Maxwell explained that the Home Office was under pressure from the Americans to do something about prostitution but that the police had difficulties enforcing laws in the black-out.[37] Ministry of Labour officials stood firm in the face of this plea. Charles McAlpine argued along the line already suggested by Riesner: "This problem is primarily one of health and public order and I think that we should try to avoid being mixed up in it. It is difficult to believe that any special measures we might take to place these women in industry would be worthwhile from the production point-of-view."[38] Couching a recommendation in such terms implies that the Ministry of Labour would not have been interested in any other point-of-view.

The next week Smieton reported that the Home Office had been approached by the American Army, the Archbishop of Canterbury and the Westminster City Council. Anyone would tremble in front of such an assemblage, and Smieton expressed some anxiety that such pressure would result in ill-conceived action, such as "large scale enforced registration of people it would [be] quite impossible for us to place in employment."[39] Other Ministry of Labour officials agreed with this view. Harold Wiles, for instance, disapproved of the training center scheme, describing it as "a measure of social reform" that would not increase production and therefore did not come under the Ministry of Labour's purview.[40] Another Ministry of Labour official concurred, pointing out yet more difficulties: "I see no possible means of identifying prostitutes or of preventing prostitution by direction into work."[41]

The issue of wartime prostitution also stimulated some public concern during 1943. A letter sent to the Home Secretary early in the spring by the Hon. Lancelot William Joynson-Hicks, son of a prominent English politician, summed up the sentiments evoked by the issue. Joynson-Hicks wrote:

> Walking home along Piccadilly tonight at 11:30 I have been accosted 11 times between Park Lane and Berkeley Street.
>
> It being a fine and and moonlight night there were many American soldiers taking a stroll, presumably they too had run the same gauntlet. I could not

help feeling that it was not very edifying for visitors to the most famous street in the greatest capital city in the world.

Could not the Ministry of Labour be persuaded to harness the energies of these ladies to the war effort?[42]

The writer's father, William Joynson-Hicks, Home Secretary during the 1924-1929 Conservative government, had displayed a keen interest in furthering social purity during his tenure in office. His successful suppression of Radclyffe Hall's Well of Loneliness in 1928 illustrates the political power of social purity.[43] Despite this additional pressure, the response originally articulated by Riesner the previous January continued to form the basis of the Ministry of Labour's official position.

At the end of the summer of 1943 government policy took shape. During July, Smieton attended a meeting with the Home Office and the Ministry of Health on prostitution. She reported that she had convinced them that the Ministry of Labour could not provide a solution for the problem.[44] Smieton attended another meeting in September. This time women officers met to consider the issue. They concluded that professional prostitutes could not be placed in work because employers would not accept them because of the effect they might have on their fellow workers. Those at the meeting considered the possibility that special separate work places could be set up for them on an experimental basis. Discussion of this "novel" and "controversial" idea concluded that the Ministry of Labour should take no action. Officials thus achieved a bureaucratic success; they avoided having to do anything at all.

At the Ministry of Labour in the midst of World War II, prostitution, an issue that concerned women, was largely left in the hands of women. That women were then in a position to take on this task represented an important gain for their sex, even though the idea that women should deal with women's questions had formed part of civil service practice since the beginning of the twentieth century. The women officers who fielded the problem of prostitution for the Ministry of Labour revealed themselves to be hard-working and competent. Their behavior proved that they had become model bureaucrats; but, as professionals, they showed no awareness of their identity as women. The discussion between Smieton and Neilans about prostitution demonstrated that these two had much less in common with one another than Smieton had with her male colleagues.

One example cannot be more than suggestive. Nevertheless, such a result should come as no surprise. Virginia Woolf had anticipated this possibility when she warned women who sought professional careers that "you will have to lead the same lives and profess the same loyalties that professional men have professed for many centuries."[45] The measure of success that Smieton and Riesner managed to achieve depended upon their ability to work within an apparatus and to conform to norms devised by men. Contrary to the hopes of those who, like Alison Neilans, believed that women in government would make a material difference in developing government policy, allowing women to participate and to compete does not, by itself, call into question the operation of the apparatus or the nature of the norms.

This is not to say that women civil servants could completely submerge their identity as women. Indeed, how could they do so when they encountered discrimination at every turn; in promotion, for instance, and in the operation of the marriage bar? The three women who held the position of Director of Women's Establishments at the Treasury from 1925 until 1941--Maude Lawrence, Hilda Martindale, and Myra Curtis--showed themselves to be strong advocates for women within the civil service. Their position enjoined such advocacy upon them, but also required them to enforce policies inimical to the interests of women, such as differential rates of pay. Again, the conversation between Neilans and Smieton best illustrates the irony of this situation. Neilans could do nothing because she lacked power. Smieton had power, at least the power to recommend; but, in order to obtain it she had to give up the will to use it on behalf of her sex.

Syracuse University
November 1987

NOTES

ABBREVIATIONS

PRO   Public Records Office

LAB   Ministry of Labour

MAF   Ministry of Agriculture and Fisheries

MH   Ministry of Health

T   Treasury

*Thanks to Karen Offen and Standish Meacham for helpful advice about earlier drafts of this essay. Thanks to Patrick Thevenard for his help collecting the data and for preparing the graphs.

[1]Richard Crossman, The Diaries of a Cabinet Minister: Vol. I 1964-66, (New York: Holt, Rinehart and Winston, 1975), 616.

[2]Helen Martindale, Women Servants of the State 1870-1938: A History of Women in the Civil Service, (London: George Allen & Unwin, 1938); Mary Drake McFeely, "The Lady Inspectors: Women at Work 1893-1921," History Today (Nov. 1986): 47-53.

157

[3]R. K. Kelsall, Higher Civil Servants in Britain (London: Routledge and Kegan Paul, 1955), 167-70.

[4]31 May 1920, PRO, LAB 2/1719 CEB/591.

[5]PRO, MH 78/60.

[6]8 April 1921, PRO, MAF 39/27.

[7]After the First World War the government set up Whitely Councils to advise government departments on staff relations. These bodies included representatives of staff organizations. E. N. Gladden, Civil Services of the United Kingdom, 1855-1970 (London: Frank Cass & Co., 1967), 128-33.

[8]Jan. 1936, PRO, MAF 39/96.

[9]PRO, MAF 39/97.

[10]23 March 1938, PRO, MAF 39/98. 10.

[11]PRO, T 162/581/E3754/012/01.

[12]Haynes to Small, 2 Feb. 1939; Nathan, 7 Jan. 1942; Matthews to Toye, 12 Sept. 1942; Toye, 10 July 1942, PRO, MAF 39/49.

[13]In 1936 the Council of Women Civil Servants addressed a long memorandum to the Treasury detailing the inequitable differences between the pay of men and women, many of which introduced since the First World War. "Memorandum on Certain Feature of the Pay to Women Civil Servants," PRO, T162/674/E12471/6. In 1948 the Civil Service Legal Society argued for equal pay for men and women barristers and solicitors, citing the example of equal pay for doctors. A Treasury official observed that this point was "obviously true and calls for no comment except that the B.M.A. is a powerful body." Abbot to Thompson, 3 Feb. 1948, PRO, T215/36.

[14]25 Mar. 1927, PRO, LAB 2/1991/S & E 980/1931.

[15]8 Mar. 1927, ibid.

[16]14 Mar. 1927, ibid.

[17]29 Mar. 1927, ibid.

[18]11 Nov. 1928, ibid.

[19]8 Oct. 1929, ibid.

[20]Meta Zimmeck, "Strategies and Stratagems for the Employment of Women in the British Civil Service, 1919-1939," The Historical Journal, 27 (1984): 908.

[21]Virginia Woolf, Three Guineas (New York: Harcourt Brace Jovanovich, 1966), 52.

[22]PRO, T162/329/E 22833.

[23]Evelyn Sharp, 6 Mar. 1945, PRO, T248/10.

[24]PRO, T162/980/E35805.

[25]PRO, T162/822/E3754/03/01.

[26]Evelyn Sharp, PRO, T248/10/115038.

[27]Ray Strachey, The Cause: A Short History of the Women's Movement in Great Britain (London: G. Bell and Sons, 1928), 376, 379-80; Brian Harrison, Prudent Revolutionaries: Portraits of British Feminists Between the Wars (Oxford: Clarendon Press, 1987), 174.

[28]See Jane Lewis, "Beyond Suffrage: English Feminism in the 1920s," The Maryland Historian 6 (1975): 1-17 for a discussion of these two variants of feminism. Other discussions of the divisions among interwar feminists include Harold Smith, "Sex vs. Class: British Feminists and the Labour Movement, 1919-1929," The Historian (1984): 19-37 and Harrison, Prudent Revolutionaries, 311-15.

[29]Alison Neilans, "Changes in Sex Morality" in Our Freedom and Its Results, ed. Ray Strachey (London: Hogarth Press, 1936), 200.

[30]See John Costello, Love, Sex and War: Changing Values 1939-45 (London: Pan Books Ltd., 1986).

[31]Neilans also participated in the militant campaign for suffrage as a leader in the Women's Freedom League prior to the First World War. Vera Brittain, Lady into Woman: A History of Women from Victoria to Elizabeth II (London: Andrew Dakers Limited, 1953), 152; Who Was Who, 1941-1950; London Times, 13 Aug. 1942, 7.

[32]Kelsall, Higher Civil Servants, 172.

[33]30 Oct. 1941, PRO, LAB 8/109 EM 1061/1942.

[34]Founded in 1924, this organization engaged in large-scale propaganda campaigns to alert the population to the dangers of venereal disease. It enjoyed a quasi-official status since it received funding from the government, but its approach to the problem of prostitution and venereal disease did not put any particular stress on the role of the double standard. Edward J. Bristow, Vice and Vigilance, Purity Movements in Britain Since 1700 (Dublin: Gill and Macmillan Ltd., 1977), 149-53.

[35]29 Oct. 1942, PRO, LAB 8/109 EM 1061/1942.

[36]8 Dec. 1942, ibid.

[37]15 Jan. 1943, ibid.

[38]28 Jan. 1943, ibid.

[39]5 Feb. 1943, ibid.

[40]15 Feb. 1943, ibid.

[41]27 Feb. 1943, ibid.

[42]1 Mar. 1943, ibid.

[43]Bristow, Vice and Vigilance, 223-24.

[44]17 Mar. 1943, PRO, LAB 8/109 EM 1061/1942.

[45]Woolf, Three Guineas, 70.

The John L. Snell Prize Seminar Paper

The Politics of Opposition: German Socialists and the Tirpitz Plan 1898-1912

Dennis Sweeney

Shortly after Alfred von Tirpitz was summoned to head the German Imperial Naval Office in March, 1897, he set in motion a plan for naval construction that fundamentally altered Germany's position among the great powers of Europe. Kaiser William II hoped to use this new naval force in his efforts to obtain Germany's "place in the sun." Some historians have focused a great deal of attention on the foreign policy implications of this new battle fleet. More recently, others have argued that the new naval program was to be used as a vehicle to solve both the foreign and domestic problems facing the German Empire at the turn of the century.[1]

German historian Volker Berghahn has argued that the navy was one of the main elements holding together the two dominant factions in Wilhelmine society: the heavy industrialists and the large landowners or Junkers whose estates lay primarily east of the Elbe River.[2] As the major plank in the program of the so-called alliance of "iron and rye"--the political alignment mentioned above--the navy was used, Berghahn maintains, as a means by which to create a common set of interests between the industrialists and the Junkers. By agreeing to support the new naval construction, the agrarians would receive help from the industrialists in erecting tariff barriers to protect the former from foreign grain competition. The industrialists, meanwhile, would benefit from the new foreign markets secured with the help of the enlarged fleet.[3] Presumably, the heavy industrialists expected to enjoy a certain amount of profit from new military contracts for ship-building materials and ship construction.

The new navy plan would also form the basis of this domestic political alliance which sought to maintain the dominance of the Junkers and the industrial elites in German society.[4] The agrarians, according to Fritz Fischer, at first rejected the new naval construction since it was favored by the free-trade groups whose economic policies were inimical to the protective tariff policy of the Junkers. "But as their own social position now seemed threatened," Fischer continues, "they were glad to support the new imperialism as a way of diverting attention from domestic problems."[5] Threatening their position, of course, was the rise of German Social Democracy. To meet this threat from below, the imperial government, Berghahn contends, proposed the new navy which would create renewed prosperity and full employment by securing new overseas markets. As a consequence, the working class would benefit from this prosperity and thus jettison their socialist convictions. The government also conceived the new battle fleet as a means to infuse the working-class movement with a new spirit of patriotism. In this way the influence of the Social Democratic Party (SPD) would be effectively undermined. Thus, Berghahn concluded, the government meant to use the navy program to secure new markets while maintaining the ascendancy of the German elites by combatting the efforts of the SPD.[6]

Though historians have begun to question to concept of the new navy plan as the glue cementing the alliance of "iron and rye,"[7] few have tried to determine whether the navy plan had its intended effect upon German Social Democracy. That is, few have examined the effectiveness of the Tirpitz plan vis-à-vis the SPD as a policy of national integration or social imperialism. In order to assess this effectiveness, this essay attempts to measure the reaction of the SPD to the navy bills of 1898, 1900, 1906, 1908 and 1912. If the navy plan was indeed meant as a palliative to reduce the influence of the SPD, it was in the long run a failure. Aside from its growing electoral support, which indicated increasing (as opposed to decreasing) support for Social Democracy, the SPD expressed its steady opposition to the navy bills in the Reichstag, at its party congresses, and through its press organs throughout the years 1898 to 1912.

SPD opposition to the naval program, however, should not be interpreted as another indication that German Social Democracy represented a separate subculture, ideologically, socially, and politically removed from mainstream German society in the years 1898 to 1912. Historians have long focused on those elements in German Social Democracy which have isolated workers from other segments in Wilhelmine Germany.[8] Increasingly, however, historians have begun to question the subculture classification. Vernon Litdke has demonstrated that the SPD cultural activities--clubs, festivities, songs, and schools--all, to varying degrees, drew on the overall German cultural milieu, especially as the party expanded rapidly in the last decade of the nineteenth century.[9] Thus, ". . .segmentation and conflict in the Reich were multidimensional, not unidimensional." Imperial Germany would be more accurately described as an "agglomeration of separate segments" rather than an "integrated system" with a well-defined "dominant culture."[10] There existed, then, no simple polarity of a dominant culture on the one hand and a Social Democratic culture on the other.

Indeed, the emphasis placed by historians on SPD exclusion from the party-political arena in the post-Bismarckian era seems to be linked to at least two persistent themes in modern German historiography. The first theme or assumption is that there existed deep cleavages in German politics and society which prevented any measure of "normal" (that is, based on western models) integration in the political and social spheres; thus, the state apparatus was increasingly less able, and in fact was never allowed by the ruling elites, to provide a framework for any successful negotiation of conflicts.[11] Since the SPD was a veritable pariah, workers' organizations were denied a participatory role in Wilhelmine politics by the imperial government, the bourgeois parties, and by the SPD's ideological self-isolation.

The second theme which requires the use of the "isolation" or subculture classification appears to be based on the SPD's lack of success in the Weimar period. The argument is as follows: SPD exclusion from the political sphere meant that later, when it came time to take a leading role in government, the SPD, crippled by its prior isolation, was politically inexperienced and historically unfit to assume the role of responsible government.[12] Aside from the teleology intrinsic to this line of argument, this theme, when unaccompanied by a discussion of the effects of the First World War, fails to explain adequately the complexity of the problems the SPD faced after 1918.

Thus, these underlying premises have informed many analyses of the SPD and have led historians to emphasize the isolated character of German Social Democracy in Wilhelmine Germany. Moreover, in view of the authoritarian nature of the imperial and state governments in Germany, the constant suspicion of the socialists on the part of political and business elites, and the official socialist party doctrine, the insistence upon SPD isolation is understandable. Yet to focus on the socialists as pariahs without examining the actual behavior of the party and without allowing for the possibility of change over time, is to gloss over the complexities of SPD political behavior and to ignore many aspects of the role and position of the SPD in prewar Germany. Indeed, by examining the SPD's position on the naval issue from 1898 to 1912 some of these complexities come to light. The SPD's activity in the political sphere during this period involved more than a simple rejection of the new battle fleet and a subsequent refusal to discuss the naval issue on the basis of socialist or Marxian theory. On the contrary, SPD political concerns reflected a growing interest in most of the key issues facing the imperial government, including foreign policy issues.

The SPD's response to the naval program, then, corroborates Litdke's thesis that imperial Germany was an "agglomeration of separate segments" without a well-defined polarity between a dominant culture and subordinate Social Democratic subculture. This is especially true when the party's response is examined over the entire span of the naval buildup prior to the First World War. During these years the SPD's position altered gradually but significantly. The SPD rejected the first two navy bills on the grounds that they represented an effort on the part of the propertied classes to maintain the existing capitalist economic system, since the goal of the navy was to seek new markets and profits. The SPD claimed that the navy would only benefit the propertied elites and not the working class. Throughout the decade prior to the First World War, however, the SPD gradually modified its stance. Overwhelmingly, its opposition began to be expressed in terms of day-to-day foreign and domestic political concerns. SPD rejection of further naval construction increasingly took the form of conventional parliamentary opposition as opposed to class hostility. Their views more accurately came to represent the expressions of one segment of the "agglomeration of separate segments" in German politics.

The First and Second Navy Bills

On June 15, 1897, Tirpitz presented William II with his new plan for constructing a battle fleet. The first navy bill called for the construction of nineteen new battleships, eight coastal armored ships, twelve large cruisers, and thirty small cruisers. It also fixes the active life for each ship and committed the Reichstag to appropriate replacement funds for the new and existing ships when needed.[13] The estimated costs for the new program, which was to be completed by 1905, amounted to approximately 410,000.000M for construction plus added annual expenses of 4,200,000M for the increases in personnel costs. The cost of the torpedo boats, mentioned vaguely in the second section of the bill, came to another 44,100,000 (though this latter cost was not revealed in the presentation of the bill to the Reichstag).[14]

Tirpitz saw the role of the new battle fleet as twofold: it was meant to enhance Germany's great power status in the international sphere and to promote German economic interests abroad. The two roles, Tirpitz maintained, were to be inextricably linked, since German power required a firm economic base and overseas economic interests were protected only by a strong fleet:

> The development of Germany into an industrial and commercial power is irresistible like a law of nature. . . . In case of such commercial and industrial development, points of contact and conflict with other nations increase. Naval power is essential if Germany does not want to go under.[15]

It is also clear the Germany sought to strengthen its navy to offset the dominance of the British navy. Tirpitz formulated a "risk" strategy by which he hoped to combine both offensive and defensive elements in the navy plan. Specifically, Tirpitz theorized that the stronger navy would both defend the Baltic and North Sea coasts from possible British attack and provide diplomatic leverage in drawing Britain into alliance with Germany.[16] Finally, Tirpitz sought to use the navy for internal political purposes. Only the fleet, he claimed, possessed the "power to reinvigorate the national feeling of the classes" and the power to "inspire patriotic love for the Emperor and nation."[17] Indeed, the German navy was in one sense the institution ideally suited to promote national unity; unlike the Prussian army, the navy drew its officers from all of Germany (though most came from the northern regions). These officers were mainly recruited from the[18] middle classes in Germany; thus the naval officer corps enjoyed more popular support than the exclusive army officer corps. Furthermore, the navy was peculiarly an imperial as opposed to Prussian institution and as such was a "symbol of national unity."[19]

When, therefore, Tirpitz presented the first navy bill to the Reichstag in December, 1897, he included a direct plea to the Social Democrats to gain their support for the passage of the bill: "There are many honorable Social Democrats and radicals who are true to the fatherland and understand its national necessities."[20] Furthermore, in presenting the bill Tirpitz was careful not to characterize the new navy as a battle fleet designed to pursue a policy of world power but as a "sortie" fleet designed to protect German coastlines and shipping.[21]

166

The SPD proved unresponsive to Tirpitz's demarche. Bruno Schönlank led the SPD Reichstag delegation in the debate over the bill. Schönlank began his attack on the new proposals by citing the dangerous consequences the new fleet would pose for German foreign policy. The new fleet, he argued, would only further destabilize German relations with the other European powers. Schönlank viewed the new bill as an outgrowth of the "absolutist" style regime which currently governed in Germany, since, as with most military legislation, the proposal was written with no consultation from members of the Reichstag. Schönlank also decried the excessive costs of the "extravagant" navy bill; costs which, he claimed, were too great a fiscal burden. And, finally, Schönlank objected to what he feared was an effort on the part of Tirpitz and William II to challenge the budgetary powers of the Reichstag. Although the new plan would require fiscal approval from the Reichstag each year, the bill would in effect commit the Reichstag to a six-year building program, and it was unlikely that the Reichstag would deny the government the funds for necessary annual fleet improvements. Like the army, then, the navy would be removed from the Reichstag's purview. Schönlank considered this attack on parliamentary control another act carried out by the "personal regime (Personalregiment)" of the Kaiser.[22] Indeed, evidence suggests that Tirpitz sought to remove the navy bills from the purview of the Reichstag in order to promote long-term stability in the navy program and to strike a blow against the Reichstag's budgetary powers.[23]

At the party congress in Stuttgart in 1898, the SPD drew up a resolution condemning the new bill after it had been passed in the Reichstag. At the congress the SPD repeated Schönlank's charges but went even further. The resolution cited the threat to the Reichstag's budgetary powers and ultimately its control over the naval bills. Furthermore, it condemned the 410 million mark cost of the program. Since these new expenditures would be raised through indirect taxes--for example, taxes on meat, tobacco, and liquor--the new fiscal burden would fall heaviest upon the lower classes. The party adamantly rejected these new burdens since they claimed that only the propertied classes would benefit from the new naval policy and its attendant policy of colonial conquest. The workers would be left to pay for the new navy in "belongings and blood (Gut und Blut)".[24]

Two years later Tirpitz presented the second of his navy bills to the Reichstag. This second navy bill was designed to upgrade further the naval forces in order to carry out Germany's foreign policy objectives. That the new bill was specifically intended to counter possible British aggression and to increase the effectiveness of Tirpitz's "risk" strategy was made clear by the Navy Secretary's reference to Great Britain in the preface to the bill:

> In general this naval power would not be in a
> position to concentrate its entire naval forces
> against us. Even if it succeeds in encountering
> us with a superior force, the destruction of the
> German fleet would so much damage the enemy that
> his own position as a world power would be brought
> into question.[25]

The new bill called for a battle fleet of two flagships, four squadrons of eight ships of the line each, eight large and twenty-four small cruisers, an overseas fleet of three large and ten small cruisers, and a reserve of four ships of the line to include three large and four small cruisers. Construction of this new fleet, which would in effect be twice the size of the existing fleet, was to be completed by 1920.[26]

Immediately the SPD's Reichstag delegates took up the opposition. Karl Frohme began by declaring the new navy proposal a threat to world peace. He saw in the new fleet the beginnings of a destabilizing arms competition with the other European powers, but with Britain in particular. Rather than a guarantee of peace and security, he claimed, the new fleet was a threat to peace. In addition, Frohme saw in the new proposal an effort by the privileged classes to gain material advantages. "The workers," he maintained, "will never benefit from such a naval policy or world policy."[27] Frohme argued that the workers would also bear the brunt of the costs for the navy. Instead of a naval policy which sought to protect German citizens and interests overseas, the government, according to Frohme, should be trying to protect and ensure the rights of Germans in Germany--an implied reference to the lack of popular participation in Wilhelmine politics.[28]

Like Frohme, SPD delegate Paul Singer also drew a connection between the state and imperial officials supporting the navy program and the private industrialists who would gain from the new navy contracts.[29] Faced with accusations of lack of loyalty to the German state, however, Singer shifted ground. He denied that Social Democrats sought to "bring about the collapse of the German Empire."[30] "Agreement with the government," Singer had explained earlier in the debates, "was not the only yardstick with which to measure loyalty and patriotism."[31] Finally, SPD delegate Hermann Molkenbuhr, responding to similar charges, reminded the Reichstag delegations that many of the workers who would build the new ships were SPD members: "If all Social Democrats at the shipyards were laid off today [because of their political convictions], tomorrow [ship] production would be impossible."[32]

During the debate over the bill in February, 1900, the editors of Vorwärts took up the SPD opposition. In response to an article in the Frankfurter Zeitung invoking the "spirit of 1848" in support of the navy, Vorwärts sarcastically recommended requiring the German princes to make their voluntary contributions to ease the financial burden on the people.[33] Vorwärts criticized the arms makers and suppliers Krupp and Stumm for their enthusiastic support for the navy bill, noting the profits those firms would make.[34] Finally, Vorwärts reported organized workers' protests against the new bill in Kiel, Lübeck, Cologne, Saalfeld, and other cities. The newspaper claimed 1500 workers organized in Kiel and 200 protested in Lubeck, both coastal cities with shipping related industries employing many workers.[35]

At the party congress in Mainz later that year, the SPD drew up its most comprehensive statement to date regarding the first navy bills. The party's resolution cited many of the same arguments presented by its Reichstag delegation. The resolution claimed the navy program was quite likely to lead to war: "Land hunger, desire for conquest and chauvinism form the foundation of this kind of policy." The party congress rejected the notion that the navy would help pursue German interests by securing the Empire's colonial possessions. It charged that the domination and exploitation of the native populations in the colonies was contrary to "German culture." Statistics were given that revealed Germany's income from its colonies was unaffected by the size of its battle fleet; the percentage increase in income from 1872 to 1899, the resolution claimed, was higher than that of Britain, whose fleet was the largest in the world. Finally, the party called the costs of the fleet "objectionable and unjust--the propertied classes do not pay their share and the propertyless shoulder most of the burden."[36]

Mainz made it clear that the SPD viewed the navy as another means by which the working class was subordinated to the propertied elites. It revealed their steadfast opposition to the new navy program, rejecting all blandishments from Tirpitz and the government officials to join in support for the navy bills. The party refused to accept the arguments that the new navy would create jobs and prosperity which would benefit the working class: "If the governing class is truly concerned about jobs for workers, then they should build educational institutions (Bildungs-anstalten), schools, and hospitals. . . ."[37] Though the socialist theory regarding imperialism as the last stage of capitalism had yet to be worked out, it is clear that the SPD suspiciously viewed the first two navy bills in class terms. Their persistent claims that the construction of a new fleet could only benefit the industrialists at the workers' expense and that the new policy was another way to shore up the capitalist forces arrayed against them,[38] bear this out. Thus, the SPD's rejection of the first two navy bills was primarily ideologically inspired, stemming from doctrinaire socialist precepts.

As we shall see, the nature of their opposition to the navy bills changed during the decade prior to the First World War. The SPD, as mentioned, rejected the buildup of the navy right up through the passage of the navy bill of 1912; but, increasingly, it turned away from a position of primarily class hostility toward a position of parliamentary opposition. From 1906 to 1912 the SPD began to fear most of all the threat to peace posed by the new fleet and the concomitant arms competition. This concern was expressed in the earlier debates, but it was clearly not the dominant concern. Furthermore, charges of profit-making against industrialists persisted up through 1912. This is not to suggest that the party experienced a sudden volte-face with regard to the navy. The dominant tone of the party did change, however. This change very likely grew out of the intensified arms competition between Germany and Britain after 1906. But it also stemmed from changes which were taking place within the party itself.

As Carl Schorske points out, the incipient fractionalization within the SPD by 1905 adumbrated the ultimate schism of the party in 1917.[39] The party congress at Mannheim in 1905, which firmly established the influence of the reformist trade unions in the party, signalled the decline of revolutionary enthusiasm in the SPD and pre-figured the fracture of the party in 1917, when a significant portion of party members broke away from the majority socialists to form the Independent Social Democratic Party.[40]

In the SPD, reformism--the tendency of socialist parties to abjure the immediate goal of proletarian revolution and seek practical reforms within the existing order--can be traced back to the Erfurt party congress in 1891. The Erfurt program represented a synthesis of reformist and revolutionary aims. It outlined a dual approach: the SPD would seek pragmatic reforms--for example, higher wages for workers and the eight-hour work day--while maintaining proletarian revolution as its ultimate goal. The SPD Reichstag delegate Georg von Vollmar was the first at Erfurt to cite the need to strive for limited and practical objectives which would gradually lead to socialism.[41]

Eduard Bernstein introduced a new brand of reformism in 1898 when he published his essay Voraus-setzungen des Sozialismus und die Aufgaben der Sozialdemokratie. Bernstein noted what he considered were the flaws in Marxian theory: the working classes were not becoming more and more impoverished and the capitalistic economic system was not on the verge of collapse as Marx claimed. On the contrary, workers' wages and standards of living were on the rise and capitalism appeared to be on the upswing. Bernstein argued, therefore, that it was necessary to concentrate on obtaining pragmatic concessions for the workers. "The goal is nothing to me," Bernstein wrote, "the movement everything!"[42] Bernstein hoped that democratic regimes would ultimately establish themselves universally and "organically grow into socialism."[43] Bernstein's "revisionist" challenge provoked the longest and most polemical debate in the SPD prior to the war.[44]

Reformism, then, emerged as a result of the vast growth and influence of the trade unions, the relative prosperity in Germany, and the growth and impressive electoral gains of the SPD in the decades before the war. By 1907, at the Socialist International in Stuttgart, the SPD had renounced the use of the mass strike by European socialist parties as a way to prevent war. At the Socialist International in 1910 the SPD again rejected the use of the mass strike, as they feared such a declaration, which the government could construe as treason, would provoke a retributive response from the Kaiser and his ministers.[45] Indeed, by 1912 the SPD showed few signs of revolutionary ambition. Its goal of electoral victory and its size meant in increasingly recognized its stake in the existing system. In 1914 the SPD had 4,100 paid party functionaries, 11,000 salaried employees, and 20 million marks invested in profit-making businesses (e.g., newspapers). One historian has called the SPD a "nation-wide corporation."[46]

As a result of its reformism the party was undergoing fissure, particularly after 1905.[47] The left wing of the party, formed around Karl Liebknecht and Rosa Luxemburg, held firmly to the Marxian goal of imminent proletarian revolution and agitated aggressively for the use of the mass strike to bring this goal about. A center group was forming around August Bebel and Karl Kautsky. This group professes a devotion to Marxian theory but saw the struggle for true parliamentary democracy in Germany as the essential immediate struggle of the socialist revolution. It set aside the demand for the overthrow of capitalism for the time being.[48]

The emerging right wing of the SPD included those party members who adopted the reformist position. Foremost among the new right wing party members were Eduard David, Gerhard Hildebrand, Ludwig Quessel, Karl Leuthner, Max Schippel, Max Maurenbrecher and Wolfgang Heine. These men tended to be the most outspoken members of the SPD in support of national defense and German great power status. Their nationalistic views were most aptly expressed by the economist Richard Calwer in the revisionist party journal Sozialistische Monatshefte: "If Germany gives up its position as a politically important country, it will decline economically and this creates a threat to the working population."[49]

Indeed, the right-wing revisionists were the staunchest supporters of Germany's colonial policy prior to the First World War. Many saw in the overseas markets the mission of a greater Germany to enjoy a new prosperity through developed industry, a colonial empire, and abundant world markets.[50] Furthermore, they maintained Germany's right to secure and protect these new markets. In 1911 Hildebrand wrote in the Sozialistische Monatshefte: "No nation that is unnaturally curtailed or threatened in its individual development need succumb without resistance to a strangulation of its economic freedom simply for the sake of peace. . . ."[51] At the 1911 party congress in Jena he pursued this argument claiming ". . .the German SPD, in unison with other sections of the German people, will oppose all attempts of other colonial powers unilaterally to enlarge their already disproportionately valuable areas of colonial influence in systematic disregard for Germany's economic requirements."[52] The revisionists within the SPD would more readily accept the burdens of a large fleet if this meant Germany could enjoy equal status with England and France with respect to markets and colonies, though this support was never unconditional.

The right wing's views concerning colonial policy and imperialism represented, however, the thinking of only a minority of the SPD.[53] Their motions and resolutions were usually voted down within the party, which maintained a steady opposition to the more aggressive foreign policies of certain individuals--including Hildebrand--within the right wing. Karl Liebknecht argued that imperialism and the arms race in general were the concomitants of the capitalist system and by virtue of this connection the SPD should oppose any and all manifestations of imperialism. Paul Lensch, anticipating Lenin's theory that imperialism represents the highest stage of capitalism, claimed that as nations seized more and more colonial markets, the chances to realize a profit would shrink and the resulting conflicts of interests between nations would bring about the fall of capitalism; thus "capitalism suffocates in its own fat." For this reason, firmly opposing imperialism became unimportant.[54]

Beginning in 1898 a different current emerged in the debate over colonialism within the party. August Bebel outlined a new brand of colonialism or "socialist world policy" which took as its aim the enlightenment of the native peoples in the German colonies. colonization could be "civilizing work," Bebel claimed, as long as it maintained no connection with capitalism.[55] Underlying this thesis, of course, was a basic acceptance of Germany's participation in the quest for overseas colonies. Indeed, Karl Frohme went so far as to concede this point during the Reichstag debate over the second navy bill. Frohme admitted that the SPD recognized the need for Germany to pursue a "world policy," but, he continued, that policy should be a "cultural world policy" rather than a "world power policy."[56]

Clearly, after 1905 the SPD was splitting into different factions over some of the key issues facing the party. By rejecting the use of the mass strike and the belief that proletarian revolution was imminent, the party was already on the path to reformism. Increasingly it acted as a party of parliamentary opposition in the Reichstag. In the field of foreign policy the SPD was forced to abandon its reticence. The new naval arms competition and the rising international tensions which had set in by the turn of the century presented the SPD, as one of the largest parties in the Reichstag, with new questions it could no longer ignore.[57] The right wing's aggressive colonialism and Bebel's "cultural world policy" were the new manifestations of this attempt to deal with the new aggressiveness in foreign relations. Thus, the party's attitude toward the navy bills adopted after 1906 should be examined and explained in light of the growing reformism within the SPD and in the context of an increasingly dangerous arms competition among the European powers.

The Navy Bills of 1906, 1908 and 1912

By 1906 Tirpitz's naval policy and "risk" theory were being called into question. From 1898 to 1904, the German navy had grown dramatically. But Great Britain had not reacted as expected; instead of recognizing the growing naval power of Germany and seeking some kind of rapprochement with the latter, Britain reached an agreement with France--the Entente Cordiale. Furthermore, Britain began enlarging the size of its navy while introducing a qualitative change in its fleet by launching the new Dreadnought in 1906.[58] This new ship with a displacement of 18,000 tons made all existing ships of the line obsolete.

Tirpitz took up the challenge laid down by Britain. The new navy bill of 1906 authorized the construction of a double squadron of eighteen ships of the line so that by 1920 Germany would possess fifty-seven ships of the line--more than the British navy had in 1906.

172

Moreover, Germany would start building sixteen ships of 18,000 tons within the next four years. The first two Dreadnought-type ships would be launched in 1908.[59]

The SPD press once again took up the opposition to the new naval buildup. The Leipziger Volkszeitung called on the bourgeoisie to end its naval policy and "world power policy." These policies of "business and industry" would bring disastrous consequences, the article claimed.[60] In January another article rejected the notion that the fleet was properly serving its original purpose of protecting industry and trade: "All overseas trade would be crippled in one blow if war broke out between Great Britain or the United States and Germany. Our fleet policy, which is leading up to such a war, will [in fact] ruin German business and German industry."[61]

While the SPD tied the fleet buildup to business and industrial interests, its main concern was not that the fleet was serving only to bolster the capitalist system; instead the risk of war inherent in the Anglo-German naval competition was the chief target. In urging an end to the fleet and world power policy, the SPD claimed, "the proletariat represents the national interests: a world policy of freedom, free trade, and peace."[62]

This desire to speak in terms of national interests no doubt was in part a response to the growing accusations from the nationalist press and political parties regarding the unpatriotic behavior of the SPD. Social Democratic opposition to the fleet program often induced these accusations. The SPD castigated the "bourgeois" press for making light of workers' class consciousness "simply because we [the working class] do not agree completely with the bourgeois classes in questions of war and peace."[63] Georg von Vollmar, SPD Reichstag Delegate, argued that the workers reserved their right to help decide "whether a war against a foreign 'enemy' should be prosecuted or not," since the difference between "offensive" and "defensive" wars was not at all obvious.[64] The SPD denied charges that the working classes were "without a fatherland (Vaterlandslos)": "When it comes to protecting the country in the case of an enemy attack, one will see that the Social Democrats love their fatherland no less than others and will make not the poorest soldiers." However, "we are grown men--not calfs (Kalber)--who will not allow themselves to be led off to battle without knowing why."[65]

As the Anglo-German naval race progressed and international tensions grew, the SPD was not only forced to confront foreign policy issues, it actively sought to influence the decisions regarding those issues. Their desire for influence, however, did not mean they hoped to seize control of the state apparatus. The SPD was simply demanding that its interests be taken into account.

The Anglo-German naval race intensified as Tirpitz introduced a new navy bill in the Reichstag in 1908. The new plan called for an increase in the German fleet to forty-five ships of the line and twenty-two larger cruisers plus thirty-three capital ships--Dreadnought-type ships of the line and battle cruisers.[66] Again, the SPD opposed the new increases. The Reichstag delegates criticized the excessive costs of the new ships. This was, in fact, the chief criticism of the fleet at the party congress at Nuremberg.[67] Also, SPD delegates raised the issue of parliamentary control over the foreign policy decision-making process. The SPD increasingly protested the complete dominance the government maintained over the direction of the navy program and foreign policy in general. As international affairs seemed more threatening the SPD placed more and more emphasis on establishing a government responsible to the Reichstag.[68] They recognized the meager progress made toward parliamentary government since the death of Bismarck: "It is a telling symbol that in these years the debates over foreign policy take place without the public finding out about them."[69]

This concern was present through the passage of Tirpitz's last significant navy bill in the Anglo-German naval race introduced in the Reichstag in 1912. By then the naval race was reaching crisis proportions. After 1908 the British feared that the German fleet would soon rival the British navy in size, especially since German production of Dreadnought-type ships had accelerated. Indeed, after the Agadir Crisis in 1911 the British prepared their fleet, fearing a German attack.[70] In the aftermath of this crisis, British Minister of War Richard Haldane left for Berlin in February, 1912, to negotiate an agreement with Germany which would in some way limit the size of both the British and German navies. The announcement of the new navy bill early in 1912 was largely responsible for the failure of this last attempt at an Anglo-German naval accord.

Tirpitz's new bill called for a 2:3 power ratio between Germany and Britain; that is, the German fleet would be increased to two-thirds the size of the British fleet. Specifically, this would require increasing the German fleet to include twenty-five Dreadnought-type battleships, twenty-two pre-Dreadnoughts (forty-seven battleships in all) and fourteen Dreadnought cruisers; all together the new fleet would include sixty-one ships of the line.[71]

The SPD overwhelmingly opposed the new bill, particularly in light of the intensified naval race. In response to Winston Churchill's remarks in the British Parliament that Britain would increase its navy budget should Germany increase hers, the SPD claimed the German government must take the necessary steps to defuse the Anglo-German naval tensions. Though considerable reductions were not to be hoped for, "the German government has in its hands the ability to prevent the arms competition from continuing at its current or at an increased rate."[72] After the Haldane mission the SPD claimed Britain was doing its part to reach some agreement.[73] The SPD press, then, laid the blame for the naval race squarely on the shoulders of Germany.

The SPD maintained that it was alone in its opposition to the fleet buildup, since no other parties in the Reichstag objected to the new increases when the new bill was read aloud: "we could only express our pity that we are not strong enough to defeat this 'dangerous' (volksfeindlich) bill."[74] The SPD felt isolated in its rejection of the arms race in general and denied any responsibility for its outcome.[75]

Again the issue of parliamentary control over government policy arose. In the Reichstag Eduard David criticized the government's secretive and "absolutist" foreign policy decision-making process. He also castigated the "bourgeois" parties in the Reichstag for willingly relinquishing all control to the government. In response to claims that the SPD's opposition to the navy bill revealed their lack of patriotism, David accused all those who threatened Anglo-German relations--by advocating a larger battle fleet--of possessing a "misguided patriotism."[76] The German workers stood for world peace, David continued. They are not unpatriotic; rather they are the ones who most "favor the interests of the nation, the well-being of our fatherland."[77]

The latter claim was a familiar one. By 1912, SPD members had given ample evidence concerning their readiness to defend the fatherland. However, the party still based its foreign policy on peace and disarmament. The SPD, it seems, did not consider pacifism, in the climate of a European arms race, and patriotism inherently contradictory.

Conclusion

By 1912 the SPD's position regarding the naval buildup, though ostensibly the same as it was in 1898, had changed in motivation. Certainly, their opposition to Tirpitz's first two navy bills was based in part on the increased costs of the new ship construction, the diminution of the Reichstag's budgetary power inherent in the navy bill, and the potential foreign policy risks created by the vastly enlarged fleet. But the SPD chose to view the government's new navy program primarily in class terms. The SPD reasoned that the navy was being built by and for a propertied elite which sought to use the fleet not only to increase its profits, but also to bolster the existing capitalist system. Furthermore, the workers would suffer from the new buildup since they would pay a disproportionate share of the price of the new fleet through indirect taxes, but in the long run the workers would suffer from their continual subordination to the propertied elite.

After 1905 the SPD's position began to change in emphasis. This change found its origins in two developments: the internal evolution within the party and the increasing tensions in the international sphere. After 1905 the party's drift toward reformism was particularly pronounced; new factions emerged upon which the ultimate schism of the SPD would be based. But this new tendency to seek practical gains within the existing political framework meant the party would resemble a party of parliamentary opposition rather than a revolutionary vanguard. This new current, along with the presence within the SPD of right wing members who favored a strong colonial policy, contributed to the party's shift in position on the naval issue. To be sure, the SPD never supported the naval buildup, but its opposition to the navy by 1912 was based primarily on the threat of war posed by the Anglo-German naval race.

The Tirpitz plan was never very successful as a policy of national integration in relation to the German socialists; nor did it undermine the strength of the SPD. The party proved completely unresponsive. But the SPD's rejection of the new battle fleet was not necessarily indicative of their isolated position in Wilhelmine society. On the contrary, by 1912 the party's behavior as an opposition party in the Reichstag suggests that the SPD played an active role even though it was part of a constitutionally and politically weak parliament. Thus, the SPD's relationship to the other parties in the Reichstag and more generally in the party-political sphere was much more complex than the subculture classification claims, and the SPD was more of a participant in Wilhelmine politics and society than has often been assumed.

NOTES

[1]See Volker Berghahn, Der Tirpitz Plan: Genesis und Verfall einer innenpolitischen Krisenstrategie unter Wilhelm II (Düsseldorf: Droste Verlag, 1971); Herbert Schottelius and Wilhelm Deist, eds., Marine und Marinepolitik im kaiserlichen Deutschland, 1871-1914 (Düsseldorf: Droste Verlag, 1972); Eckart Kehr, Schlachtflottenbau und Parteipolitik, 1894-1901 (Berlin: E. Ebering, 1930); Fritz Fischer, War of Illusions, German Policies from 1911 to 1914 (New York: Norton, 1975); Holger Herwig, The German Naval Officer Corps: A Social and Political History, 1890-1918 (Oxford: Clarendon Press, 1973), 4-16; Alex Hall, Scandal, Sensation and Social Democracy: The SPD Press and Wilhelmine Germany, 1890-1914 (New York: Cambridge University Press, 1977), 7.

[2]Volker Berghahn, "Der Tirpitz-Plan und die Krisis des preussisch-deutschen Herrschaftssystems," in Schottelius and Deist, eds., Marine und Marinepolitik, 93.

[3]Ibid.

[4]Berghahn, Der Tirpitz Plan, 15-16.

[5]Fischer, War of Illusions, 248-49; Berghahn, "Der Tirpitz-Plan und die Krisis," 91.

[6]Berghahn, "Der Tirpitz-Plan und die Krisis," 91. For an earlier exposition of this thesis see Kehr, Schlachtflottenbau, 7, 146, passim.; and Kehr, "The Social and Financial Foundations of Tirpitz's Naval Propaganda," in Economic Interest, Militarism, and Foreign Policy, ed. and with an introduction by Gordon Craig, trans. Grete Heinz (Berkeley: University of California Press, 1977), 82. This thesis has also been incorporated into more general works. See, for example, Hans-Ulrich Wehler, The German Empire, 1871-1918 (Leamington Spa: Berg Publishers, 1985), 164-70.

[7]Geoff Eley, "Sammlungspolitik, Social Imperialism and the Navy Law of 1898," in Eley, From Unification to Nazism: Reinterpreting the German Past (Boston: G. Allen & Unwin, 1986), 114-15. See also Eley, Reshaping the German Right: Radical Nationalism and Political Change After Bismarck (New Haven: Yale University Press, 1980), 9, passim., in which the author demonstrates the popular origins of the rapid growth of the Navy League and significantly challenges the view propounded by Kehr, Berghahn and others that the government and other ruling elites were able to manipulate the masses by using social imperialist techniques such as naval propaganda. For a more general attack on the theme of manipulation by Wilhelmine elites, see Richard J. Evans, ed., Society and Politics in Wilhelmine Germany (London: Croom Helm and New York: Barnes & Noble, 1978), 27, passim.

[8]Guenther Roth, The Social Democrats in Imperial Germany: A Study in Working-Class Isolation and National Integration (Totowa, N.J.: Bedminster Press, 1963), 159-61; W. L. Guttsman, The German Social Democratic Party, 1875-1933: From Ghetto to Government (London and Boston: Allen & Unwin, 1981), 142-43; Dieter Groh, Negative Integration und revolutionärer Attentismus: Die deutsche Sozialdemokratie am Vorabend des Ersten Weltkrieges (Frankfurt am Main: Ulstein, 1974); Alex Hall, Scandal, 16-17, 189-90, passim.; Hans-Josef Steinberg, Sozialismus und Deutsche Sozialdemokratie: zur Ideologie der Partei vor dem I. Weltkrieg (Hanover: Verlag fur Literatur und Zeitgeschehen, 1967), 146-49; Wehler, The German Empire, 81-83; Hagen Schulze, "Die SPD und der Staat von Weimar," in Michael Sturmer, ed., Die Weimarer Republik: belagerte Civitas, 279-83; Roger Fletcher, Revisionism and Empire: Socialist Imperialism in Germany, 1897-1914 (London and Boston: Allen & Unwin, 1984), 20-23.

[9]Vernon Lidtke, The Alternative Culture. Socialist Labor in Imperial Germany (New York: Oxford University Press, 1985), 60. Other historians have also challenged the subculture concept. See, for example, Richard J. Evans, "Introduction: The Sociological Interpretation of German Labour History," in Evans, ed., The German Working Class, 1888-1933 (London: Croom Helm, 1982); Gerhard A. Ritter, "Workers' Culture in Imperial Germany: Problems and Points of Departure for Research," Journal of Contemporary History 13 (1978): 165-89; Peter Domann, Sozialdemokratie und Kaisertum unter Wilhelm II. Die Auseinandersetzung der Partei mit dem monarchischen System, seinen Gesellschafts- und Verfassungspolitischen Voraussetzungen (Wiesbaden: Steiner Verlag, 1974).

[10]Ibid., 10.

[11]A good example of this viewpoint can be found in Wehler, The German Empire, 244-45, passim. See David Blackbourn and Geoff Eley, The Peculiarities of German History (Oxford and New York: Oxford University Press, 1984), 127-43, for a useful discussion of this theme.

[12]See, for example, Hall, Scandal, 190, Wehler, The German Empire, 226, Schulze, "Die SPD und der Staat", 279-82, and Fletcher, Revisionism and Empire, 21.

[13]Jonathan Steinberg, Yesterday's Deterrent: Tirpitz and the Birth of the German Battle Fleet (London: Macdonald, 1965), 144-45.

[14]Ibid., 147.

[15]Quoted in Ivo Lambi, The Navy and German Power Politics, 1862-1914 (Boston, Mass.: Allen & Unwin, 1984), 139.

[16]Steinberg, Yesterday's Deterrent, 20-21; Lambi, The Navy and German Power Politics, 140; Herwig, The German Naval Officer Corps, 11-12.

[17]Berghahn, "Der Tirpitz-Plan und die Krisis," 93.

[18]Herwig, The German Naval Officer Corps, 40-42, 59-60; see also the same author's "Zur Soziologie des kaiserlichen Seeoffizierkorps vor 1914," in Deist and Schottelius, eds., Marine und Marinepolitik, 74-76.

[19]Jonathan Steinberg, "The Kaiser's Navy and German Society," Past and Present, 28 (1964): 104.

[20]Quoted in Steinberg, Yesterday's Deterrent, 58.

[21]Despite the fact that a sortie fleet would consist primarily of fast cruisers while Tirpitz was calling for the construction of nineteen battleships.

[22]Vorwärts, 7 Dec. 1897.

[23]On 3 February 1898 Tirpitz told William II that he would "remove the disturbing influence of the Reichstag on Your Majesty's intentions concerning the development of the navy." Quoted in Herwig, The German Naval Officer Corps, 20-21. See also Berghahn, Der Tirpitz Plan, 111; Lambi, The Navy and German Power Politics, 149.

[24]Protokoll des Parteitages, 1898, 51.

[25]Quoted in Lambi, The Navy and German Power Politics, 147. See also Berghahn, Der Tirpitz Plan, 226-27.

[26]Lambi, The Navy and German Power Politics, 146; Herwig, The German Naval Officer Corps, 8.

[27]Stenographische Berichte des Deutschen Reichstags, 10. Legislatur Periode, I, Bd 5, p. 3967.

[28]Ibid., p. 3966.

[29]See Kehr, Schlachtflottenbau, for a discussion of the connections between big business and government officials in the authorization of naval contracts and in the formation of naval policy in general.

[30]Stenographische Berichte des Deutschen Reichstags, 10. Legislatur Periode, I, Bd 5, p. 520.

[31]Vorwärts, 22 Feb. 1900.

[32]Stenographische Berichte des Deutschen Reichstags, 10. Legislatur Periode, I, Bd 5, p. 520.

[33]Vorwärts, 25 Feb. 1900.

[34]Ibid.

[35]Ibid., 21-22 Feb. 1900.

[36]Protokoll des Parteitages, 1900, 70-71.

[37]Ibid.

[38]Ibid.

[39]Carl Schorske, German Social Democracy, 1905-1917. The Development of the Great Schism (Cambridge, Mass.: Harvard University Press, 1955), passim.

[40]Ibid., 52. See also John Snell and Hans Schmitt, The Democratic Movement in Germany 1789-1914 (Chapel Hill, N.C.: University of North Carolina Press, 1976), 294-95.

[41]William H. Maehl, "The Triumph of Nationalism in the German Socialist Party on the Eve of the First World War," Journal of Modern History, 245 (1952): 16-17.

[42]Quoted in ibid., 18.

[43]Protokoll des Parteitages, 1899, 123-24.

[44]See Peter Gay, The Dilemma of Democratic Socialism: Eduard Bernstein's Challenge to Marx (New York: Collier Books, 1962).

[45]Maehl, "The Triumph of Nationalism," 18; Snell and Schmitt, The Democratic Movement, 301. There is a rich body of literature on SPD reformism prior to the First World War. For an introduction to these works and the relevant debates, see Geoff Eley, "Joining Two Histories: The SPD and the German Working Class, 1860-1914," Radical History Review, no. 28-30 (1984): 13-44.

[46] Maehl, "The Triumph of Nationalism," 27.

[47] There are, of course, problems with characterizing amorphous ideological groupings within the SPD as representing homogeneous factions. Clearly, the use of terms such as "left wing," "center," and "right wing" obscures, to a certain extent, the variety and complexity of political alignments within the SPD (see especially Fletcher, Revisionism and Empire). But for heuristic purposes it is necessary to assess the ideological similarities among these groups in order to classify the different positions which were emerging within the party. Indeed, on many issues there was a convergence of opinion within the respective groupings.

[48] Maehl, "The Triumph of Nationalism," 19-22.

[49] Fischer, War of Illusions, 250.

[50] Maehl, "The Triumph of Nationalism," 30.

[51] Quoted in ibid.

[52] Ibid., 31.

[53] And, in fact, a pro-naval policy was not pursued by many members classified as right-wingers within the SPD. For example, Eduard David was a persistent critic of Tirpitz's navy bills.

[54] Abraham Ascher, "Imperialists within German Social Democracy, 1912-1918," Political Science Quarterly, 76 (1961): 559-60.

[55] Ibid., 165.

[56] Stenographische Berichte des Deutschen Reichstags, 10. Legislatur Periode, I, Bd 5, p. 3967.

[57] Max Victor, "Die Stellung der deutschen Sozialdemokratie zu den Fragen der Auswärtigen Politik (1869-1914)," Archiv für Sozialwissenschaft und Sozialpolitik, 60 (1928): 158-59, 164.

[58] Berghahn, "Der Tirpitz-Plan und die Krisis," 93.

[59] Lambi, The Navy and German Power Politics, 275-76.

[60] Leipziger Volkszeitung, 5 Feb. 1906.

[61] Ibid., 30 Jan. 1906.

[62] Ibid., 5 Feb. 1906.

[63] Ibid., 5 Jan. 1906.

[64] Ibid., 15 Jan. 1906.

[65]Ibid., 5 Jan. 1906.

[66]Lambi, The Navy and German Power Politics, 284.

[67]Protokoll des Parteitages, 1908, 231.

[68]Vorwärts, 25 Mar. 1908.

[69]Vorwärts, 31 Mar. 1908.

[70]William Carr, A History of Germany, 1815-1945 (New York: St. Martin's Press, 1969), 213.

[71]Lambi, The Navy and German Power Politics, 365.

[72]Hamburger Echo, 15 Mar. 1912.

[73]Ibid., 26 Mar. 1912.

[74]Protokoll des Parteitages, 1912, 134.

[75]Hamburger Echo, 26 Mar. 1912.

[76]Vorwärts, 19 May 1912.

[77]Ibid.